Museums and the Shaping of Knowledge

D1050724

Museums have been active in shaping knowledge over the last 600 years. Yet what is their function within today's society? At the present time, when funding is becoming increasingly scarce, difficult questions are being asked about the justification of museums.

Museums are actively re-organising their spaces and collections, in order to present themselves as environments for self-directed learning based on experience, often to new audiences. This critical review of past and current practices and theories will provide a valuable point of reference for museum professionals planning future policies. It will also provide powerful insights for academics and students in the fields of cultural studies, archaeology and material cultures, for it shows how context has determined the interpretation of objects.

Eilean Hooper-Greenhill is Lecturer in Museum Studies at the University of Leicester.

THE HERITAGE
CARE
PRESERVATION
MANAGEMENT

Editor in chief Andrew Wheatcroft

The Heritage: Care–Preservation–Management programme has been designed to serve the needs of the museum and heritage community worldwide. It publishes books and information services for professional museum and heritage workers, and for all the organisations that service the museum community.

Forward Planning: *A handbook of business, corporate and development planning for museums and galleries*
Edited by Timothy Ambrose and Sue Runyard

Heritage Gardens: *Care, conservation and management*
Sheena Mackellar Goulty

Heritage and Tourism: *in 'the global village'*
Priscilla Boniface and Peter J. Fowler

The Industrial Heritage: *Managing resources and uses*
Judith Alfrey and Tim Putnam

Museum Basics
Timothy Ambrose and Crispin Paine

Museum Security and Protection: *A handbook for cultural heritage institutions*
ICOM and ICMS

Museums 2000: *Politics, people, professionals and profit*
Edited by Patrick J. Boylan

Museums Without Barriers: *A new deal for disabled people*
Fondation de France and ICOM

The Past in Contemporary Society: Then/Now
Peter J. Fowler

The Representation of the Past: *Museums and heritage in the post-modern world*
Kevin Walsh

Museums and the Shaping of Knowledge

Eilean Hooper-Greenhill

London and New York

First published in 1992
by Routledge
11 New Fetter Lane, London EC4P 4EE

Simultaneously published in the USA and Canada
by Routledge
29 West 35th Street, New York, NY 10001

Reprinted 1993

© 1992 Eilean Hooper-Greenhill

Printed in Great Britain by Butler & Tanner Ltd,
Frome and London

All rights reserved. No part of this book may be reprinted or
reproduced or utilised in any form or by any electronic,
mechanical, or other means, now known or hereafter invented,
including photocopying and recording, or in any information storage
or retrieval system, without permission in writing from the
publishers.

British Library Cataloguing in Publication Data

Hooper-Greenhill, Eilean
   Museums and the shaping of knowledge. – (Heritage).
   1. Museums
   I. Title
   069

Library of Congress Cataloging in Publication Data

Hooper-Greenhill, Eilean
   Museums and the shaping of knowledge/Eilean Hooper-Greenhill.
      p.   cm.—(Heritage)
   Includes bibliographical references.
   1. Museums—Management. 2. Museum techniques. 3. Museums—
Educational aspects.   I. Title.   II. Series.
   AM7.H66   1992
   069′.5—dc20   91–17628

ISBN 0–415–06145–8
ISBN 0–415–07031–7 (pbk)

Printed on permanent paper in accordance with American NISO Standards

For my family, with love

Contents

List of plates

What is a museum? 1

What is a museum? Museums are no longer built in the image of that nationalistic temple of culture, the British Museum. Today, almost anything may turn out to be a museum, and museums can be found in farms, boats, coal mines, warehouses, prisons, castles, or cottages. The experience of going to a museum is often closer to that of going to a theme park or a funfair than that which used to be offered by the austere, glass-case museum.

The last few years have seen a major shifting and reorganisation of museums. Change has been extreme and rapid, and, to many people who loved museums as they were, this change has seemed unprecedented, unexpected, and unacceptable. It has thrown previous assumptions about the nature of museums into disarray. The recent changes have shocked most those who felt that they knew what museums were, how they should be, and what they should be doing.

This fixed view of the identity of museums has sometimes been firmly held and, until recently, little has disturbed it. But it is a mistake to assume that there is only one form of reality for museums, only one fixed mode of operating. Looking back into the history of museums, the realities of museums have changed many times. Museums have always had to modify how they worked, and what they did, according to the context, the plays of power, and the social, economic, and political imperatives that surrounded them. Museums, in common with all other social institutions, serve many masters, and must play many tunes accordingly. Perhaps success can be defined by the ability to balance all the tunes that must be played and still make a sound worth listening to.

At the present time, in many areas where decisions are made about the funding and maintenance of museums, hard questions are now being asked about the justification of museums, about their role in the community, and their functions and potentials. Where the answers are not forthcoming, or where perceptions of the value of museums are low in relation to other priorities, collections are sold, staff dismissed, and buildings closed. In most cases the answers that are given are that museums are educational institutions. Today, the educational role of museums is claimed as a major justification. The director of the Museums Association, for example, argued to Derbyshire County Council on the occasion of their decision to sell some of their collections, that:

> Museums and their collections are a valuable and irreplaceable community service and have immense educational value. To show no interest in keeping the museum collection is to show no interest in education and in preserving an awareness of Derbyshire and its history and culture.
>
> (The Independent 6 September 1990)

Knowledge is now well understood as the commodity that museums offer. An example makes this clear. As part of the new ethos of corporate involvement in museums and galleries, the opportunity to change one's perception or knowledge of the world through a visit to an art gallery is offered by those whose funding makes exhibitions possible. In an advertisement in *The Independent* Colour Supplement (8 September 1990), for example, a sponsor of the Monet exhibition at the Royal Academy in the autumn of 1990, proclaimed:

> Discover how one man's vision can change the way you look at the world.
>
> In every series, no two pictures are exactly alike. A single theme. The same object. But enveloped in varying light, changing seasons and atmosphere. This is Monet in the '90s.
>
> Digital Equipment Corporation and its employees are proud to sponsor the exhibition that brings together, for the first time, the series paintings of Claude Monet.

This, in the form of an advertisement, and used to celebrate corporate values, is a proclamation about how knowing can alter seeing. Our perception of the world, we are told, will be different once we know and are familiar with these paintings. The statement is a recognition of the way in which museums and galleries can alter perception, and can contribute to knowledge.

But if museums are places in which we may come to know new things, and where our perceptions may radically change, what is the nature of this knowing, and how are these changes brought about?

It is only fairly recently that museums have been subjected to any rigorous form of critical analysis. In the past, museums have somehow escaped the careful study to which schooling, or the media, for example, have been subjected. The hidden curriculum and the unseen and unspoken but powerful, underlying assumptions that construct what counts as knowledge in school curricula have been exposed (Young, 1975). Television programmes have equally been closely observed and the ideological, economic, and cultural elements that have formed the apparently seamless products that we consume daily have been exposed (Glasgow University Media Group, 1972; 1980; 1982; Williams, 1974). The study of the way in which knowing is enabled, constructed, and consumed in schools, through films, in television, and in literature, is well established. However, the analysis of the various elements that together make up the 'reality' that we call 'the museum' has barely begun.

This book asks some very basic questions. What does 'knowing' in museums mean? What counts as knowledge in the museum? Or to put it another way, what is the basis of rationality in the museum? What is acceptable and what is regarded as ridiculous, and why? Does this change over time? How are individual people expected to perform in museums? What is the role of the visitor and what is the role of the curator? How are material things constructed as objects within the museum? How are individuals constructed as subjects? What is the relationship of space, time, subject, and object? And, perhaps the question that subsumes all the others, how are 'museums' constructed as objects? Or, what counts as a museum?

There have been very few critical studies in relation to the museum and virtually all of these have been written from outside a direct experience of the museum as a profession. Museum workers have, until recently, remained unaware of their practices, and uncritical of the processes that they are engaged in every day. Within the practices of the museum, the aspect of criticism, or of developed reflection on day-to-day work, has been very weak indeed. Critical reflection is, indeed, still actively resisted by some curators who see themselves as practical people who have no time to waste on this unproductive activity. Most museum work, until very recently, proceeded without identified objectives, without generally agreed and understood institutional policies, and in a context of received opinion (Burrett, 1985; Miles, 1985; Prince and Schadla-Hall, 1985).

The lack of examination and interrogation of the professional, cultural, and ideological practices of museums has meant both a failure to examine the basic underlying principles on which current museum and gallery practices rest, and a failure to construct a critical history of the museum field. The structure of rationality that informs the way in which museums come into being, both at the present time and in the past, is taken as unproblematic, and therefore as a given.

Most explanations of museums do not take the concept of rationality as problematic, although it might be argued that the museum in its role as the 'Classifying House' (Whitehead, 1970; 1971) is and has been actively engaged over time in the construction of varying rationalities. 'Rationality' is understood as something which is self-evident and which needs no explanation:

> The fundamental role of the museum in assembling objects and maintaining them within a specific intellectual environment emphasizes that museums are storehouses of knowledge as well as storehouses of objects, and that the whole exercise is liable to be futile unless the accumulation of objects is strictly rational.
>
> (Cannon-Brookes, 1984: 116)

But if museum workers have been unaware of the effects of their practices, others have not been so blind. Michel Foucault points graphically to the extraordinary effect of systems of classification in the Preface to *The Order of Things*, where he points out that:

> This book first arose out of a passage in Borges, out of the laughter that shattered, as I read the passage, all the familiar landmarks of my thought - *our* thought, the thought that bears the stamp of our age and our geography - breaking up all the ordered surfaces and all the planes with which we are accustomed to tame the wild profusion of existing things, and continued long afterwards to disturb and threaten with collapse our age-old distinction between the Same and the Other. This passage quotes a 'certain Chinese encyclopedia' in which it is written that 'animals are divided into: (a) belonging to the Emperor, (b) embalmed, (c) tame, (d) sucking pigs, (e) sirens, (f) fabulous, (g) stray dogs, (h) included in the present classification, (i) frenzied, (j) innumerable, (k) drawn with a very fine camel-hair brush, (l) *et cetera*, (m) having just broken the water pitcher, (n) that from a long way off look like flies'. In the wonderment of this taxonomy, the thing that we apprehend in one great leap, the thing that, by means of this fable, is demonstrated as the charm of another system of thought, is the limitation of our own, the stark impossibility of thinking *that*.
>
> (Foucault, 1970: xv)

The system of classification, ordering, and framing, on which such a list is based is so fundamentally alien to our western way of thinking as to be, in fact, 'unthinkable', and, indeed, 'irrational'. But presumably the list was regarded as rational, and as a valid way of knowing. How can we be sure that there is not a rationality that explains the sense of the list?

To be able to make sense of such a list would be mind-expanding and would offer new possibilities of classifying the world, and even new ways of living in it. It would certainly demand new ways of organising museum and art gallery collections. The separations we know between 'fine and decorative art' and 'natural history' for example, would collapse. Many of the taxonomies that we use to explain the interrelationships of objects and species would need to be rewritten, and collections would need to be reordered; paintings, artefacts, and specimens would need to be placed differently within display cases, their records and documentation would need to be re-examined and amended; their positions in storage drawers, cabinets, and racks would need to be changed. In other words, if we accepted as 'true' the classification that Foucault describes, the work of curators in identifying, controlling, ordering, and displaying their collections would have to begin all over again.

If new taxonomies mean new ways of ordering and documenting collections, then do the existing ways in which collections are organised mean that taxonomies are in fact socially constructed rather than 'true' or 'rational'? Do the existing systems of classification enable some ways of knowing, but prevent others? Are the exclusions, inclusions, and priorities that determine whether objects become part of collections, also creating systems of knowledge? Do the rituals and power relationships that allow some objects to be valued and others to be rejected operate to control the parameters of knowledge in the same way as the timetabling rituals and the power relationships of teachers, governors, pupils, and the state operate to make some school subjects more valuable than others?

Taxonomies within the museum have not been considered in relation to the rational possibilities that they might enable or prevent. Classification in the museum has taken place within an ethos of obviousness. The selection and ordering processes of museums are rarely understood as historically and geographically specific, except at a very rudimentary level:

> Collecting is a very basic activity, in that food-gathering is a characteristic of all animals, but, setting aside the activities of certain species of birds, the systematic collecting of objects which fulfil a cerebral, as against bodily, function is confined to a limited number of cultures and societies of man.
>
> (Cannon-Brookes, 1984: 115)

Museums and the Shaping of Knowledge

In the same way as the signification of the identity of collections and museums is taken as a given, so too is the identity of specific material things. The construction of material things as 'objects' of a particular character is not perceived as problematic. Things are what they are. There is little idea that material things can be understood in a multitude of different ways, that many meanings can be read from things, and that this meaning can be manipulated as required. Although we are familiar with the way in which advertisements, for example, select and manipulate images of material objects in relation to their associative and relational potentials, it is not understood that the ways in which museums 'manipulate' material things also set up relationships and associations, and in fact create identities (Barthes, 1977).

Similarly, the divisions and classifications of objects have not been explored in relation to the way in which this ordering interrelates with the divisions and orderings of spaces and of individuals. If a museum accepts a new collection, for example of nineteenth-century mechanical banks or of sixteenth-century sedan chairs, this will immediately create a need for either a new subject position (a new professional post) to be created, or, if this is impossible, an existing subject role will have to be modified through fragmentation. The curator of social history (or decorative art) will have to split his/her existing workload to accommodate the demands of the new collection. Research must be done and new knowledge must be created through the writing of catalogues and monographs, and the mounting of exhibitions. New spaces must be found, or old ones adapted. Perhaps there will be less room for the Chippendale chairs, particularly if the sedan chairs are in excellent condition and used to belong to significant people, and the Chippendale chairs are not in good condition. New systems of priority must be determined. As this process goes on, the identity of the museum shifts and modulates.

Decisions in museums and galleries about how to position material things in the context of others are determined by a number of factors including the existing divisions between objects, the particular curatorial practices of the specific institution, the physical condition of the material object, and the interests, enthusiasms, and expertise of the curator in question.

Although the ordering of material things takes place in each institution within rigidly defined distinctions that order individual subjects, curatorial disciplines, specific storage or display spaces, and artefacts and specimens, these distinctions may vary from one institution to another, being equally firmly fixed in each. The same material object, entering the disciplines of different ensembles of practices, would be differently classified. Thus a silver teaspoon made during the eighteenth century in

Sheffield would be classified as 'Industrial Art' in Birmingham City Museum, 'Decorative Art' at Stoke-on-Trent, 'Silver' at the Victoria and Albert Museum, and 'Industry' at Kelham Island Museum in Sheffield. The other objects also so classified would be different in each case, and the meaning and significance of the teaspoon itself correspondingly modified.

Within museums there is much discussion in relation to location and retrieval of things, that is, the control of the artefact within the space of the museum and in relation to other artefacts and specimens (Thompson, 1984: 113–376), but these spatial divisions are not problematised in terms of what they enable and what they conceal. The axis of visibility that operates in relation to subject, object, and space is not interrogated as to the representations that are constructed. In many cases the axis is not itself perceived. Relationships of subject and object are taken as given, as natural. A strong public/private division is in operation which positions subjects either as 'members of the public' or as 'museum curators'. Although many museums are concerned to 'broaden the audience', this is generally seen as an extension of the already existing distinctions between individual subjects. A rigid division is maintained between the collecting subject as curator, and the viewing subject as visitor, even though in other articulations of practices these distinctions might be reversed. In visiting museums other than their own, for example, curators are invisible as professionals unless they so declare themselves by playing out a particular ritual that secures specific privileges such as being taken 'behind the scenes', being allowed to handle or get closer to objects, or perhaps even give an opinion about the identity of an object.

Power relations within museums and galleries are skewed towards the collecting subject who makes decisions in relation to space, time, and visibility; in other words as to what may be viewed, how it should be seen, and when this is possible. For the public, interaction with the collections other than at the level of looking at fully completed and immaculately presented displays is generally severely curtailed, and because of this, definitions of the meanings of the collections are restricted to the private sphere of the museum worker. Those curators who under-stand how these practices place them in positions of power, and who wish to reduce this personal power, are finding ways to offer more opportunities to others to construct and impose their own interpretations (Fewster, 1990). Interestingly, this generally means that curatorial prac-tices, which were after all designed to keep objects out of the public view, have to be completely reworked.

On the whole, however, the existing make-up of museums with its rather rigid relationships is taken as given. These givens are projected back in time to explain the identities of museums at other historical moments and in other geographical spaces. Thus the writing of museum history up until now has consisted in taking the existing relationships in museums and placing them as far back in time as possible, and then identifying a forward linear development of these relationships. 'Museums' from other historical periods are seen as the 'direct ancestors' of the forms of museum that exist at the present time (Taylor, 1987: 202). 'The modern museum effectively dates from the Renaissance.... Even at that time, however, one can already see the dual role of museums: to exhibit objects and to provide a working collection for scholars' (Whitehead, 1981: 7).

This 'blind' history, and this failure to analyse, understand, and articulate the practices of the present, has some serious consequences. Firstly, there is a difficulty in accommodating a plurality of histories. This is particularly acute in relation to museums, as there is an extreme diversity of forms, with varying funding and administrative arrangements, varying 'collections', and varying scales of operation. Each of these different material manifestations can be related to a different set of constraints and possibilities.

A second difficulty with an impoverished understanding of the past is the lack of a historical specificity. The search for 'origins' and a 'tradition' means a search for similarities rather than differences, and the specific set of political, cultural, economic, and ideological relations that characterises different historical manifestations is rendered invisible, and is therefore effectively lost.

Thirdly, concepts of change are in themselves difficult to articulate. If the aim is to show how things have remained the same, then how is change to be understood? The inability to understand the possibility of change within the museum entails an inflexibility in the understanding of the present. The conditions that exist in the present are seen as immutable, justified by a single, undifferentiated history. The existing articulations of practices are seen as the only possible ones and the radical potentials of museums as sites for critical reflection on the past and the present are lost. At a time when all other social fields are in a period of rapid change, which willy-nilly impinges upon the practices and possibilities of museums, the lack of a flexible model for museums leads to severe problems in accommodating and working with the new elements that are imposed upon the existing field. Without this ability to adapt, to find new ways of being museums, and new ways of recruiting support, museums are being closed down, collections sold, and staff dismissed. If present-day museums and galleries can be seen as not the only form in which museums can exist, but merely the form which the play of various powers has permitted to emerge, then shifts in this play of powers can be seen as part of an unceasing, jostling process to gain the high ground. If the process is continuous and inevitable, as the play of powers must be, then the choices are clear: enter the arena, fight for the power to impose meaning and definition, or stay out of the game and allow others to impose meaning and to define limits.

Effective history

This book interrogates the present-day givens of museums in order to find new ways of writing and understanding the history of this present. In order to do this, insights from the work of Michel Foucault will be used.

Foucault's work is interesting in a number of ways. For example, Foucault calls into question the rationality which grounds the establishment of a regime of acceptability (Foucault, 1980a: 257). In other words, the common-sense world within which we all live is not taken as a given, but is questioned in all its aspects, including the very basic notions that we understand to be reasonable, or 'true'. Foucault understands reason and truth to be relative, rather than absolute concepts, and he proposes that both reason and truth have historical, social, and cultural contexts. Rather than accept the traditional philosophical tenet that an absolute rationality exists, Foucault rejects the familiar rational/irrational split, and proposes that forms of rationality have a historical specificity. What counts as a rational act at one time will not so count at another time, and this is dependent on the context of reason that prevails.

Foucault examines how forms of reason have modified over time and how they have been constituted at specific historical moments. He has also examined how forms of rationality and regimes of truth inscribe themselves in practices or systems of practices, and has asked what role they play within these practices (Foucault, 1981a: 8). How has reason, truth, or knowledge been produced and how do people govern both themselves and others by the limitations and specifics of particular forms?

Foucault's work shows that the origin of what we take to be rational, the bearer of truth, is rooted in domination and subjugation, and is constituted by the relationship of forces and powers (Hoy, 1986: 225). He offers us a set of tools for the identification of the conditions of possibility which operate through the apparent obviousnesses and enigmas of our present. These tools suggest techniques that open the ensemble of practices, understood as givens, to interrogation, and thereby to understanding and subsequently, to modification (Foucault, 1980a: 258). If we can use these tools to analyse, understand, and evaluate the reasons why museums are as they are now, through analysing other ways in which they have been in the past, then perhaps new horizons open, and new possibilities for radical action emerge.

One of Foucault's most useful tools is his approach to history. Foucault rejects the notion of a continuous, smooth, progressive, totalising, developmental history. He works instead with 'effective history', a view of the past that emphasises discontinuity, rupture, displacement, and dispersion (Foucault, 1974: 4). The targets of Foucault's work are not 'institutions', 'theories', or 'ideologies', but 'practices', with the aim of grasping the conditions which make these acceptable at a given moment (Foucault, 1981a: 5).

One of the ways in which the history of truth is discovered is by focusing on the history of error. Those things which appear to us now to be most irrational may, through careful open-ended analysis, reveal the identity of the contemporary structures of knowledge. If the structures of rationality do in fact change, it is in fact more than likely that what we now know to be reasonable was not so known in the past, and will not so appear in the future. Our familiar common-sense practices, brought about and sustained by our own social, cultural, and epistemological contexts, are tomorrow's quaint and misguided errors, explained by our lack of knowledge and sophistication. Just as we see the sixteenth-century apothecary's application of pigeons' wings to the patient's chest as both useless and incomprehensible in curing a fever, so some of our own everyday actions (and who knows which) will appear equally incomprehensible in the future to others whose knowledge and truth is founded on other structures of rationality.

The basis of 'effective history' is an opposition to the pursuit of the founding origin of things, and a rejection of the approach that seeks to impose a chronology, an ordering structure, and a developmental flow from the past to the present. History must abandon its absolutes, and instead of attempting to find generalisations and unities, should look for differences, for change, and for rupture. 'Knowledge is not made for understanding; it is made for cutting' (Foucault, 1977c: 154). The differences between things, rather than the links, become significant. The question to be asked, therefore, is not 'How have things remained the same?' but 'How are things different; how have things changed; and why?'

Foucault's approach to history is informed by the 'general history' of Fernand Braudel and the *Annales* school, which proposes a synthesising and interdisciplinary research programme involving the specialisms of geography, economics, demography, sociology, ethnology, and psychology (Gordon, 1980: 230). The tools of each of these fields of analysis applied in the historical field have revealed the slow movements of 'material civilisation', the movements of accumulation and slow saturation that traditional history has covered with a layer of events (Foucault, 1974: 3).

Effective history thus focuses on those very long-term movements that span the centuries, which are often ignored by normal history which prefers to look at more immediate and shorter-term activities. Effective history also prioritises the breaks and ruptures which signal abrupt endings and painful new beginnings, violent change, and disruption. These too are often not analysed, precisely because links and continuity are sought in order to justify and sustain present-day practices. Thus in the history of museums we have our attention drawn to the Medici Palace in fifteenth-century Italy as 'The first museum of Europe' (Taylor, 1948: 69) and as an example that we should still be following (Alsop, 1982: 339).

Foucault suggests that the old questions of normal historical analysis such as 'What links may be made between disparate events?' and 'How can a causal succession be established between them?' should be replaced by questions of another type. These new questions ask 'Which strata should be isolated from others?', 'What types of series should be established?', and 'What criteria of periodisation should be adopted for each of them?' – understanding that different events and different knowledges have their own times (Lemert and Gillan, 1982: 16). Questions of systems of relations, series of series, and large-scale chronological tables have now become relevant. A focus is developed on the history of error rather than the history of truth. The failures rather than the successes of history are examined.

A 'history of the museum' written from the standpoint of effective history should reveal new relationships and new articulations. Focusing on when and how 'museums' in the past changed, and in which way and why long-standing practices were ruptured and abandoned, may provide a context for today's apparently all too sudden cultural shifts.

The usefulness of examining the history of error in order to discover the history of truth is demonstrated, for example, in the discussion of the 'cabinets of curiosity', a set of practices and relations characterised by 'normal' museum history as 'irrational', 'miscellaneous', and 'confused'. The peculiarly illuminating results of 'effective history' are revealed through the attempt to grasp the conditions and the regime of practices under which these 'errors' did in fact, at the time, count as 'truths'. The specific logic and self-evidence of the 'cabinet of the world', once identified and explored, will later be shown to reverse the judgements of normal history.

The structures of knowledge

'Effective history' provides some tools for rereading the past. Foucault also offers other tools, some of which are peculiarly relevant in the analysis of the ways in which museums have shaped knowledge. In *The Order of Things* (Foucault, 1970), the structures of knowing are described as they shift from the Renaissance to modern times. Just as rationality is not absolute, but relative and shaped by culture, so what counts as knowing has varied across the centuries. To describe the context of knowing, Foucault offers us the concept of the *episteme*; the unconscious, but positive and productive set of relations within which knowledge is produced and rationality defined (Foucault, 1974: 191). It is suggested that what counts as knowing is largely dependent on specific elements, including cultural, social, political, scientific, and other elements (ibid.: 7, 53). These elements interrelate and work with or against each other in a state of constant flux, so that meaning is continually defined and redefined (Laclau and Mouffe, 1985: 106, 113). The elements themselves will also vary, as 'science' or 'culture' changes and is redefined. However, within this constant flux of meaning, Foucault discerns large-scale congruence in the intellectual activity of certain periods. This congruence, constituted through elements in relation, forms the basis for the identification of the *episteme*.

Foucault discovered and describes three major *epistemes*. These are the Renaissance, the classical, and the modern *epistemes*. Each of these had quite specific characteristics, and the shift from one to the next represented a massive cultural and epistemological upheaval, a rupture that meant the complete rewriting of knowledge.

The basic characteristics of the Renaissance *episteme* were interpretation and similitude, with things being read for their hidden relationships to each other. These hidden relationships could be endlessly rewritten, which made this form of knowing 'a thing of sand' (Foucault, 1970: 30). It was resemblance that made it possible to know things that were both visible and invisible, that enabled the interpretation of texts, and that organised the endless play of symbols.

Resemblance was positioned as a form of repetition and reflection, with the earth echoing the sky, and faces reflected in the stars (Foucault, 1970: 17). The world and all the things in it were conceived as being continuously and endlessly related in many different ways, which were

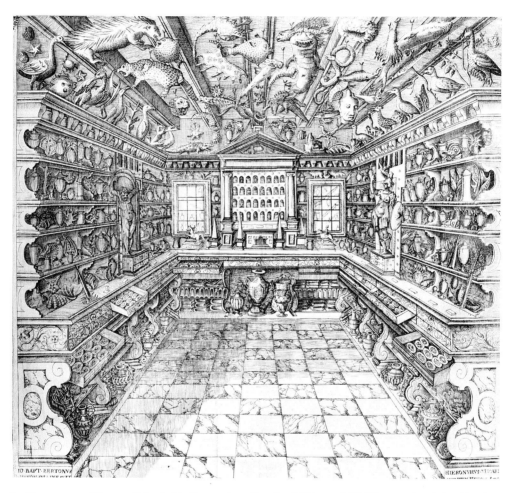

1   The museum of Frances Calceolari in Verona, from Ceruti and Chiocco, 1622. What are the relationships that linked the divers objects in the museum of Frances Calceolari in Verona at the beginning of the seventeenth century? 'Readings' of the collections must have revealed many complex, and possibly secret, webs of resemblances. The function of the museum was to enable the interpretation and reinterpretation of the similitudes, made manifest in the collections, which demonstrated how Art and Nature echoed each other.

in fact hidden and secret. These secrets would be revealed if the surface signs, the indications inscribed on the visibility of things, were correctly related to that which they signified. Visible marks existed to indicate invisible, and often secret, analogies (ibid.: 26). Herbs, plants, and other natural things that issued from the bowels of the earth were seen as so many magic books and signs (ibid.: 27).

The activities that constituted the process of knowing were those forms of interpretation that revealed some aspect of the similitude of things. Foucault describes these in some detail. There are four similitudes. The first is *convenientia*, which indicates the adjacency of things that are 'convenient' enough to be placed in conjunction to each other, with their edges touching. The Elizabethan Great Chain of Being is an example of the notion of *convenientia* (Tillyard, 1943). The second similitude is *aemulatio*, which is a form of *convenientia* that has been freed from the need for proximity and may operate at a distance, so that things with no apparent relation of juxtaposition may in fact answer each other from a long way off. The third form of similitude is *analogy*, which is a complicated superimposition of *convenientia* and *aemulatio*, which may give rise to an endless number of relationships from one single starting point. The final form of similitude is provided by the play of *sympathies*, which span the universe in a free way, with no limitations and prefigurations laid down in advance. *Sympathy* is a play of movement, attracting that which is heavy to the earth and those things which are light to the air. For example, it is *sympathy* which enables the sunflower to turn towards the sun, and makes the roots of a growing plant seek out water. A basic task for *sympathy* is the drawing together of things, the revelation of the sameness of things. This is counterbalanced by *antipathy*, which maintains the isolation of things and prevents their total assimilation. The movement created by the interplay of the *sympathy–antipathy* pair gives rise to the other three forms of similitude, and the whole volume of the world is held together, supported, and reproduced by this space of resemblances. In this way, Foucault suggests, the world remains the same (Foucault, 1970: 25). Resemblance, sameness, links, and relationships are a basic structure of knowing. To know is to understand how the things of the world are the same, however different they may look.

And it is in the signatures inscribed upon the surface of things that these similitudes, this sameness, can be recognised. The world is a world of signs to be read and the endless task of interpretation is the basic structure of knowledge.

The fundamental epistemological configuration is the reciprocal cross-referencing of signs and similitudes. Knowledge was *divinatio*. Magic and the occult were integral parts of knowledge. As a consequence of this endless reading, words and things were understood as the same. There was as much language, and as much to be read, in stones, animals, and herbs as there was in books. Reading and writing were privileged activities.

Foucault describes the Renaissance *episteme* as plethoric, but poverty-stricken: limitless, because resemblance was never stable, but consisting of endless relationships. This was a knowledge which could and did proceed by the accumulations of configurations that were all dependent on each other. There was, therefore, no real substance, and no means of verification. Legend, stories, hearsay, and material things all offered possibilities for discovering likenesses and relationships. None could be discarded, as all were potentially 'true'.

The Renaissance forms of knowing, which Foucault describes as the great circular forms within which similitude was enclosed, were abruptly ruptured in the early years of the seventeenth century. The attenuated and expanded medieval forms of knowing, with their dependence on endless accumulations of dubious and unverifiable 'proofs', and with no distinction between what had been seen and what had been read, could no longer be sustained at a time when the voyages of discovery, and experiments with natural materials, were making new information available. In the seventeenth century, 'all that was left of the Renaissance *episteme* were games – the fantasies and charms of a not yet scientific knowledge' (Foucault, 1970: 51). Resemblance, as a primary function of empirical knowledge, was now perceived as muddled, confused, and disordered.

The classical *episteme* set itself a more restricted project. Its founding structure was that of order, through measurement and the drawing-up of hierarchical series. The classificatory table emerged as the basic structure of knowledge (Foucault, 1970: 74). The activity of mind, knowing, was no longer to consist of drawing things together, but in setting things apart, in discriminating on the basis of difference, rather than in joining on the basis of similitude. To know was to discriminate, and this discrimination took place through a separation of the endless world of resemblances into two parts: on the one hand the taxonomies, the classifications, and the hierarchies of knowledge; and on the other hand, the infinite raw material provided by nature for analysis into divisions and distributions. Theory and nature, being and knowing, become two parts of the world, which was now to be known through objective analysis rather than through subjective experience.

A table of classification was posited, and on it, all natural things were arranged, grouped into families on the basis of their visible features.

This visual grouping resulted in 'sets', with their relationships described through their specific positioning on the table. Thus, in menageries, for example, the animals were arranged in cages that were positioned in such a way as to demonstrate their family relationships through their placing. In libraries, books were arranged to form classifications through their physical relationships. The space of the two-dimensional classificatory table presented all the possible relationships in advance, which were then visually scanned in order to identify the sequences of order.

The classical age rejected the complexity of the Renaissance *episteme*, and attempted to present a simplified, but utterly verifiable knowledge. On the classificatory table, order was presented through the visible features of things. The botanical model of the identification of plant families was transposed on to other forms of knowledge. Thus doctors botanised in the garden of pathology. Knowledge, which was previously thought to be without limit, was now felt to be definable and controllable. Limits could be drawn through the correct identification of hierarchies and sets. If the exact relationship of one thing to another, or of one word to one thing, could only be established, once and for all, then a firm foundation for knowing would come into existence. This could be used with confidence, in a way in which the knowledge which had been passed down from the sixteenth century could not. For this knowledge to be truly effective, the basic relationships and identities needed to be agreed by all scholars. With the increasing use of vernacular languages, scientists and scholars could not speak to each other. The project of a universal language was proposed, where the fixed and agreed taxonomies of words were to be supported by a similar taxonomy of natural things.

This form of knowing, however, was also flawed. It did not prove possible to relate all the things of the world to each other on the basis of visible difference, in a great flat table of difference. Nor was it possible to devise a language where each word had its counterpart in a material object. This, to us today, living at the end of Foucault's modern age, seems a ridiculous thing to try to do. We no longer understand language as representing *things*. We 'know' that words represent *thoughts*. Language relates to the activity of mind rather than the materiality of nature.

At the end of the eighteenth century, the space of knowledge was ruptured yet again. We have seen how the great circular forms of sixteenth-century similitude collapsed into the flat tables of identity and difference (Foucault, 1970: 217). Now this flat table of difference mutated into a three-dimensional space where 'the general area of knowledge was no longer that of identities and of differences, that of non-quantitative orders, that of a universal characterisation, of a general taxonomia, of a non-measurable mathesis, but an area made up of organic structures, that is, of internal relations between elements whose totality forms a function' (ibid.: 218).

The modern *episteme* does not understand natural objects (or any other things) simply because of how they look on the surface, but wishes to know why it is that things came to look as they do. Things are no longer simple visual pieces to be moved about on a board of one-level hierarchies, but are understood as organic structures, with a variety of different levels of complexity, and a variety of different relationships to each other, some at one level and some at another. The organising principles of the new three-dimensional space are analogy and succession. The link between one organic structure and another is no longer the identity of several parts, but the identity of the relationship between the parts, and of the functions which they perform. In this questioning of the relationships of parts, philosophy was born.

In the seventeenth and eighteenth centuries, classifiers measured difference by comparing visible structures: in the nineteenth century, organic structure provided the organising principle. Organic structure was manifested through, in relation to the great natural families of plants and animals, those characteristics most basic to their existence, rather than the most visible. These characteristics were linked to functions (Foucault, 1970: 228). The visible features of plants and animals were now to be explained in terms of their functional role. Thus links were made between the structure of the teeth of a carnivore and the corresponding structure of its toes, claws, and intestines.

The notion of life became indispensable to the ordering of natural beings. Superficial manifestations had to be understood in relation to the depths of the body. The visible had to be related to the invisible. Classifying was no longer to mean the referring of the visible back to itself, nor was the task of representing all the elements to be the responsibility of one; classifying would now mean, in a move that swings the mode of analysis into the third dimension, relating the seen to the unseen, and then moving again from unseen structures back to the visible signs displayed on the surface of bodies and things. These invisible structures, these deeper causes, are not now understood as secret texts or hidden resemblances, as they were in the sixteenth century: these depths are now to be understood as features of a coherent, organic structure. The search for causes and organic structures meant that, in the knowing of the natural world, for example, natural history came to an end and biology opened up.

The idea that a complete and unified corpus of knowledge was possible still had validity at the beginning of the nineteenth century, as is demonstrated by the work of Descartes, Diderot, and Leibniz

(Foucault, 1970: 247). But the encyclopedic project which these scholars proposed, which was grounded in the notion of the complete classificatory table, was, Foucault states, 'reduced to a superficial glitter above an abyss' (ibid.: 251).

In the abyss were the complex interrelationships of analysis and philosophical thought. The modern age made possible the sciences of man. The human sciences questioned objects and relationships. Problematics were raised; new methods and approaches were developed. A new form of knowing, based on the questioning of why things were how they were, made its appearance. The activity of knowing was the questioning, the analysis, and the exposition of organic and functional relationships between material things. It was no longer enough to merely place objects in physical proximities in order to reveal their immediate links. Now, knowledge required the revelation of deeper, more intimate, and more fundamental relationships. And as deeper relationships between things were demanded, so the philosophical questions were asked about the nature of man.

In many ways, Foucault's three *epistemes* appear remarkably improbable. They certainly raise issues and approaches that have not been used to explore any history of museums. And yet, there are resonances here that are tantalising. In some instances, Foucault comes close to discussing museums. He talks about natural history collections, and menageries. The encyclopedic project is mentioned. And *The Order of Things* is, of course, entirely concerned with the way in which objects have been known and understood. If Foucault's extraordinary *epistemes* could in any way be feasible, what kind of museums would be revealed? With what functions? As has been pointed out, someone who accepts Foucault's descriptions of the different *epistemes* in *The Order of Things* will look for explanations of a very different kind from those required by other descriptions of the 'objects' that stand in need of explanation (Davidson, 1986: 223).

In relation to the 'history of the museum', very little historical work has been undertaken from any theoretical perspective at all, but those histories that have been produced to date have not been written either to take account of the epistemological context of museums, or from the standpoint of effective history.

The 'histories' of museums

Two forms of 'histories' of the 'museum' can be currently identified. One is the all-encompassing 'encyclopedic' account that attempts to produce

2 A young visitor at the African culture exhibition at Bruce Castle Museum, Haringey, London, 1990. In the modern age, the function of the museum is to research and demonstrate the social and cultural context of artefacts and to foster relationships between objects and people.

chronological, incremental descriptions of the 'development' of museums. These histories include Alexander (1979), Bazin (1967), Taylor (1948), Van Holst (1967), Murray (1904), and Wittlin (1949; 1970). Alongside these accounts are narratives concerning either single individuals as collectors (Alexander, 1983; Edwards, 1870) or focusing on the history of single institutions (Bazin, 1959; Caygill, 1981; Gould, 1965; Klessmann, 1971; MacGregor, 1983). These are all written from within 'traditional' history (Foucault, 1977c: 153) and retain its dependence on absolutes and its belief in the transcendental creative subject.

In each case, the narrow focus of description demanded in order to satisfy the constraints to place particular themes within an already existing fully fixed identity (the museum) leads to a lack of critical analysis of the specific features under discussion. This results in the construction of a 'safe' and uncontentious history, which is of course the object of the exercise all along. To take one example, Caygill writes: 'The "father" of the British Museum was Sir Hans Sloane (1660–1753), a physician said to have been born at Killyleagh, County Down and graduated MD at Orange in 1683. Sloane's passion for collecting accelerated following his appointment as personal physician to the new Governor of Jamaica, the Duke of Albemarle, in 1687' (Caygill, 1981: 5). The account goes on to point out how Sloane was noted for 'promoting the practice of inoculation against smallpox and popularising the consumption of milk chocolate'.

This 'normal history' does not question the specific conditions under which Sloane's 'passion for collecting' was able to be accelerated in Jamaica, nor the relationship between two such apparently diverse practices as inoculation and drinking chocolate. A more recent account (Dabydeen, 1987) identifies an articulation between the marriage of Sloane to a Jamaican heiress, his participation in the slave trade, and his financial abilities to collect. An effective history of the British Museum would select a specific time-frame and would identify all the various elements that together made up the identity of the 'museum' at that particular time. The effects of the different elements, such as the participation in the slave trade, the acquisition of large financial resources, the travel to the West Indies, and so on, would all be assessed as to their particular functions. In addition, those aspects not generally considered 'historical' (love, conscience, instincts, egoisms, bodies) would be isolated, and their roles assessed (Foucault, 1977c: 140, 149).

Recently more detailed, scholarly work has begun to be produced by curators engaged in research, where the writers are often enmeshed in the practices whose histories they are reconstructing (MacGregor, 1983; Impey and MacGregor, 1985; Simcock, 1984; Hill, 1986; Nicholson and Warhurst, 1984). In many cases this work is more useful than the generalised, all-encompassing 'museum history' in that it focuses on and gives considerable detail of specifics. One example is the paper on Joseph Mayer, who gave Liverpool Museum (now part of the National Museums and Galleries on Merseyside) its largest single donation in 1867. This is described as consisting of about 14,000 items, including prehistoric, Egyptian, classical, Etruscan, Peruvian, and Mexican antiquities; medieval and post-medieval manuscripts, ivories, enamels, embroideries, pottery, clocks and watches, arms and armour, and ethnological objects. (Nicholson and Warhurst, 1984). Another example of this sort of work is the examination of the cabinet of Bonnier de la Mosson (1702–44) in Paris in about 1740, which is reconstructed through the survival of a set of drawings, a contemporary description, and a sale catalogue (Hill, 1986).

In some cases this research is relatively exploratory and in its focus on contemporary records (for example, Welch, 1983) might well provide some useful material for an effective history, but in very many cases the slanting of the questioning of these contemporary documents (Foucault, 1974: 6) has failed to remark on quite critical points made by the documents themselves. Thus MacGregor, for example, writes of John Tradescant: 'Three years later he made his first visit to Virginia, when it was recorded that: "In 1637 John Tredescant [*sic*] was in the colony, to gather all rarities of flowers, plants, shells" ' (MacGregor, 1983: 11). The documents are interrogated from the point of view of reconstructing a history of John Tradescant, the 'father' of the Ashmolean Museum, a history that is premised on the centralised and transcendental subject. An effective history, working on the documents from within, and asking what series present themselves for analysis, would not assemble the documents to provide a descriptive biography of a single 'collector', but might put together a series that demonstrated how colonisation enabled the emergence of a particular range of subject positions, or a particular set of technologies, that together partly accounted for the transformation of existing practices of the collection of material things within a specific geo-historical site.

Where very genuine and detailed archival research has been carried out, this is susceptible to being presented in a way that tends to underplay the precise specificity and the difference of the findings. Recently, much work has been carried out in Europe as a whole on the 'museums' of the late sixteenth and early seventeenth centuries. Some of these were collated following a conference on *The Origins of Museums* (Impey and MacGregor, 1985). The unique conclusions and originality of much of the research presented in the papers is denied by the editors in their introductory statements which seek to establish the unity of a linear progressive history of an essentialist 'museum'. The editors assert that since the sixteenth century, 'with due allowance for the passage of years, no difficulty will be found in recognizing that, in terms of function, little has changed' (ibid.: 1). 'Function' is understood as 'keeping and sorting the products of Man and Nature'. This ignores the fact that in the processes of 'keeping and sorting' it is precisely the principles of selection and classification that have radically changed. Most museums today, for example, collect almost exclusively from among old things, and have extreme difficulty integrating new things into current practices (Bourne, 1985; Jones, 1987). The endless debates over 'twentieth-century collecting' or 'contemporary collecting' (Green, 1985; Suggitt, 1985; Davies, 1985; Ambrose and Kavanagh, 1987; Schlereth, 1989) show the difficulty that some museums have in conceptualising their 'functions' as other than in relation to the past. In the 'museums' of the sixteenth century, as the collected papers amply indicate, many of the main items collected were in fact contemporary, including, for example, finely worked recently imported precious materials (Scheicher, 1985: 33); ornaments, weapons, and clothing from recently 'discovered' parts of the world (Aimi *et al.*, 1985); and tools made to order for many contemporary crafts and professions (Menzhausen, 1985: 71).

Menzhausen further points out that the *Kunstkammer* of the Elector Augustus in Dresden in the seventeenth century was 'not a museum in the sense of an exclusive exhibition: it was a working collection', with places to work, particularly at technical processes, within the *Kunstkammer*. In addition, the collection contained many pieces made by the elector himself and his son. It is further recorded that tools, books, and materials were loaned from the *Kunstkammer* to craftsmen who were producing items for the collection (Menzhausen, 1985: 73). This is very dissimilar to museums today. Searching for the unity in relation to an essential identity conceals the rich diversity of things and disguises possible opportunities for the present.

Other current museum practices are discovered in the 'museums' of the sixteenth century. 'Reference collections were essential tools for the fundamental research undertaken by early naturalists' (Impey and Mac-Gregor, 1985: 1). 'Scholars benefited instantly from the publication of specimens held by their contemporaries - an arrangement which retains equal importance today' (ibid.: 2). Both these statements seek to replicate the present in the past. 'Normal' history seeks to show how things have not changed, how things have remained the same from one century to the next. How will these histories change if 'effective' history, informed by Foucault's *epistemes*, is employed?

The first museum of Europe? | 2

The Medici Palace: a narrative

> The house was in reality the first museum of Europe and, so far as the art of Italy and Flanders of the fifteenth century is concerned, has never been equalled since, nor can it be again.
>
> (F. H. Taylor, 1948: 69)

> The Medici (Riccardi) Palace in the fifteenth century was in a sense a private museum.
>
> (Alexander, 1979: 20)

> Quite demonstrably ... this Italian magnates' art collecting, for which the fifteenth century Medici partly set the example, then exercised an influence on Western art itself which lasted for another three hundred years.
>
> (Alsop, 1982: 339)

These remarks demonstrate how the Medici Palace, in fifteenth-century Florence, is cited and celebrated as the identity of origin for European 'museums' and for European collecting practices. This complex combination of subjects, objects, spaces, and practices is our first case-study, and some of the existing evidence that describes it will be reread and reanalysed, using both the methods of 'effective history', and Foucault's description of historic epistemic configurations. Will Foucault's method reveal a new Medici Palace, a Medici Palace that can be understood in new ways?

The rereading will begin with a 'narrative' of the Medici Palace, which has been reconstructed from readily available sources. This will be followed in this chapter by a discussion of the broad context of thought and social action within which the Medici Palace had its existence. This broad context is external to the specific reality of the Medici Palace, but its constituent characteristics are inevitably present in its formation. Chapter 3 will discuss specific elements and factors that together make up the identity of the Medici Palace, looking at both what counts as 'knowledge' and who is enabled to 'know'.

The Medici Palace emerged at a time in Florence when the success and rapid growth of banking, trading, and mercantile activities were producing large fortunes for the most powerful of the merchant class. The networks of power and influence that were constituted through these activities were adapted from use in the economic field to use in a newly developing cultural field. Culture, connoisseurship and ostentatious display began to be used to support the positions of the dominant merchants to underline their economic power. Through the collecting together of expensive goods and the construction of elaborate spaces, a new subject position emerged. Initially brought about through the possession of wealth, networks of communication, and an existing relation of superiority within the city population, this new subject position soon became autonomous, and a marker of power and knowledge in its own right.

One of the reasons for the emergence of the Medici Palace was the desire on the part of the Medici family, the most successful of the merchant families, to create a technology of space that would emphasise their newly acquired dominant status in Florence. The building of the Medici Palace constituted both a major political decision and a new form of power.

During the 1440s Cosimo de Medici (1389–1464) judged that the political moment had arrived to build himself a new *palazzo* in Florence. Up until then he had been cautious in personal display (Gombrich, 1985a: 44) and careful to appear a plain citizen like any other Florentine (Alsop, 1982: 365), while at the same time quietly amassing an enormous fortune through the enterprises of the Medici bank (Burke, 1974: 314). However, Cosimo took pains not to appear too ostentatious in his new use of space, and rejected an elaborate design by Brunelleschi in favour of a plainer building designed by Michelozzo, an architect he had used on other occasions (Gombrich, 1985a: 44; Wackernagel, 1981: 236).

The impact of this palace in the context of the contemporary plain, undecorated, fortress-like buildings in Florence must have been enormous. The first Renaissance palaces, built around 1420–40, were undecorated both on the exterior (Wackernagel, 1981: 240) and in the interior spaces. There were few household possessions other than the strictly utilitarian (Burke, 1974: 147; Alsop, 1982: 361). The Medici Palace in the Via Largo (also sometimes known by the name of later owners as the Riccardi Palace), was the first house in Florence to be built on what are now seen

3   Michelozzo: Palazzo Medici, Riccardi, Florence, *c.* 1440. The 'first museum of Europe', the home of the Medici family at the height of their social, cultural, and political dominance in Florence.

as Renaissance principles, and must have been unique at the time in its size and height, its use of decorative motifs on the exterior walls and spaces, in the richly decorated interior spaces, and in the extensive accumulation of material goods.

Cosimo de Medici first set about commissioning the house for himself and his family in 1444 when he was 55 years old. The building proceeded leisurely, and Cosimo himself spent only the last few years of his life there (Wackernagel, 1981: 236). His son Piero (1419–69) and grandson Lorenzo (The Magnificent, 1448–92) were to reap the benefits of Cosimo's work.

In 1459 the young Galeazzo Sforza, son and heir of the ally of the Medici, the Duke of Milan, visited Florence. One of his party sent home an account in a letter of the Palazzo Medici which partly indicates the arrangement of spaces and things. It describes:

> the studies, chapels, salons, chambers and garden, all of which are constructed and decorated on every side with gold and fine marbles, with pictures and inlays done in perspective by the most accomplished and perfect of masters down to the very benches and floors of the house; tapestries and household ornaments of gold and silk; silverware and bookcases that are endless without number; then the vaults or rather ceilings of the chambers and salons, which are for the most part done in fine gold with diverse and various forms.
>
> (Alsop, 1982: 366)

The outside of the palace carried a number of decorative devices: above the door of the palace was the inscription 'The Nurse of All Learning' (Taylor, 1948: 69); marble medallions, roundels, which combined both the Medici arms and classical designs, were placed in 1452 above the arcades in the semi-public courtyard. The designs for these were drawn from existing cameos that belonged to Cosimo (Wackernagel, 1981: 102, 236). A series of busts of ancient Roman emperors decorated the rear façade of the new *palazzo*. A number of sculptures were produced by Donatello for the exterior spaces; the bronze *David*, which stood in the centre of the courtyard (ibid.: 236) and a *Judith with the Head of Holofernes* which was created as part of the fountain in the garden (ibid.: 237).

The interior spaces were carefully ordered, richly decorated, and planned to produce a harmonious overall effect (Wackernagel, 1981: 163). An inventory of the contents of the palace, drawn up in 1492 after the death of Lorenzo, has enabled researchers to reconstruct to some degree the organisation of these internal spaces. The large ground-floor room, the '*camera terrena di Lorenzo*', was panelled in various expensive woods,

4 Posthumous portrait of *Cosimo de Medici* (Pater Patriae), by Pontormo. Cosimo was trained as a merchant and spent much of his time dealing with banking and business affairs, but his portrait shows him as the father of a dynasty.

into and against which were set some pieces of immovable furniture: a cupboard, a large chest, and two highly decorated beds, one larger than the other. A large table on heavy carved feet stood in the middle of the room. Two small chests (*cassoni*) were embellished with the Medici arms. Above the panelling the walls were decorated with a number of paintings. Six large paintings in gold frames, each about 2 metres high with a total length of 25 metres, included three episodes from the battle of San Romano and a battle between lions and dragons, painted by Uccello (Alsop, 1982: 382), a judgement of Paris, and a hunting scene. Several smaller pictures were also displayed in the room; these included a round Epiphany by Fra Angelico, a head of St Sebastian by Squarcione, and a group of smaller paintings which were probably incorporated into the frame moulding, which included a *Last Communion of St Jerome*. There were also two portraits, one of Galeazzo Maria Sforza by Pollaiuolo, and another of the Duke of Urbino (Wackernagel, 1981: 164–5).

An upstairs room, the *camera di Lorenzo*, contained several pieces of large furniture, including a large bed (five and a half *braccia*, that is, 3.2 metres long) decorated with panelling with carved and gilded heads and figures, and a pair of chests which were gilded and painted with scenes from Petrarch's *Trionfi*. In the middle of the room stood a large table with a valuable cover spread over it, and a velvet tapestry 7 metres wide hung on the wall (Wackernagel, 1981: 165–6).

The upper wall areas were decorated with various pictures and sculptures, including a marble Madonna relief in a carved gilt frame; a round painting of *The Triumph of Fame*, which was a '*desco da parto*' (a birth salver); and a small cupboard ornately painted with images of a lady and two other figures. Marble busts of Lorenzo's father, Piero, and his mother, Lucrezia Tornabuoni, were each set up above the two doors in the room; and a small, rectangular, alabaster relief in a frame decorated with bone inlay was probably placed nearby.

The inventory lists other movable pieces in addition to the ones itemised above. These include a series of small mosaics, two of Christ, three of saints, one of a young girl and the impresa of Lorenzo's brother Giuliano; three marble sculptures, two of which are nude figures, one sitting and one standing, in high relief; a clockwork in gilded copper; four copper sconces decorated with leafwork; a gilded copper lily (a palio prize from the feast of St John the Baptist); an ostrich egg; and a mirror-glass sphere which hung on a silken string.

From this inventory and the work of various scholars (Gombrich, 1985a; Wackernagel, 1981; Alsop, 1982; Gilbert, 1980) it is possible to gain some idea both of the Palazzo Medici as a building and of its contents. Further documents reveal something of the appearance of another room, and of the way in which its occupant used its contents.

Piero de Medici, the son of Cosimo and the father of Lorenzo, had a room in the palace designated for his personal use, the *scrittoio*, or studio. This private room had a high vaulted ceiling which was covered with coloured majolica tiles by Luca della Robbia. The walls were also treated in this way (Wackernagel, 1981: 239), and the room had a corresponding tile pavement (ibid.: 146).

Antonio Filarete (*c*.1400–69) describes how Piero, a man who was largely immobilised by arthritis, spent his time:

> Piero takes great pleasure in whiling away his time by having himself carried to his studio ... there he would look at his books as if they were a pile of gold ... let us not talk about his readings. One day he may simply want for his pleasure to let his eye pass along these volumes to while away the time and give recreation to the eye. The next day, then, according to what I am told, he takes out some of the effigies and images of all the Emperors and Worthies of the past, some made of gold, some of silver, some of bronze, of precious stones or of marble and other materials, which are wonderful to behold. Their worth is such that they give the greatest enjoyment and pleasure to the eye. . . .
>
> The next day he would look at his jewels and precious stones, of which he has a marvellous quantity of great value, some engraved in various ways, some not. He takes great pleasure and delight in looking at those and in discussing their various powers and excellencies. The next day, maybe, he inspects his vases of gold and silver and other precious material and praises their noble worth and the skill of the masters who wrought them. All in all when it is a matter of acquiring worthy or strange objects he does not look at the price. . . . I am told he has such a wealth and variety of things that if he wanted to look at each of them in turn it would take him a whole month and he could then begin afresh, and they would again give him pleasure since a whole month had now passed since he saw them last.
>
> (Gombrich, 1985a: 51)

How can we understand the meaning of these activities in these elaborately decorated spaces? What did they mean in the mid-fifteenth century? What are the conditions of knowledge within which they were happening? What counts as knowing and doing in this house at this time?

The present and the past

Italy in the 1440s was neither a social nor a cultural unit. The concept of 'Italia' existed, but the city republics were the dominant form of organisation and had been since the twelfth and early thirteenth centuries (Burke, 1974: 13). There was no concept of national identity, and the rivalry between the city states was at times intense. The new political form that replaced the feudal system was that of the absolute prince, relying for his power on the support of the merchants, and who might even be an ennobled merchant himself, as was the case with the Medici family.

A rapid extension of trade was made possible by improvements in shipping and navigation, and by a greater available surplus of goods, especially in the products of agriculture and cloth-making (Bernal, 1969: 380–1). Throughout the fifteenth century the main current of trade, which consisted in luxury goods (Bronowski and Mazlish, 1970: 42), flowed from the east through Venice and into Italy and Germany. New forms of wealth and power emerged at this time. The new wealth of the merchants made possible the development of conspicuous consumption, which then became an expression of power. However, the voyages of discovery to the New World, that would bring many strange and unknown things back to Europe, had not yet begun. After 1500, when the Americas were discovered, large quantities of treasure were imported into Europe (Bronowski and Mazlish, 1970: 46) and would be incorporated into the expression of conspicuous consumption. In the mid-fifteenth century, this expression was largely limited to the use of sumptuous materials.

Along with economic independence and greater wealth, came an emphasis on the importance of a life in the present rather than the contemplative ideal of earlier times. There was an emphasis on the secular, the visible, and the manual, rather than the contemplative and the spiritual.

A new element in the early Renaissance was its deliberate rejection of older forms of thought and its seeking out of new ideas. This was the work of a small, self-conscious group of scholars and artists, who no longer wished to see the ancients through the eyes of the Arabs and the medieval schoolmen, but with their own eyes, reading the texts directly (Bernal, 1969: 383). This involved digging up statues from the ground and placing them where they could be studied; recovering neglected manuscripts from the monasteries; and going back to the original Greek and reading first-hand the works of Plato, Aristotle, and Archimedes. It depended too on the construction of a new gaze, one that no longer saw the statues that emerged from the ground as the bearers of pagan curses

5   Marble bust of *Piero de Medici* by Mino da Fiesole, 1453.

(Alsop, 1982: 304) and which saw the codices of the ancients as capable of supplying a new philosophy for a newly emerging society.

The new emphasis on contemporary active life expressed itself in the rapid growth of the secular arts, including the arts of ornamentation and display: painting, sculpture, poetry, and music. Those practices that provided for the twin needs of war, metal mining and metal working, were regarded as particularly important (Bernal, 1969: 386). Technicians and artists were essential to the making and the spending of money (Wackernagel, 1981: 243), which affected the social status of this group. Respect was newly accorded to the practical arts of spinning, weaving, pottery, and glass-making.

A newly reawakened consciousness of the importance of the direct observation of natural effects grew out of the pursuit of technical trades (Wackernagel, 1981: 243). The Middle Ages had laid some basis for this. Following the Aristotelian doctrine of *emperia*, the medieval schoolman Roger Bacon had demanded the *argumentum ex re*, the observation of the things themselves, instead of the *argumentum ex verbo*, opinions based on the incremental accumulation of words (Heidegger, 1951: 6). This attention to materiality was one of the elements that had led to the emergence of an aesthetics of the organism based on proportion, luminosity, and relativity (Eco, 1986: 69).

A new sense of temporal change began to emerge during the fifteenth century. In the Middle Ages the past was not regarded as different, but was seen in terms of the present. Where this was impossible, and difference had to be acknowleged, there were two possible recourses. One was to use the idea of 'foreign-ness'. A sense of space was substituted for the sense of time; a Roman tomb becomes 'the tomb of a Saracen'. A second possible explanation was in terms of the supernatural: thus castles were seen as the work of giants. This notion was, in fact, linked to the first, as foreigners were often regarded as not quite human (Burke, 1969: 6).

The lack of causal history may be observed in the structure of medieval histories, which were related to chronicles, narrative accounts of what had happened during the year. Histories were also organised around concepts such as the four empires, or the six ages. This form of division relates to the cosmological divisions of the world through numerology (Burke, 1974: 209) and is concerned with description rather than analysis.

It was not until the fifteenth century that people in Italy began to be aware of temporal differences. *Rome Restored*, written during the period 1440–6 by Flavio Bondi, is one of the first accounts that indicate a rupture, a new way of seeing already existing material things. The writer studied the ruins of Rome, copied inscriptions, and described baths, gates, and obelisks, and discussed their material features rather than rehearsing the myths and stories that formerly explained their existence. Thus marble, glass, gilded wood, and other building materials are mentioned, and measurements are given in terms of numbers of pillars required and numbers of men that could be contained (Burke, 1969: 26).

In the reactivation of the past, the events of the immediate past in Italy were rejected in favour of a classical past and the events of antiquity (Burke, 1974: 39). Across many contemporary practices, the models of antiquity were emulated: in architecture Vitruvius was studied and the vocabulary of classical form taken up; in sculpture the equestrian statue and the portrait bust were revived; in narrative poetry there was a move from romance to epic; in the theatre, comedies imitated Plautus and Terence, tragedies imitated Seneca. A capitalist economic climate, and an active progressive society keen to celebrate the secular present, sought its intellectual justification in the old classical texts, seen as the testimonies of the great men of the past.

Princes, merchants, and scholars began to establish collections that would demonstrate their knowledge of the classical past and, equally, their new wealth. Classical coins, medals, intaglios, inscriptions, fragments of buildings, and sculptures were actively sought and collected for their legible importance along with codices, texts, and illustrated volumes from classical times. Statues were dug out of the ground, and new building sites were eagerly scanned for the pieces that might emerge. As Rome was rebuilt, pieces of classical buildings were retrieved that would be reused in the palaces of the merchants. Emissaries were despatched to search for the old neglected classical manuscripts that lay rotting in the cellars of the monasteries and cathedrals (Alsop, 1982: 346). The portraits on the carved antique gems were read as the historical documents of successful past societies that could become the models for the newly powerful mercantile Florence.

Gradually, during the Renaissance, individuals began to be aware that many things, such as buildings, clothes, laws, and words, had changed over time. In the 1440s, however, this must have been a new idea, and the descriptive and explanatory power of the concept of temporal change must have coexisted with other, older, explanations of the nature of the world.

Cosmology and magic

Foucault suggests that 'Up to the end of the sixteenth century, resemblance played a constructive role in the knowledge of western culture' (Foucault, 1970: 17). Foucault discusses the various forms of similitude in detail, in relation to the doctrine of signatures, but is not very helpful when trying to place these resemblances within a general cosmological framework. This he takes as given and does not explain. Thus *convenientia, aemulatio, analogy*, and the play of *sympathies* are difficult to place. Other writers have tried to explain in more detail the concepts of the world that were operational in the 1440s.

Renaissance similitude proposed a converging centripetal world of order. The order of the macrocosm (the world) resembled that of the microcosm (man) (Lowe, 1982: 10). The mental universe that was organised by resemblance was animate rather than mechanical, moralised rather than objective, and organised in terms of correspondences rather than causes (Burke, 1974: 208).

The world was understood as 'an animal'. Leonardo da Vinci (1452–1519) wrote: 'We can say that the earth has a vegetative soul, and that its flesh is the land, its bones are the structure of the rocks ... its blood is the pools of water ... its breathing and its pulse are the ebb and flow of the sea. (Burke, 1974: 208). Artefacts were also understood as animate; Antonio Filarete(1400–69) wrote: 'A building ... wants to be nourished and looked after, and through lack of this it sickens and dies like a man' (Burke, 1974: 208).

The operations of the universe were described in anthropomorphic terms, thus the magnet is so greatly loved by the iron that in spite of the size and weight of the iron, it moves to find the magnet. Love is a form of *sympathy*, one of the principles of mobility (Foucault, 1970: 23). *Antipathy* is its opposite: 'It is fairly widely known that the plants have hatreds between themselves ... the olive and the vine hate the cabbage' (ibid.: 24). Love and hate, elements that we would understand as emotions only attributable to the human subject, are understood as principles of mobility between metals and plants.

The perception of the animate nature of things that would now be seen as inanimate is matched by attitudes to animals that would now be called irrational. The ancient Greeks had held that a murder committed by a human subject, or an animal, or even an artefact, unless properly expiated, could arouse the furies and bring plagues and other devastations (E. P. Evans, 1987: 9). The medieval church taught the same doctrine, although substituting the demons of Christian theology for the furies of classical mythology. Animals could therefore be arrested, tried in a full court of law, convicted, and executed (ibid.: 2). In 1386 in Falaise, Normandy, for example, a sow that had killed a child was tried, found guilty, and executed by hanging. The event was represented in a fresco on the west wall of the Church of the Holy Trinity (ibid.: 16).

Animals were sometimes seen as evil spirits in disguise, and although all animals had the potential of being invaded by a devil in search of a home, some animals were more often seen as intrinsically contaminated, notably the asp, the dragon, the serpent, the leviathan, and the basilisk. Tales of fabulous beasts were common in Italy as elsewhere in Europe during the fifteenth century and for a long time thereafter.

The universe was 'moralised' in the sense that it was divided into different strata with higher or lower status, with the higher levels being seen as better, and more desirable. Thus the warm was better than the cold: 'the warm is much more noble and perfect than the cold, because it is active and productive'. In the same way, it was better not to change, like the heavens, than to change, like the earth; better to be at rest than to move; better to move in a circle than in any other way; better to be a tree than a stone, an animal than a tree, a human being than an animal, a man than a woman, a nobleman than a peasant (Burke, 1974: 209).

The conventional picture of the cosmos worked with a fundamental distinction between the heavens and the earth. The earth was surrounded by seven 'spheres' or 'heavens', in each of which moved a planet. The planets were animate, and each moved by an 'intelligence', sometimes represented by the appropriate classical god or goddess, but sometimes relating to the pagan gods. Lives were subjected to planetary influences; in the carnival song written by Lorenzo de Medici, the planets sing: 'from us come all good and evil things' (Burke, 1974: 211).

The paths of the planets were divided into twelve sections, each represented by one of the signs of the zodiac, and were subdivided into thirty-six decans. Astrology was used extensively to discover both the future and how to act in the present, as the days of the week, for example, were also subject to planetary influences. Filippo Strozzi had the foundations of his palace laid on 6 August, 1489, after consulting 'a man learned in astrology'. Contemporary writers advised on the choice of a 'good constellation' for the laying of the foundations of a building (Burke, 1974: 211). It is highly likely that the building of the Medici Palace would not have been undertaken without some sort of verification of support from the planetary influences. The tiles in the study of Piero de Medici with the images of the months indicate the constant presence and context of the astrological.

For each planet it was possible to make an appropriate talisman, an image engraved on a precious stone under a good constellation. Mars, for example was susceptible to an image of a young man with a girl (Burke, 1974: 212). These talismans might enable some control over the all-important planetary influences and would therefore be regarded as valuable and necessary. Gombrich points out that part of Piero de Medici's pleasure in looking at his jewels was in the discussion of their powers (Gombrich, 1985a: 51). It is likely that Piero was in fact trying to exercise some control over the planets through his 'collections'.

The parts of the universe were related to each other symbolically rather than causally, through the play of resemblances and the system of 'correspondences' (Burke, 1974: 209; Foucault, 1970: 17; Dijksterhuis, 1961: 280). The relationship of 'microcosm' to 'macrocosm' established links between 'man' and the 'universe'. Thus Filarete wrote that a man's right eye corresponded to the sun, his left eye to the moon, his ears to Jupiter and Mars, his nostrils to Mercury and Venus, and his mouth to Saturn. Numerology was taken as one basis for analogy: if two sets contained the same number of units, a correspondence was discovered. There were twelve apostles and twelve signs of the zodiac, therefore an apostle was linked to each sign. It was thus 'convenient' to discover that there were twelve Roman emperors, and that correspondences could be sought.

Astrology was allowed by the church and it was not considered incompatible with Christianity, although it might be argued that theology and astrology formed two systems that did compete in practice. The saints presided over certain days, but so too did the planets. Which of these should be attended to? Some attempts were made to combine the two; thus it was said that the angels dwelt in the signs of the zodiac and moved the planets (Burke, 1974: 212). Different contradictory concepts of the world existed alongside each other, and discussions concerning the differing articulations of the relationships occupied both scholars and laymen for much of their time.

The relationship between the church and magical practices was more problematic. In relation to some forms, the clergy were the most powerful practitioners; they were the custodians of objects of great magical power, the relics of holy events, and in addition they were trained in exorcism. The church was closely linked to other magical objects, such as the Lamb of God (usually a wax image, that protected its owner from shipwreck, storms, and the dangers of childbirth) or the images of the Virgin, which had magical powers (Burke, 1974: 218). However, in relation to practices that could be characterised as black magic, the church could vary in its response from the suspicious and disapproving to viciously prohibitive.

Foucault points out that although the ancient hermetic notion of the microcosm (Dijksterhuis, 1961: 106, 280) was revived at the beginning of the Renaissance by 'a certain neo-Platonic tradition' (presumably the early humanists), by the sixteenth century it played a more fundamental role. Firstly, as a category of thought, it applied the idea of duplicated resemblances to all realms of nature, thus ensuring that every material investigation would find a stronger echo; and secondly, as a general configuration of nature, it imposed real limits to the endless search for resemblances (Foucault, 1970: 31). We should expect to find at the beginning of the period, the 1440s, that the role of the microcosm/macrocosm correspondence is weaker than at the later period.

During the fifteenth century the moralised animate universe, combined with the doctrine of signatures, entailed articulations of the inter-relationship of human subjects, animals, artefacts, and words that are very difficult indeed to understand today. In addition, in the move away from the Renaissance *episteme* at the beginning of the seventeenth century, many of these articulations were felt to be fanciful, irrational, and untrue, and in the shift towards a more 'scientific' epistemic configuration, they were written out. 'Similitude is no longer the form of knowledge but the occasion of error' (Foucault, 1970: 51). Similitude as a form of knowing appears equally erroneous, not to say ridiculous, to the modern *episteme*, and thus histories of this period cannot accept the evidence as 'sensible'.

One of the most useful aspects of the Renaissance *episteme* is that Foucault takes magic and the supernatural seriously. The neutrality of his approach, stemming from the basic questioning of the 'positive uncon-scious' of knowledge (Foucault, 1970: xi) enables him to 'accept magic and erudition on the same level' (ibid.: 32). Where other writers on the Renaissance stress the move away from superstition and tend to either ignore or play down these elements, Foucault provides a description of them. The prime role in the structure of knowledge during the Renaissance given to interpretation, organised through the system of correspondences, made divination a major part of epistemology. The fundamental con-figuration of knowledge consisted of the reciprocal cross-reference of signs and similitudes, and the form of magic was inherent in this way of knowing. The world was covered in signs that had to be deciphered, and those signs, however strange they may have appeared to be, were in fact no more than various forms of similitude, linked to that which was known by resemblances and affinities (Foucault, 1970: 32). However strange a thing might be, and wherever on the face of the earth it might actually have come from, it would have a relationship with things that were known, if this could only be discovered. Foucault quotes from Paracelsus, *Archidoxis magica*:

But we men discover all that is hidden in the mountains by signs and outward correspondences; and it is thus that we find out all the properties of herbs and all that is in stones . . . There is nothing in the depths of the seas, nothing in the heights of the firmament that man is not capable of discovering. There is no mountain so vast that it can hide from the gaze of man what is in it; it is revealed to him by corresponding signs.

(Foucault, 1970: 32)

This emphasis on knowing as discovering and interpreting, and on the power of the gaze of man to decipher even the most distant of things from the bottom of the sea, the heights of the sky, or the depths of the earth, places both magic and erudition on the same epistemological plane. Divination is a crucial part of knowing. Herbs and stones and other things, both made by man and made by nature, were there to be read and to be drawn into a vast cosmology, where each one, through the interpretation of its secrets according to the marks that it bore upon its face, would find its pre-appointed place.

Although Paracelsus was writing later than the 1440s, many of his ideas are developments of ideas that are in fact much older. There is no doubt that these 'supernatural' interpretations are very dense and have their own spatio-temporal significance (Dijksterhuis, 1961: 280). Paracelsus develops his own mode of analysis that has its particular specificity (Bernal, 1969: 301). The structures of understanding in relation to magic and the occult that are used are very complex, and often so strange to us now that it is difficult to grasp their complexities or the efficacy of their use. However, an acceptance that aspects of the supernatural provided a rational explanation of the world during the Renaissance will offer a new way of understanding the Medici Palace as a space where subjects, spaces, material things, activities, and knowledge were formed in a complex inter-relationship.

It will become clear that a reading of things in this way leads to new ways to review and to order the evidence. New series will be enabled. Earlier readings of the contemporary documents are shown as constructed to exclude, either intentionally or unintentionally, any discussion of the explanatory power of the supernatural.

An example will draw this out. Any translation of early Renaissance documents is bound to require a selection of terms. This selection will be influenced by the attitudes and ideas of the knowing subject (the translator). If the supernatural is regarded as irrational and nonsensical, this will lead to a particular rendering of specific words which may well totally conceal the possibility of the explanatory potential of a belief in the supernatural. A comparison of two versions of the same document, the text of Antonio Filarete introduced earlier, makes this clear. The second translation includes the word 'powers' in relation to the gems, while the first excludes it.

> Another day he looks at his jewels and precious stones. He has a marvellous quantity of them of great value cut in different ways. He takes pleasure and delight in looking at them and in talking about the virtue and value of those he has.
>
> (Alsop, 1982: 375)

> The next day he would look at his jewels and precious stones, of which he has a marvellous quantity of great value, some engraved in various ways, some not. He takes great pleasure and delight in looking at those and in discussing their various powers and excellencies.
>
> (Gombrich, 1985a: 51)

The idea of a discussion of the 'powers' of the stones leads us to consider the stones in the light of the supernatural, the universe understood as animate, the prevailing cosmology, all of which may imbue specific stones with particular 'powers'.

The importance during the fifteenth century of the explanatory power of the supernatural linked to the belief in correspondences can be gauged by the following comments which record the events that preceded the break-up of the Medici Palace in 1494:

> In Apulia, at night, there were three suns in the middle of the sky but cloudy all about them and with horrible thunder and lightning; in the territory of Arezzo, for many days infinite numbers of armed men on great horses passed through the air, with a terrible noise of trumpets and drums; in many places in Italy holy images and statues sweated openly; many monstrous men and other animals were born everywhere.
>
> (Burke, 1974: 210)

The perceptual field

It has been persuasively argued that an aesthetic sense existed during the medieval period even though a fully developed aesthetic theory did not (Eco, 1986). There are two aspects of this that have relevance to the discussion of the Medici Palace. These are a quantitative and a qualitative aesthetics.

The quantitative aesthetics was an aesthetics of proportion, which began with the musical theories of late antiquity and the early Middle Ages. Later it was extended to literature and the plastic arts, and was aligned with mysticism, where the number of parts relating to a whole would have, for example, a religious significance (ibid.: 39).

The qualitative aesthetics was an aesthetics of light, which was related to the experience of colour, and was manifested in the lively sensuous appreciation of gems, flowers, and materials, and, for example, in the emergence of the 'art' of stained glass. Philosophers and mystics made constant reference to luminosity and the light of the sun. The image of God as light had descended from the Baal of Semitic paganism, from the Egyptian Ra, and from the Persian Mazda to the Platonic 'Sun' of the Ideal (Eco, 1986: 47). Rainbows and mirrors were regarded as wonders because of their properties of light and the symbolic power of luminosity. Many different words were employed in the discussion of light: *lux* was light 'in itself', the origin of motion, which penetrates to the bowels of the earth to form its minerals and sow the seeds of its life, *lumen* was the light that travels through space; *colour* or *splendour* was reflected light (ibid.: 50).

In the thirteenth century, greater attention was paid to the concrete reality of things and ideas began to emerge concerning the subject–object relation and the 'beautiful'. 'We call a thing visually beautiful when of its own accord it gives pleasure to spectators and delight to the vision' (ibid.: 67). The highest pleasure is when a luminous object encounters the luminous nature within the human subject. This pleasure is partly based on proportion and in particular the adaption of mind and world to each other. An aesthetics began to emerge based on the visual perception of material things.

Two types of visual perception were distinguished: 'a grasp of visible forms ... through intuition alone ... and perception 'through intuition together with preceding knowledge [where] an act of reason ... compares the different forms perceived with one another', which are complemented by memory, imagination, and reason to form a complex but swift synthesis (ibid.: 69).

Two principles of relativity were introduced. The first suggested that visual properties possess a quality of suitability (*convenientia*) which is not the same everywhere. 'Each person makes his own estimate of beauty according to his own custom.' The second was that the subjective side of sense experience is an accurate measure of how to evaluate and enjoy the object aesthetically. Some things should be viewed from a distance; others, such as miniatures, should be looked at very closely to discern the detail, the hidden intentions, the decorum of the line, and the beautiful ordering of parts. Distance, nearness, and in addition axis of vision were all essential features in aesthetic experience (Eco, 1986: 69). It is likely that these ideas of proportion, luminosity, and relativity were still considered as part of the pleasure of aesthetic experience in the 1440s and that the way of looking itself was considered in as much detail.

'Art' as a distinct body of experiences and particular classifications of material things did not exist at this time. The 'visual arts' had no place in any epistemological system and no collective identity. The ancients had understood 'art' as something that was 'teachable' (Kristeller, 1951: 498) and in Europe, 'art' had had the meaning of 'skill' since the thirteenth century (Williams, 1976: 23). The grouping of the 'fine arts' that we know now did not come into existence until the eighteenth century (Kristeller, 1951: 497).

A scheme of seven mechanical arts, corresponding to the seven liberal arts was formulated in the Middle Ages. These were: *lanificium, armatura, navigatio, agricultura, venatio, medicina, theatrica*. Architecture and various branches of sculpture and painting are listed, along with several other crafts, as subdivisions of *armatura*, thus occupying a low position even among the mechanical arts. Music appears in relation to mathematics, while poetry is linked to grammar, logic, and rhetoric, within the liberal arts. Thus painting and sculpture are placed very lowly indeed in the hierarchies of disciplines during the Middle Ages. Even though there are many different schemes that group the disciplines variously during this and earlier periods, in relation to the practices of painting and sculpture, the general pattern is persistent and continues to influence later thought (Kristeller, 1951: 508).

In the fifteenth century the grouping of disciplines (including grammar, rhetoric, arithmetic, geometry, astronomy, and music) that came within the liberal arts was seen, in terms of practices, as appropriate to and indicative of a higher social status. The mechanical arts, on the other hand, were related to a low social status (Williams, 1976: 148). During the later Middle Ages, poetry and music were among the subjects taught in schools and universities, while the teaching of the visual arts was confined to the artisans' guilds, in which painters were sometimes associated with the druggists who mixed their paints, the sculptors with the goldsmiths, and the architects with the masons and carpenters.

Although the concept of 'art' did not develop until the late Renaissance, from the late fourteenth century until the end of the sixteenth century, painting and the other visual arts steadily grew in importance. The patronage of the Medici and the place given to painting in the Palazzo

Medici contributed to a new way of seeing the visual arts and a new status for the artist. At the end of the fourteenth century it is documented that Michelangelo's family resented his taking up sculpture as a career as it was one of the mechanical arts, but were persuaded by the support of Medici patronage. The patronage of Lorenzo de Medici and the close association of artists and the wealthy contributed to this rise in status (Burke, 1974: 90).

During the fifteenth century, technological innovations enabled a more precise response to both time and space. The old way of measuring time was to divide the day according to what was happening in it. Short amounts of time were counted in 'Aves', that is the amount of time it took to say a 'Hail Mary'. In the later fourteenth century, mechanical clocks came into use and the division of time into hours and minutes became possible. There are records of various public buildings having clocks installed throughout the fifteenth century, and towards the end of the century portable clocks were made (Burke, 1974: 235). Lorenzo de Medici's 'clockwork in gilded copper' (Wackernagel, 1981: 156) must have been one of the first of these.

The idea that time was like money and should be 'spent' carefully and prudently is linked both to this change in technology and to contemporary mercantile attitudes. Time was 'precious', as coins and jewels were. There is an emphasis in the contemporary documents on the careful spending of money and the pleasures of doing this in relation to the earning and accumulation of money (Burke, 1974: 243).

Just as the control of time became more precise, so the control of space, through more precise measurement, became possible at this time. At the beginning of the Renaissance, measurement was still vague: the large bed in Lorenzo's room is five and a half 'braccia'. The 'braccio', or arm's length, tended to vary between 22 and 26 inches (Burke, 1974: 237). The development of perspective in the painting of the later fifteenth and early sixteenth centuries is one indication of a more calculating approach to the measurement of space, which is then combined with an aesthetics of proportion.

The gaze of the fourteenth- and fifteenth-century Florentine was one that was skilled in visual measurement and the exact estimation of quantity, weight, and scale. When commodities came in non-standard containers, this was an essential business skill (Baxandall, 1972: 86). This discriminatory skill extended to looking at paintings. The exercising of the skill of the visual estimation of quantity was an essential part of looking at a painting. Piero della Francesco produced both a practical mathematical handbook for merchants, as well as paintings that depend on a sophisticated mathematical vernacular that is foreign to the modern world (ibid.: 87).

The viewer of a painting in the fifteenth century would exerise skill in relation to the mathematics inherent in the perspectival composition, and also to the monetary value of the materials used, and the skill of the painter displayed. A very precise calculation would be possible in relation to these factors relating to value. It was taught that the cultivated beholder of paintings would be able to make these exact discriminations, and sometimes, to make them verbally (Baxandall, 1972: 34). In addition, looking, as we have seen, was constituted as a detailed and specific skill. Thus the viewing subject was calculating, interpreting, estimating, and verbalising. Each material thing was looked at in a way appropriate to its form. It is without doubt that this skill of active, interpretive, evaluative looking was also appropriate in relation to other material things, and also to the human subject.

The gaze of the viewer assessed a painting and a courtier with the same calculating and measuring look. Castiglione's *Courtier* (published in 1528) stresses the necessity to act with style, and compares the courtier to the painter, who knows how to control his work. The self is discussed as a carefully crafted work of art. The same emphasis can be detected in the advice that Lorenzo de Medici gave to his lady: 'Whether you are walking, standing or sitting, try always to do it with style' (Burke, 1974: 230). A precise, rational, and evaluative gaze that was exercised in relation to people, things, and practices was characteristic of the period.

The epistemic elements in articulation

In the fifteenth century, the groupings of disciplines that were in operation were very different from those we know in modern times. This is particularly the case in relation to art. The merchants, scholars, and the aristocracy would be familiar with the liberal arts. With technological innovation, a more precise view of the world became a possibility. This precision extended to the gaze, which was calculating, prudent, and evaluative. It is likely that the aesthetic sense and the understanding of aesthetic experience that emerged during the Middle Ages would still be a strong factor in the understanding and appreciation of the concrete domain. Thus proportion, luminosity, and relativity would be important factors.

The emphasis on a contemporary, secular life, which was to spread later to other parts of northern Italy, can be observed early in Florence. An emerging capitalist economy produced new forms of wealth which were expressed through conspicuous consumption, a consumption carried out 'with style'. An extension of trade led to the appearance of new commodities on the market which fed this new desire, although the extensive journeys of discovery that would bring many new and strange things to Europe from Africa and the Americas had not yet begun.

The increasingly secular, enquiry-oriented way of knowing entailed the rejection of the immediate past, which was seen as limited and irrelevant, and prioritised the search for a grander classical past that celebrated the power of the present through the undoubted success of the ancients. Classical artefacts of all kinds started to become objects of desire, and were collected, and reinterpreted, in the spaces of the newly wealthy.

The world was conceived as articulated through correspondences, identified through *analogy*, *aemulatio*, and the play of *sympathies*. Animals and artefacts were animate as opposed to inanimate and were therefore likely to be thought of in human terms. The universe was both hierarchised and moralised, but contradictory pictures of its constitution existed as different interpretations and correspondences were evoked. 'To know about things was to bring to light the system of resemblances that made them close to and dependent upon one another' (Foucault, 1970: 41). The hidden relationships could be endlessly rewritten, and therefore 'This knowlege will be a thing of sand' (Foucault, 1970: 30). But underneath the endless interpretation runs the promise of the eventual revelation of the 'primal Text', the 'original Text' (ibid.: 41). Knowing meant deciphering the secrets of the universe that would bring the knower closer to God.

Divination and magical practices formed an integral part of the structure of knowledge in the middle of the fifteenth century. Belief in the magical powers of certain images ran alongside their precise assessment in terms of style. Equally, the interpretation of the meaning of the images on the carved jewels, for example, might relate either to perceived correspondences between the past and the present, or the natural and the supernatural.

Burke suggests that, in a long perspective, it is possible to distinguish traditional from modern views within the period, although he stresses that within the period itself, the articulations of these views might well be contradictory. The idea of God's direct intervention in the universe, of correspondences, of the animate universe, of the moralised universe, are all characterised as 'traditional'. The ideas of the universe as subject to natural law, of causes, of the mechanical universe, of the objective universe, these are modern (Burke, 1974: 245).

The target of Foucault's methods (Foucault, 1977c; 1981a), in privileging a detailed and neutral analysis of a specific regime of practices, produces more emphasis than 'normal' histories on the supernatural and magical practices. 'Normal' histories of this period tend to emphasise the newer elements at the expense of the old, celebrating the move towards a modern form of 'truth'. It is clear, however, that the newer elements found an articulation in the context of the old, and that therefore a separation is not possible.

Once it is accepted that material practices within the epistemic context of the mid-fifteenth century will be constituted through both old and new elements, it becomes relevant to ask what the effect of this articulation might be. These old and new elements are in articulation at precisely the moment which signals the beginning of modern times, as distinct from medieval times (Heidegger, 1951: 10). Heidegger suggests that the concept of the 'world view' is a phenomenon of modern times. The objective concept of the world as picture, constituted as a view, entails the transformation of man into the centre to which such a view relates. Man as 'subject' is not possible before the transformation of the existent into a 'world picture' (Heidegger, 1951: 9). At this period, in the mid-fifteenth century, the world is not yet pictured as an object. The human individual is still, to a large extent, enmeshed in older processes, in understandings of the world that position man as fixed in a hierarchical position between the angels and the plants, and as at the mercy of magical and supernatural powers that are not controllable by man.

At this stage of the early Renaissance, the idea that the world may be at once represented, and thereby controlled, by man, has not yet emerged. Later, at the end of the sixteenth century, it will be seen that efforts are made to collect and assemble the world, to represent the entirety of nature, to picture the world through the arrangement of material things, both natural and artefactual. Foucault describes just such an encyclopedic project, the desire to represent all the languages of the world in a vast space where the texts are ordered in such a way that, in their visual arrangement, they reflect the order of knowing as both library and encyclopedia at once (Foucault, 1970: 39). At the same time, as we will see later in the discussion of the 'cabinet of the world', many similar projects existed that were not limited to the representation of language, but which sought to represent the world view of the 'collector', as collector-prince, collector-scholar, collector-teacher, and so on. 'Museums' were to become central to the task of the representation of the world as a view. The collection and display of material things that represented in themselves many different and complex combinations and articulations would later enable the individual subject to draw up the world before his constitutive gaze. But in the mid-fifteenth century, the constitution of an encyclopedic world view was *not* the aim of 'collectors'. The Medici Palace did not attempt to present a world picture through its collections and its spaces. However, it did seek to develop subject positions that would enable the Medici to become, and to be seen to become, more powerful, more knowledgeable, and more wealthy than their fellow citizens.

This chapter has concentrated on the identification of some general factors that were constitutive of knowledge and knowing in the middle of fifteenth-century Italy. These general epistemic elements formed part of the context within which the Medici Palace was formed. These elements include: beliefs in the real effects of the correspondences, the animate nature of the universe, the powers of the supernatural, a tension between the long, slow movements of the past and the quickening sense of the present, the construction of a new past drawn from the ancient world, and the new calculating and evaluative gaze of mercantilism. It is accepted that there may be other elements at the epistemic level that are also important and that the context of rationality constructed here may well not be complete. However, it is judged that enough of the context has been constructed to be of use in a rereading of the Medici Palace.

The palace of the prince 3

The Medici Palace combined in a new way earlier practices, including the treasure gathering of the medieval princes, and the newer practices of collecting classical things (for example, sculpture, manuscripts, fragments of buildings, and coins) which emerged as scholarly interest turned very slowly to the past of ancient Greece and Rome. These two elements combined within a shift in the practices of patronage from the older, public, religious forms where buildings or works were commissioned, often by groups of patrons, to glorify God, to a newer form that was private, singular, secular, and dedicated to the glory of man, specifically the patron. Although the two forms ran together in fifteenth-century Florence for some time, the emergence of the newer practices constituted subject positions that positioned families like the Medici in new relations of advantage/disadvantage, as more wealthy, more powerful, more knowledgeable than their fellow merchants. By establishing themselves in this higher social position, they established themselves, within a hierarchised universe, as more worthy than their former peers, thereby legitimising their unconstitutional rule.

Shifts in the practices of collecting and of patronage articulated with new attitudes to the past, and with older understandings of the nature of the universe as the creation of a supernatural being. Material things were made meaningful within this complex discourse of multifaceted and often contradictory factors.

Meanings articulated were in constant movement. Changes in the field of possibilities, which included political changes, changes in the operation and management of the Medici banks, wars, shifts in trading patterns, deaths, movements of finances, as well as cultural changes, led to a constant oscillation of meaning and practices within the Medici Palace. Considerable changes of all sorts can be identified during the fifty-year period under discussion.

Our discussion of the Medici Palace covers the period 1450–1500, that is the time of three generations of the Medici family: Cosimo (1389–1464), his son Piero (1419–69), and his grandson Lorenzo ('The Magnificent') (1448–92). Changes in the nature of the Medici Palace can be observed in the three generations of the Medici, from Cosimo 'Pater Patriae' to Lorenzo 'El Magnifico'. It is possible to identify the specific articulations that characterise and enable a move in subject position from merchant (Cosimo) to prince in all but name (Lorenzo).

The specific articulation of practices that clustered around the spaces, objects, and subjects collectively referred to as the Medici Palace can legitimately be seen as an abrupt break with previous practices. The Medici Palace embodied practices and activities that were distinctive at the time and which later, because of both the decisiveness of the break with earlier practices, and the strength and effectiveness of the Medici Palace itself, came to be seen as a model for the future.

Treasure hoards and banks: the old and the new

Two distinct modes of operation can be seen in the Medici Palace in relation to the generation and maintenance of wealth. The older practices of hoarding treasure, which already have their own specific histories, are adapted as part of the identity of the Medici Palace, while the newer practices of banking, in large part emerge here as specific activities for the first time.

During the Middle Ages the marks of sovereign power were 'realm, people and treasure' (Wittlin, 1949: 16). Wealth was measured by weight of precious metal. 'Treasure hoards' were a feature of both secular and religious princely sites. The treasure chambers held items made out of gold or silver, jewels and gems of many sorts, coins and medals: a rich source of tales of wonder and amazement (ibid.: 18). Both the material things and the legends that accrued to them constituted a technology for the maintenance of power relations.

Precious metals represented value that could be negotiated inter-nationally; they were durable, divisible without loss of value, and portable. 'Treasures' were artefacts made out of these precious materials that could be melted down, broken up, or sold in times of war or other expense-creating crises. In addition to being expendable, the treasure hoards were also often portable and would be carried with their owners as they went from one to another of their residences.

Before the standardisation of prices, the measure of wealth depended on

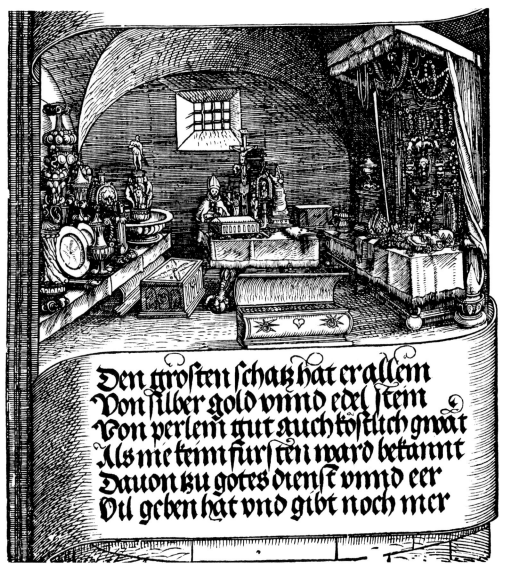

Den grösten schatz hat er allem
Von silber gold vnnd edel stein
Von perlein gut auch köstlich gwat
Als nie keim fürsten ward bekannt
Dauon zu gottes dienst vnnd eer
Vil geben hat vnd gibt noch mer

6 School of Albrecht Dürer, *Maximilian's Treasure*, woodcut, 1512–15. The Habsburg Emperor Maximilian's treasure hoard, probably kept securely in a fortress, represented a reserve of liquid assets, and in this respect, performed some of the functions of a bank. Although the objects would have been used from time to time, display was not one of the main tasks of this collection.

the material reality of the thing itself. Metal could only, later, act as a sign for wealth because it was itself wealth.

> It [metal] possessed the power to signify because it was itself a real mark. And just as the marks of living beings were inscribed upon their bodies in the manner of visible and positive marks, similarly, the signs that indicated wealth and measured it were bound to carry the real mark in themseves. In order to represent prices, they themselves had to be precious. They had to be rare, useful, desirable.
>
> (Foucault, 1970: 169)

'Treasures' were valued first and foremost for the intrinsic value of their raw materials, which were precious metals and minerals. The plate, vessels, chalices, crowns, and weapons that these raw materials were made up into represented a useful form in which to keep bullion. These items were therefore temporary manifestations, holding forms only, for the valuable metals and jewels that might be sold or re-formed when necessary. Many of these temporary forms were, in fact, melted down soon after they had been produced. The works of Benvenuto Cellini, for example, can only be gauged by the descriptions he (Cellini) and others give of them, as only one piece remains, the 'Salt' that he made for the French King François I (Alsop, 1982: 56). There are many other examples from the medieval period up to the time of the French Revolution of the realisation of the intrinsic value of these 'treasures'. In 1458, the tiara of Pope Eugenius IV, made by Ghiberti, was melted down by Pope Calixtus III to pay for the war against the Turks. The gold and jewels were valued at 38,000 florins (ibid.: 53). At the same time, the richly bound volumes in the Vatican library were stripped of their gold and silver (ibid.: 55). Most of the medieval treasures of the French royal abbey of St Denis were melted down during the French Revolution to finance the wars of Napoleon. One object which would have been used for Mass, the Eagle of Abbot Suger, a silver gilt vessel formed round an antique vase of porphyry, with the later addition of an eagle's head, neck, wings, tail, legs, and feet, has survived, and is now regarded as one of the most important objects (treasures) of the Louvre.

Gold and silver artefacts were generally classified and kept with the stores of coin and bullion. Plate and vessels might be used on the table or the altar or might act as display items on a temporary basis, but when not in use would be stored in the vaults with the other liquid assets (Alsop, 1982: 54). These practices from the early Middle Ages continued well into the Renaissance and in some cases into the early eighteenth century (Wittlin, 1949: fig. 1; Alsop, 1982: 55).

These temporary holding forms were temporary in a further sense. They might be redeemable for their material value, but equally they could be re-formed, made up again in a more modern style, or a style more in keeping with the requirements of the current owner. The original functions of objects might be changed in this process. Gems might often be set as rings as Ghiberti describes in his *Commentarii* (Alsop, 1982: 355).

The Medici were, of course, bankers. The banker often started, as was probable in their case, as a trader. Purchasing goods in one town and selling them in another, where a different sort of money prevailed, soon led to the transfer of credit rather than coin. Gradually, branch banking emerged. The Medici had branches in Venice, Rome, Milan, Bruges, and London. Princes of state and church became their debtors. The Medici added silk and wool workshops in their home town of Florence to their enterprises in banking and trading. When deposits of alum, necessary to fix dies, were found near Rome, the Medici entered into an agreement with the papacy to exploit them. Thus a complex of banking, trading, and manufacturing was built up that was to provide a fabulous fortune (Bronowski and Mazlish, 1970: 43).

The Medici were very wealthy in 1450; and during the years up to Cosimo's death their wealth augmented. After this period, through bad management, failure to reinvest, and excessively high household expenses as the family rose to princely status, their fortune began to fail (de Roover, 1948: 60). The Medici bank, in the later years of the century, contributed little to economic growth and its funds, instead of being invested productively, were mainly used to finance either the conspicuous consumption of royal courts or military campaigns. The general financial crisis in the 1470s and 1480s that caused other more prudent bankers to withdraw from banking found the Medici bank unable to react in a constructive way. The catastrophic collapse of the Medici bank coincided with the general collapse of Florentine banking (de Roover, 1963: 374).

The management of the Medici bank and their other enterprises was crucial in building up the fortunes of the family (de Roover, 1948: 6). In contrast to contemporary Florentine companies, the Medici banking house comprised not one, but a combination of companies. A separate partnership was formed for each of the Medici enterprises. According to a statement prepared for the Florentine property tax in 1458, Cosimo de Medici was a partner in eleven different enterprises, including cloth-manufacturing ventures in his home town, and branches of the bank at home and abroad. Clearly, delegation and control were essential to the structure of these businesses. Cosimo had evolved complex technologies that involved the managers of the branch banks and other businesses as partners with a share in the profits, and with considerable, but controlled, personal decision-making capacities. Bearing in mind the distances involved and the slowness of communications, the managers of the branches were crucial in the network that the Medici had established, and Cosimo maintained a strong directing role. His successors, Piero and Lorenzo, relaxed their grip on the branch managers, who were thereby allowed much more leeway than previously, with ultimately disastrous results for the prosperity of the Medici house (de Roover, 1948: 9).

At the beginning of the period under review, the practices of accumulation in the Medici Palace were modelled on medieval treasure gathering, with desires focused on anything made from precious metals, and on coins, medals, and carved gems. Some of these artefacts were from 'the ancient world', and later, as the practices of the activation of the past of Greece and Rome began to emerge, collecting practices themselves were modified and the percentage and range of collected classical items grew.

Very large quantities of antique gems, carved precious stones, and coins and medals were accumulated at the site of the Medici Palace from the early years of the century to the collapse in 1494. The old economic function of bullion was still in operation, and at times, particularly in the later years of the century, these liquid assets were realised. The contents of Cosimo's collection can be partly gauged by two inventories taken of the possessions of Piero Il Gottoso, one in 1456 and one in 1465 after the death of his father, Cosimo (Alsop, 1982: 360). The later inventory reflects the acquisition of at least part of Cosimo's collection. Gold medals (classical coins and medals) increased from 53 to 100, silver medals increased from 300 to 503, and antique carved gems and hard-stone vessels were also proportionately augmented.

The newer practices of mercantile banking articulated with the older practices of treasure gathering. In fact, the accumulation of bullion (the collecting of precious things) underpinned the newer, less certain practices, and these older practices were reverted to in times of stress and rupture.

Information as to the financial values that were placed on some of the items of 'treasure' can be gained from the very detailed inventory of the Palazzo Medici that was made after the death of Lorenzo in 1492, which lists all the interior contents (including the furniture, the paintings, the bedding, oils, and spices) and gives estimations of their worth (Alsop, 1982: 395–409). The most valuable items were the antique jewels, and the carved Greek and Roman gems. The larger gold and silver mounted vessels of 'hard stones' range in value from 500 to 2,000 florins apiece; the 'Seal of Nero', which had been mounted by Ghiberti as a ring, was valued at 1,000 florins.

A point of comparison is that 8,000 florins was the entire working capital of the Medici branch bank in Venice at the same period, and that 3,700 florins comprised the dowry of a bride from the Medici family, and this was regarded as lavish (Alsop, 1982: 382). Interestingly, a richly mounted unicorn horn was valued at 6,000 florins and was, therefore, one of the most valuable pieces in the entire list. Unicorn horns were attributed with the power to sweat in the presence of poison, and the great emphasis placed on the magical powers of some material things is revealed in this inventory.

Gems as representative of wealth are part of a long tradition and this acts as one of the older elements in this particular discursive formation. As ruptures in the family fortunes occurred, the collection of gems was used as raw capital (Alsop, 1982: 400). However, although this facet of the use of precious materials is important, other ways of seeing the carved and figured gems, some of them old and some new, were also in operation. Within the Medici Palace, the same material entity, a carved jewel, was understood in a number of different ways: firstly and traditionally, as 'wealth'; later as the classical discourse was taken up and represented, the carvings on the precious stone took on a new importance and the jewel was read as 'testimony'; at the same time, the magical and cosmological meanings of the material were of supreme importance. Thus gems were meaningful through the articulation of several factors, including wealth, testimony, and magical potency.

Shifts in the practices of patronage

In the middle of the fifteenth century in Florence, patronage and collecting began to combine. Previously, patronage had been closely linked to religious practices and had not been related to the collection of material things in the home. Occasionally, family heirlooms were kept in the family vaults in the church. The idea of the home as a spectacle of splendour, wealth, and position did not emerge until patronage turned from a public social duty to a private glorification. Private patronage articulated with subject positions to create new relations of advantage. During the fifteenth century, the display of wealth became one of the technologies of power, and ostentatious luxury one of the measures of social and economic success (Bronowski and Mazlish, 1970: 42). The opportunity to commission decorative and expensive artefacts led to the birth of notions concerned with 'taste' and 'discrimination', which entailed new subject positions and new relations of advantage/disadvantage. Later, during the sixteenth century, this was to combine with the acquisition of rare artefacts from the voyages of discovery. Later, too, the destruction and dismantling of the great palaces as political fortunes were won and lost led to the emergence of a market for the furnishings, decorations, and luxury items that, detached from their original contexts, could confer glory, worth, and prestige on new owners, partly because of their past uses, and partly because of the financial capital invested in them.

The practices of patronage are considerably transformed in the contextual shift from the religious to the secular world. In addition, patronage as a practice of the Medici Palace changes in the fifty years under consideration. These further modifications include changes in subject position combined with shifts in relations of advantage/disadvantage, and, articulated with other constitutive factors such as banking or the perception of the 'arts', new relational sequences, new targets, and new fields of possibility emerge.

Patronage was one of the chief instruments of Medici policy during the fifteenth century when they had no legal title of authority (Gombrich, 1985a: 35). The dispersal of subject positions within the practices of patronage changes from an articulation of public/religious/collective/guild to one of private/secular/individual/family. In addition the target of patronage shifts, from external to internal spaces. The Medici exemplify the shift in emphasis after the 1450s from activities external to the family as donors and public patrons, to an increasing concern with the most artistically splendid and costliest possible furnishing of private spaces, accessible only to the owners and their guests (Wackernagel, 1981: 248).

When the Medici first took up their role as patrons, their practices still fitted into the old patterns of communal, religious, guild-based activities. Patronage at this time was understood to be a public, group activity, and was intended to glorify God. In the early years of the fifteenth century, earlier generations of the Medici were involved in communal schemes such as enlarging or decorating churches (Gombrich, 1985a: 36). The differentiation between private and public life was less clear-cut then than it was later to become. These were spaces where public and private life mingled and interpenetrated as a matter of course (Wackernagel, 1981: 243).

During the period 1434–71, the Medici family paid 663,755 gold florins for charities, public buildings, and taxes (Bronowski and Mazlish, 1970: 43). As a banker, Cosimo had to atone for the sin of usury (Gombrich, 1985a: 37), and he therefore spent vast sums on public patronage. The profits of the Medici bank were abundant at this time and Cosimo was able to withdraw very large sums to display his munificence. He gave funds, for example, to erect the Church of San Lorenzo, to complete the

7   The *Tazza Farnese* was one of the most prestigious objects in the collection of Lorenzo de Medici. This sardonyx cup, one of the largest known cameos, had belonged to Pope Paul II, and was bought by Lorenzo in Rome in 1471. It probably came from the ruins of the Villa Adriana, Tivoli, and, dating back to the Hellenistic period, must have been made in Alexandria for the Ptolemies. The story represented is an allegory of the Nile with Isis and Horus. This object could be understood in a number of different ways.

Dominican Friary of San Marco, to enlarge the Badia of Fiesole, and to renovate the Church of the Holy Spirit in Jerusalem. In addition, it was Cosimo who started the collection of manuscripts that later came to be known as the Biblioteca Laurenziana (de Roover, 1963: 371). This public benefaction was represented in a new way in relation to the Medici Palace. In the memoirs of his patron written by Vespasiano, the writer represents the building of the *palazzo* as part of Cosimo's efforts to spend money for the good of the city, as the monies which he expended remained within the economy of the city (Gombrich, 1985a: 39).

Private patronage emerged partly from a shift in the field of possibilities. A hazardous and dangerous way of life in medieval Florence meant that family groups tended to cluster together in a quarter of the city of their own, which then had the character of a fortress. The fortress influence on the houses of rich men continued for over four decades into the fifteenth century, even though several major *palazzi* were constructed during these years.

The Palazzo Uzzano, for example, was constructed fairly early in the century but still had a plain and fortress-like exterior. An inventory was taken of the internal contents in 1425 which reveals a space of a functional bleakness, with limited possessions. The movable objects included a painted terracotta Madonna in a chest, four paintings of the Madonna, and two more of saints, which are described by Alsop as routine devotional works, in other words, aids to meditation (Alsop, 1982: 363). The house may have had frescoes, but these, not being movable, would not have appeared in the inventory. Many of the richer families at this time owned plate which was convenient for storing capital and making temporary display on grand occasions (Alsop, 1982: 362). In the main, however, houses were considered as defensive rather than expository spaces and artists were not yet commissioned to decorate them. A comparison of the interior contents of the Palazzo Uzzano with those of the Palazzo Medici, only thirty years later, makes the point.

While Cosimo de Medici was alive, he dealt almost exclusively with the commissioning of architecture, which was understood as a 'royal art', leaving his sons Piero and Giovanni to negotiate with painters and decorators, whose skills were less valued (Gombrich, 1985a: 46). Later during the century, the status of the artists/craftsmen were to become more highly valued as the desire for more luxurious surroundings emerged. Piero and his generation had come into contact through their business enterprises with the noblemen in France and Burgundy, and their aristocratic style of life. Where Cosimo had been concerned with public and religious buildings, with the Palazzo Medici as one of his later ventures, Piero was more interested in decorative work that would embellish the palace and accentuate the family status. The articulations of the practices, networks, and experiences of banking with the practices of patronage partly enabled the shift in the orientation of patronage through the provision of new targets and models.

By the time of the collapse of the Medici Palace, a further shift in the practices of patronage had been effected. Lorenzo was established as a private and a public arbiter of taste, to whom matters were referred by the city when judgements were required (Gombrich, 1985a: 54). Patronage and its practices had created a new subject position with new relations of advantage/disadvantage, and a new field of action, that of the connoisseur.

It has already been suggested that the shift from public to private patronage enabled the Medici to establish new subject positions and new relations of equivalence between subjects. One of the principal means of establishing these subject positions was through the manipulation of the gaze. It was suggested in the previous chapter that the character of the gaze in Florence at this time was particularly acute, and that the employment of a rational, calculating gaze was a prerequisite of social, economic, and religious life. In the operation of private patronage, and the commissioning of ever more grand, complex, and often narrative things which were imbued with many levels of meaning, the Medici directed the gaze of their fellow citizens by providing them with a target for their expertise. Visitors to the Medici Palace would, willy-nilly, have to partake of the activity of observing, reviewing, interpreting, assessing, evaluating the skill of the artist, estimating the expense of the patron, deciphering the meaning of the messages. In doing so, visitors occupied perforce a specific subject position whose possibilities and limitations had been constructed in advance.

The reactivation of the past of Greece and Rome

Towards the end of the fourteenth century, a shift in attitudes to the past emerged. Collections began to be formed, which were partly open to visitors. An account of a visit to Florence in 1432 describes this:

> Meanwhile, after Ciriaco had accompanied Carlo Aretine to see his outstanding library along with ancient coins and images, together with a remarkable gem of nicolo, carved by the famous Pyrgoteles with a figure of a Lupercalian priest, and a bronze statue of ankle-winged Mercury, they also saw many very valuable fine things of the same sort belonging to Cosimo de Medici, that richest of men. And at the houses of Donatello and Necio (Ghiberti), famous sculptors, he

saw many ancient statues, and new ones produced by them from bronze and marble.

(Alsop, 1982: 354)

The items made from precious materials and with symbolic significance are listed alongside both 'ancient statues' and 'new ones'. Interestingly, in the context of perceptions of 'museums', little separation seems to be made here between old and new: we shall return to this later. The object of attention at the present time must be the 'ancient statues'.

A further document is relevant, the letter of 1375 of Giovanni Dondi dall'Orlogio to his friend Fra Guglielmo da Cremona concerning a trip that he made to Rome during that year:

Though few of the products of ancient genius survive, yet those that are in existence here and there are avidly sought for and gazed at by those who have perception in these matters, and great prices are paid for them: and if you compare the products of today you cannot escape the conclusion that those who made them were naturally endowed with a more powerful talent and were more skilled in mastery of the art. I am speaking of ancient buildings and statues and sculptures together with other things of this kind: when contemporary artists carefully examine certain of these ancient works of art they are overwhelmed with amazement.

(Alsop, 1982: 308)

Dondi was a physician and had, presumably to support him in his work, a collection of medical books and a rare text of Vitruvius. He also owned 'a few minor treasures' (Alsop, 1982: 308). According to his friend Petrarch, he was a man of many interests, with enough talent 'to have reached the stars' if only 'medicine had not held him down'.

In another letter, Dondi refers to Rome's monuments as 'the testimonies of great men'. He sees the buildings, their fragments, inscriptions, sarcophagi, statues, and other sculptures as texts from the past, when the earth had the vigour of youth and was therefore a better place. He writes in the conviction that the decay of the ancient world is explained by the decay of nature's power, and the darkness of the Dark Ages in Europe is attributable to the failure of nature's vigour during the twilight of the classical world (Alsop, 1982: 338). The reactivation of the themes and monuments of the ancients will confer some of this vigour and energy to contemporary Italy.

The interpretation of the monuments as books to be read is an early manifestation of that characteristic of the Renaissance *episteme* that

8   Terracotta bust of *Lorenzo de Medici* by Andrea del Verrocchio (*c.* 1485?). Lorenzo was trained in the liberal arts, and spent much of his time on matters of taste, style, and patronage.

privileges writing as a basic structure and procedure of knowing. Foucault proposes that knowledge during the Renaissance consisted of making everything speak, of relating the different surfaces of language to each other (Foucault, 1970: 40). He does not point out that this concern for the interpretation of material texts that he places in the late sixteenth century could be identified two centuries before.

The beginnings of a revival of interest in classical learning gradually led to new way of seeing classical things. A gaze informed by the idea that classical artefacts were the product of a superior epoch, and that a correct interpretation of the material manifestation of that superiority could be related to contemporary notions of worth, would exercise a different perception from a gaze that was rooted in the thoughts and experience of the immediate contemporary epistemological context. Before the Renaissance, classical sculptures were feared as idolatrous and were thought to possess magical powers. Occasionally, in building, a sculpture would be found in the ground and it would be either reburied or broken. Sometimes it was thought that the ground itself had generated the sculpture, as it was known that the ground could produce all kinds of things, including frogs and the bones of giants.

A much-quoted incident in mid-fourteenth century Sienna illustrates the confused beginnings of the new way of seeing. Lorenzo Ghiberti tells the story of the discovery of a statue of Venus during the digging of a house foundation. The sculpture was initially celebrated as an example of marvellous artistic skill, the product of the ancient world, and it was erected with much ceremony in the town square, acting as a material testimony to the great antecedents of the town. Later, the city entered a period of reversal and this was attributed to the presence of the statue, as the ill-luck appeared to follow its erection in the square. The statue was taken down, smashed, and its rubble buried across the Florentine border where it might inflict its evil magical powers on the Florentines, the traditional rivals of the Siennese (Alsop, 1982: 304).

A more mundane and practical attitude to sculptures can also be detected that indicates the way in which they were seen before the Renaissance. Statues were sometimes used for worship or for decoration either at home or in the churches and chapels. If a second-hand sculpture were purchased, the buyer would expect to pay less for it because it was old and used (Alsop, 1982: 310). A great change in the gaze would be necessary before people would expect to pay more because the items were old. Nearly a hundred years passed after the incident with the statue in Sienna before one of the first Florentine collectors wrote from Greece in 1431 to complain of the Greeks using the name of Praxiteles rather too freely to inflate the price of statues (Alsop, 1982: 351).

By the closing decades of the fourteenth century, Florence was the centre of Italian intellectual life, part of which was constituted through the search for evidence of the classical past. This meant retrieving the material texts of the past, including codices, statues, coins, medals, fragments of buildings, and inscriptions from tombs or buildings. Collections of such materials were built up by the small circle of humanist scholars and by artists. Scholars compiled and interpreted the material, copying out the texts. Artists studied the carved stones in order to inform their own work. A collecting network was rapidly established, built on the existing trading and diplomatic networks. Political and merchandising expeditions were used to track down and appropriate classical material. The practices of mercantilism enmeshed with and fostered new cultural practices.

Cosimo de Medici was connected with these early collectors and collecting processes. Niccolo Niccoli was a close friend, and they travelled together to Rome in 1428. Poggio Bracciolini, the papal secretary, had served as his guide to the Roman antiquities on at least one occasion. Both Niccoli and Poggio had collections, Niccoli a fairly diverse one, and Poggio a collection of classical sculpture.

At the funeral of Niccoli, Poggio Bracciolini described some of Niccoli's possessions and pointed out how unusual it was to have things like this at that time:

> he took much delight in pictures and statues and various collections of objects fashioned in the manner of men of old. For almost alone, he had a great number of these things, and more choice ones, than practically anyone else ... [In his house] could be seen statues and pictures, likenesses of men of old, and coins dating back to that earlier age when bronze first began to be struck and coined money first began to be stamped.
>
> (Alsop, 1982: 328)

Niccoli himself was a 'noble sight', like encountering 'a figure from the ancient world' (Alsop, 1982: 325).

It is likely that Cosimo provided the means for both Niccoli and Bracciolini to acquire material, either by funding the collecting journeys, or by lending the collectors the use of his overseas agents. He also used these men as his advisers. Both of their collections were probably acquired by Cosimo on their deaths. Cosimo had effectively used Niccoli and Bracciolini as agents in the accumulation of objects of taste.

Politics, mercantilism, and the specific practices of collecting combine as aspects of the identity of the Medici Palace. The emergence of the practices of collecting entailed new uses for material things, new uses of spaces, and new subject positions. Many different things were reinterpreted, and their form and meanings were reinscribed for use in a different field of use. The codices appropriated from the northern monasteries, for example, were retrieved, re-collated, transcribed, translated, and rep-resented. Niccoli copied the classical texts and in the difficult and lengthy work changed from a crabbed medieval script to a modified version of Carolingian minuscule, thereby contributing to the fine script used in the Renaissance and to the present italic form of the modern alphabet (Alsop, 1982: 328). The images of the ancient world were reused to transform and represent contemporary rulers. A medal, now in the National Gallery of Art in Washington, presents Cosimo de Medici with his features rearranged in a deliberate approximation to the type of a Roman emperor (Gombrich, 1985a: 49).

The power of 'artists' is interesting to note in the establishment of these practices. Artists are recorded as working closely with wealthy collectors in many different instances; as agents in establishing the collections, and in directing and carrying out repairing and remaking processes, as well as in the production of their own work to commission. These different activities can be identified and exemplified in Donatello, who carried out his own commissions, including the bronze *David* sculpted for Cosimo de Medici which was placed in the courtyard of the palace. Donatello was also called in to repair Cosimo's classical pieces when he began to add this type of material. In addition, by 1432, Donatello already had a small collection of classical sculpture of his own, and his judgement on classical works was valued.

New uses of domestic spaces emerged. There is evidence to show that the houses of the collectors were open to scholars, travellers, and others who were interested in studying the collections. For example, by the end of his life Niccoli owned over 800 codices, in many of which works by various authors were bound together. This may have been the largest 'library' in Europe at the time. The house was open to students, who were able to read in the library each day, after which topics were proposed for collective discussion. This reactivation of themes from the classical discourse must have been an important factor in the modification of the gaze that enabled, among other instances, the commission for the doors of the Baptistery *all'antica* (Alsop, 1982: 315). There is also evidence of artists studying in Niccoli's house. Ghiberti says that among his other antiques, Niccoli had a chalcedony that was 'more perfect' than anything he had ever examined (ibid.: 329). The techniques, themes, and use of materials that artists observed in their study of classical artefacts were later incorporated into their own productions.

9 Terracotta bust of *Niccolo Niccoli da Uzzano* by Donatello, based on an antique bust of Cicero (between 1460 and 1480). It is fitting that he should be portrayed as a 'figure from the ancient world'.

In this reactivation of objects and texts, the form of the material statement is changed through repetition and reinscription. As the codices were collected together, transcribed, written into a more modern script, and presented in combination with related ancient texts, so a newly stabilised classical discourse was assembled. The statements, in their materiality, were recirculated, placed into new networks, and integrated into a new field of use (Foucault, 1974: 105). Gems, coins, medals, statues, and vessels were also translated and transcribed into a new discursive field. During the Middle Ages, for example, the bindings of manuscripts had incorporated precious stones. Now the stones were removed (Van Holst, 1967: 63) and instead of being part of a collective unity, they became independent units. Ancient 'hard-stone' vases had additions made to them with precious metals; classical gems were reset as rings (Alsop, 1982: 355).

There are earlier isolated examples of gems being used for the semiological power of their images rather than the financial power of their raw materials. During the twelfth century it is likely that the Emperor Frederick II of Hohenstaufen, for example, had a substantial collection of antique carved gems which he supplied to his gem carving workshop for his sculptors to copy. The classical male nudes are used to underline his claim to revive the Roman Empire (Alsop, 1982: 302). Petrarch collected antique coins and medals and in 1354 gave a part or all of his collection to the Emperor Charles IV, urging this sovereign to study and follow the example of his ancient predecessors. The depictions of famous men on the coins acted as a history lesson on the lost grandeur of the pagan Roman Empire (Alsop, 1982: 307; Wittlin, 1949: 45).

By the middle of the fifteenth century the practice of reading classical coins, medals, and gems as 'history' becomes more common. Portraits in themselves become one of the elements of a historical discourse, which will be emphasised more strongly during the sixteenth century, when collections of painted portraits, many of them copied from medals, were assembled for the historical lessons that they taught.

During the fifteenth century the propagandist use of classical images emerged strongly for the first time. The designs for the marble roundels in the courtyard of the Medici Palace were drawn from antique cameos that Cosimo had in his collection (Wackernagel, 1981: 102, 236). The images on the roundels consisted of enlarged classical scenes from the jewels, which were represented along with the arms of the Medici. In addition, a series of busts of Roman emperors decorated the rear façade of the *palazzo*. All these references to classical times underlined the links between the Medici and their adopted illustrious forebears.

This emphasis on the study and use of material things for the sake of the lessons that could be read from them, and the discourses that could be constructed out of them, is in marked contrast to the princely treasure hoards, which had a primarily mono-dimensional function, that of being wealthy through the weight of their raw materials. These hoards were private and secret, and represented one aspect of the sovereign power of the prince. The collections of the humanist scholars Niccolo Niccoli and Poggio Bracciolini enabled new relations of advantage through the construction, control, and dissemination of knowledge. This new modality of power required on the one hand that the collections should be openly available for study, and on the other created the subject positions of expert/owner and student/visitor.

By the second decade of the fifteenth century, the collecting of classical things had ceased to be merely the eccentric pastime of isolated scholars and artists and had begun to be practised by the families of the rich merchants and the princes. In the competition for classical things, prices rose and Niccoli and other more modest collectors were priced out of the market (Alsop, 1982: 333). Collecting emerged an an activity that was appropriate for those with wealth, although in the early years of the century collecting was not as important an activity as patronage. Later, in the second half of the fifteenth century, collecting as a distinct activity can be identified more strongly.

However, a difference in collecting practices can be identified, according to the subject position of the 'collector'. In the activities characteristic of the 'collector-scholar', study and the pursuit of knowledge were likely to be strongly articulated, with status represented by this strength. In the collecting activities characteristic of the 'collector-prince', the element of power and advantage represented through sheer material wealth was likely to be articulated more strongly. The poorer scholars, who had largely initiated the practices of collecting, were reduced to the status of agents and advisers once the princes and richer merchants adopted the idea. In the case of Cosimo, his own unlimited means and the far-ranging connections of his business firm enabled him, first as a pupil, then as a competitor, and later as chief purchaser of their estates, to far outstrip the older Florentine humanists and collectors (Wackernagel, 1981: 236). The 'best' collector would always be the subject with the best resources in terms of wealth and communication networks.

Magical moments

Wealth, patronage, and the use of the past have been identified as important factors in the constitution of the Medici Palace. One final aspect remains to be drawn out, and it is likely to prove the most difficult. On the one hand, most accounts of the Renaissance play down the supernatural elements that occur; in addition, the twentieth-century mind finds credulity difficult when dealing with 'superstition'. Much of what follows could therefore be dismissed as speculation, but nonetheless it has emerged that magic and occult cosmology played a dominant role in the general epistemic configuration and therefore it is likely to act as a dominant element within any specific context of knowing.

It has already been pointed out that the universe was regarded as animate and that this extended to material things, where, for example, 'a building ... wants to be nourished and looked after, and through lack of this it sickens and dies like a man' (Burke, 1974: 208). Although it is difficult to know in what sense to fully understand a comment such as this, it is reasonable to suppose that the artefacts would also require nourishing in order to maintain their potency. This 'nourishing' appears to have the function of cherishing and producing meaning from rare material statements (Foucault, 1974: 120): a carved jewel in the Medici Palace would have been given a status in the institution, its meaning would have been repeated and reiterated, and it would have attained the status of a statement in many different contexts.

Antonio Filarete's account of Piero in his studio includes a comment on how he would look at his jewels and precious stones and how he 'took delight ... in discussing their various powers and excellencies' (Gombrich, 1985a: 51). Many of these powers would undoubtedly have been magical. Jewels engraved with a specific image under a specific constellation had a power in relation to the planets concerned and might act as a talisman (Burke, 1974: 212). The importance of the influence of the planets is demonstrated by the ceramic tiles in the studio. Is it significant that Filarete suggests that Piero's re-looking at his collection 'would again give him pleasure since a whole month had now passed since he saw them last, (Gombrich, 1985a: 51)? Is Piero rereading the meaning of his jewels within a new astrological context?

Jewels and precious stones had been attributed with magical properties for a long time. Diamonds, for example, had the power to avert bad dreams and were called the gem of reconciliation because they mitigated wrath and discord (Thorndike, 1941: 315). Some particularly brilliant gems were believed to render the wearer invisible (ibid.: 320).

Piero possessed images made of many different materials which included gold, silver, bronze, marble, precious stones, and other materials. These 'images' of 'all the Emperors and Worthies of the past' must have included sculptured busts, coins, medals, jewels, relief sculptures, all classified together as 'images'. The detailed listing of the materials employed suggests that the catalogue of material has some significance, and it may be possible to surmise an attempt to represent all the important material elements that formed the hierarchised material structure of the world. Alchemy, which was part of the early Renaissance world picture, held that there was a hierarchy of metals, with gold as the noblest, and that a transformation of metals was possible (Burke, 1974: 216; Taylor, 1945: 53). The contemporary cosmological picture of the world worked partly through just such a catalogue of materials.

In addition, the gathering together of images of those who had been powerful and important in the past may have been in order to permit the transference of some of that power to the subject in the present.

Some of the material things that Piero had collected together in his studio may well have been thought of as *mirabilia*, their marvellous qualities taken as given, largely on the basis that they could not be accounted for within the existing explanations of the existent (Burke, 1969: 2). Some of the figures and images on the carved stones no doubt reiterated old 'myths' or told stories about 'giants' or 'Saracens'. The fact that the world was interpreted in terms of allegory and symbol, and that this could be endlessly reinterpreted through reversibility and shifts in emphasis (Foucault, 1970: 22) meant that each thing could be ordered and reordered as different classifications or different contexts of meaning or plays of sympathies were employed. Interpretation and divination must have gone hand in hand in Piero's 'looking' at the 'worthy or strange objects' that he possessed. In his nourishing of his precious material things, Piero gathered them together and presented them to himself and his intimates as a unified totality (Foucault, 1974: 120). This unity was relational, and was relative. Different articulated unities might be constructed according to the subjectivity of the subject. 'Each person makes his own estimate of beauty according to his own custom' (Eco, 1986a: 69).

Filarete mentions 'pleasure' several times in his account of Piero's activities: he takes 'great pleasure'; he wants 'for his pleasure'; his images 'give the greatest enjoyment and pleasure to the eye'; 'he takes great pleasure and delight'. Pleasure seems to have been an important aspect of ideas about beauty and goodness in the Middle Ages. The measure of beauty was in many ways related to the pleasure that was generated: 'we call a thing visually beautiful when of its own accord it gives pleasure to spectators and delight to the vision' (Eco, 1986a: 67). Part of the pursuit of pleasure lay in determining the correct distance, nearness, and axis of vision appropriate to each thing (ibid.: 69). The pursuit of pleasure was justified by the idea that the pleasures of sound, sight, smell, and touch, brought the human subject face to face with the beauty of the world, so that he could see in it the reflection of God (ibid.: 58).

An appreciation of a material thing was not limited to the concrete form that could be perceived, but led to a greater, more mystical, imaginative, and fundamentally religious experience. Suger, Abbot of St Denis during the twelfth century, describes the path from material appreciation to mystical and magical communion with God:

> Thus, when – out of my delight in the beauty of the house of God – the loveliness of the many coloured gems has called me away from external cares, and worthy meditation has induced me to reflect, transferring that which is material to that which is immaterial, on the diversity of the sacred virtues: then it seems to me that I see myself dwelling, as it were, in some strange region of the universe which exists neither in the slime of the earth nor entirely in the purity of Heaven; and that, by the grace of God, I can be transported from this inferior to that higher world in an anagogical manner.
>
> (Eco, 1986a: 14)

Suger is regarded as an early prototypical collector by many (Eco, 1986a: 13) and he may have provided a programmatic model on which later secular as opposed to religious princes may have based their own practices, reanimating mystical and religious themes for a newly secular and personalised discourse. During the fifteenth century it is likely that the contemplation of material things would lead to contemplation, initially on religious themes, but increasingly, on secular themes. The reactivation of the themes of imperial Rome is one example of this. Medieval practices of contemplation and mysticism were remodelled for a more active and more present-day oriented society (Burke, 1974: 241).

Other artefacts owned by the Medici may well have had magical significances that we can only guess at now. Certain paintings of Christ, of the saints, and especially of Our Lady were believed to have magical powers and to protect the owner from shipwrecks and other disasters (Burke, 1974: 218). The 'camera terrena di Lorenzo' contained several religious paintings, including some images of the saints (Wackernagel, 1981: 165). Were these paintings thought to have magical powers and to protect the Medici from evil? Piero's unicorn horn, the most highly valued item among his possessions (Alsop, 1982: 404), whose value nearly equalled an entire branch bank's annual working capital, must have been prized almost entirely because of the belief that it would sweat in the presence of poison (Thorndike, 1941: 232). The ostrich egg and the mirror-glass in Lorenzo's room may also have been credited with magical powers. Certainly mirrors were prized for the symbolic powers of their luminosity. The images, or even the materials, of the tapestries and the paintings possibly had some magical significance. Animals were viewed symbolically (E. P. Evans, 1987: 55), and may have had magical connotations. Colours and materials had their own special significance.

The Medici Palace: articulations and rearticulations

The identity of the Medici Palace is formed through the articulation of different aspects, including private domestic space, material things, wealth, patronage, mercantilism, a sense of the past, and the supernatural. Each of these elements has been discussed as part of a general epistemic field which included both old and new practices. Older practices included the amassing of bullion and medieval cosmology; newer practices included a new view of the past, mercantilism, and a new way of co-opting the gaze.

This new gaze both generated and followed new ways of being, which included the Medici seen as 'merchant-princes' (with reference back to medieval treasure-gatherers and at the time to social and intellectual leaders); and also as 'patron/connoisseurs' (through the shift from public/collective/guild to private/individual/family). Artists and agents occupied new spaces and positions in a newly emerging 'art-market'; and a new subject role appeared, that of the visitor/viewer/gazer, co-opted to appreciate and, through appreciation, to generate and to maintain the whole complex edifice. The Medici Palace could not have functioned without spectators. The expository objective acted both to reveal and to articulate other objectives. In what sense could this complex articulation be understood as 'the first museum'?

The Medici Palace consists of spaces, subjects, and things. The spaces have been deliberately constructed with a view to creating an imposing impression, and to demonstrating networks of advantage. At the same time, given the early Renaissance tendency to think in terms of allegory and symbol, the position of the palace among other Florentine houses sets a model for the understanding of the position of the Medici as a dynasty among the other powerful families of the city state. An identification of architectural space with subject position is suggested (Wackernagel, 1981: 255). The architectural space carries messages in stone and other materials that proclaim the power of the dynasty and which refers this back to other, more powerful rulers from the past. Dynastic links are created with the past, which is thereby given a new role to play.

The internal spaces of the building are used to indicate wealth and status through the presence of luxury goods, both collected and commissioned. The ornately decorated surfaces of the rooms carry overt messages through their images and their materials about the time and money spent in their construction and both overtly and covertly about the position of the family. Patronage is used as a means of articulating both internal and external spaces. Where, in the past, patronage was an opportunity to spend money and thereby glorify God, now patronage becomes an opportunity to spend money and to construct, glorify, and present a position for the family.

The articulation of spaces and things includes two categories of material things: one category is of those things which have been specially made for a particular space, a wall-hanging, a wall-painting, a tile, a chair; the other category is of those things which have been acquired from other contexts, and which have been brought into the new spaces, including gems, coins, and statues. The Medici Palace, as a building, contained a great many of the former category and probably rather less of the second. It is difficult to identify the precise proportions in terms of volume of each of the categories, but judging from the existing records it would appear that the walls, ceilings, floors, and fixed furniture were constructed from and covered entirely with specially produced material, intricately worked. This would include tapestries, tiles, sculptures, and paintings, both on the walls themselves as frescoes and incorporated into the decorative carvings as integral parts of the design. All these things were produced by contemporary craftsmen, mainly working in Florence.

In contrast, the things that must have been brought into the house from other contexts, and not specifically produced for the house, may well have been rather scarcer in quantity. These would have included the gems and jewels and carved vessels of precious stone, the classical statues in the house and, more particularly, in the courtyard and garden, and 'curiosities' like the unicorn horn, the copper clockwork, the ostrich egg, and the mirror-glass sphere. The clock probably represents the latest developments in the relevant technology; the egg and the unicorn horn were almost certainly valued for their magical properties; the mirror for its power of light.

In the discussion of the inventories of the Medici possessions, it was clear that the jewels, the carved vessels, and the 'curiosities' were valued, at least in financial terms, far more highly than the commissioned contents of the house. It is likely that the symbolic valuation followed this pattern. The 'decorative' items were probably regarded as household furniture, and although they were produced by the best craftsmen, and carried specific messages of wealth and position, they were almost certainly seen as part of a general scheme of decoration, rather than as individually selected and chosen 'objects'. The paintings by Masaccio, Uccello, Pollaiuolo, Fra Angelico, and Benozzo Gozzoli, now regarded as 'priceless treasures', were, in the Medici Palace, wall decorations and part of a unified totality. The unicorn horn, a valueless oddity today, was indeed the unique 'priceless treasure' of the palace. This interpretation of the relative values of the contents of the palace seems to be confirmed by the announcement of the sale of the possessions of the Medici following their expulsion from the city in 1494:

> Put up for sale ... besides the house furnishings ... statues of ancient workmanship, chased metal, gems and various stones distinguished by remarkable carving from the hands of ancient workmen, murrhine vases, coins in gold, bronze and silver of which the likenesses of famous commanders were to be seen – all collected by long and learned study, in years of peace.
>
> (Alsop, 1982: 408)

This inversion of values suggests that other inversions that we can no longer perceive may have existed.

A number of subject positions can be identified in the Medici Palace: they include those of the prince, who was also the patron and the principal collector, the determiner of policy and the ultimate financial controller; the junior members of the family, who would have an important but lesser controlling role; the artists, craftsmen, and workers who worked directly for the palace and its occupants, who effectively were the patronised in the nexus patron–patronised; the other 'Medici' workers, the bank or business employees who indirectly, but crucially, contributed to the continuation of the palace through their labours, but who were not directly concerned in it themselves, unless occupying another subject position; and the guests and visitors to the palace, such as the members of the other wealthy Florentine families, or other visitors to the city, perhaps scholars or agents from other courts or countries.

This ordering of subject positions was feudal and aristocratic in structure, with the prince at the apex wielding sovereign power, and a series of severely hierarchised levels beneath him. The structure is likely to have been less well established during the earlier period of the Medici Palace, as the main function of the palace was in fact to create such a structure. The space and its articulations were used to position the family and to construct the position merchant/prince/patron. The structure, although based on feudal characteristics, was new in that the 'prince' was not a hereditary ruler, and he therefore had to use persuasive power, symbol, and propaganda to establish his position of superiority. This was achieved through the emergence of new articulations of the old practices of treasure-gathering and patronage, combined with a new use of the past, largely effected through the collection and reuse of material things.

The dispersed hierarchised subject positions all entailed a subjectivity to the Medici, and a tacit acceptance of their dominating role. Although many of these positions would have been familiar (those of the junior members of the family, and those of the family retainers), a great number of them would have been new. These new subject positions would have included those of the artists, now working for a single private patron on mainly secular and private tasks, rather than for a group of patrons on public religious tasks. The status of the artist shifted with this close association with the wealthy. This was also affected by their use as cultural agents and as advisers, and 'curators' in the newly emerging practices of collecting. The tasks of the accumulation of material things, and their subsequent care and restoration, allied to their use as reiterated statements in the creative products of the artist himself, led to the occupation by artists of positions of authority. Later this would lead to the break away from working within the ambience of the patron to working directly in the marketplace.

Further new subject positions can be observed in those occupied by 'visitors' to the palace. One of the main tasks imposed upon the 'guest' or 'visitor' would be to exercise the gaze in appreciation, to observe, to measure, to admire, to evaluate the time and money and expertise expended on the spaces and the things, and by this process to adopt the subjected position: that is, to accede to and concur with the subject positions that were implicit in the space/subject/object articulation. This adoption of the subjected position also, of course, generated the position of the subjector. The hierarchy of rule and power emerges through the delineation and adoption of specific subject positions.

One of the basic functions of 'the first museum of Europe', was the establishment of a position of superiority and exteriority through the display of wealth and status. The concept of expository space, a space specifically designed to display, was born from the necessities of this task. An important element of this new expository space was its private nature. In contrast to the public spaces, such as churches, where patronage and its resulting display had been communal and open and accessible to all, this new form of space was private, and access to it was controlled. Seeing, the skill of the exercise of the gaze, which had previously been a freedom that anyone could enjoy, instead now became a privilege, meted out by the prince, the owner of the palace. Where the painted and sculpted lessons of the churches had been free for all to read, and had offered the knowledge of the scriptures to those who could not read them any other way, an essentially democratic operation, in the Medici Palace the painted and sculpted lessons were only available in so far as the prince decreed, and the lessons taught were those that supported his domination. This was an essentially aristocratic mode of operation. Thus power and knowledge acted together through control to maintain the Medici Palace.

Part of the constitution of 'serious speech acts' that work to produce 'truth' is the establishment of a discursive 'police' (Dreyfus and Rabinow, 1982: 48). The 'speech' of the Medici Palace is constructed through the articulation of spaces, subjects, and meaningful objects. The discursive police in this formation consist of the family themselves and their artists/agents, who acted as their cultural advisers. Lorenzo de Medici was regarded by his contemporaries as a man of discrimination, an 'arbiter of taste', to the extent that he would be called on to make judgements in the artistic matters of the city. His judgements were sought and had the status of 'truth'. An altar panel assigned to Ghirlandaio in 1483 was to be done 'according to the standards, manner and form as will seem good to and please ... Lorenzo' (Gombrich, 1985a: 54). This subject position within the networks of advantage/disadvantage of the city reinforced and was reinforced by the material statements of the palace, and was also sustained by the political and economic powers of the Medici.

Earlier generations of Medici had relied more heavily on their artists to police their productions of 'truth'. At the time of the emergence of the Medici Palace, the judgements of the family were less secure, and Cosimo, for example, relied on the advice of Donatello at the beginning of his collecting practices. Later, it was Donatello who reinscribed the classical images in a new field of use, and who repaired, restored, and completed the material statements themselves. As the Medici Palace matured, the prince himself took on the policing and directing role through the subject position of 'connoisseur', and separations were made in production and consumption.

The Medici Palace found its own momentum, so that the task of maintaining it became more important than the task of generating the conditions for its continued existence. Where Cosimo was trained as a merchant and spent much of his time dealing with banking and business affairs, Lorenzo was trained in the liberal arts and spent much of his time acting as a courtier, and acting much more centrally than his grandfather in reiterating the discursive practices of the Medici Palace. This led in the end to its collapse. No longer supported and empowered by a constant flow of wealth, generated through competent business and banking practices, the elements of the articulation began to disintegrate. The unity of the dispersions were fractured. Death, war, financial and political collapse led to an abrupt end.

The last decades of the fifteenth century witnessed a depression that was both lasting and profound. Demographic conditions related to the declining population in the 150 years from the Black Death to the Discoveries explain a downward economic trend, although they do not explain the trough that occurred in the last years of the century. More local factors affected this deepening depression, such as the war between the Turks and Venice which lasted from 1463 to 1479 and caused a wave of bankruptcies (de Roover, 1963: 373). Monetary instability, problems of transferring funds from northern Europe, a changing balance of power in the countries concerned with the wool trade (England, Holland, and Italy), and poorly trained and supervised branch bank managers, all contributed to the collapse of the Medici bank.

The most immediate cause, however, was the French invasion in 1494 (de Roover, 1963: 370). The Medici at this time were on the brink of bankruptcy; most of the branch banks were closed, and those that remained were unable to operate through funds immobilised by loans, or through crushing debts. The Medici banks had operated with very low cash reserves and with money substitutes. Medieval merchant-bankers tended to rely in a crisis on their private resources or treasure hoards and the Medici had already gone through this process in 1433 and again in 1478 on the occasion of the Pazzi conspiracy when Lorenzo barely escaped with his life and his brother Giuliano was killed (ibid.: 365, 371).

The Medici Palace was abruptly ruptured in 1494 when the Medici were driven out of Florence, and the city was invaded by the French King Charles VIII.

After the Medici were expelled from Florence, all their property was seized by the new regime set up by their opponents (de Roover, 1963: 370). The material things that had formed much of the discourse of the Medici Palace were thrown abruptly into new contexts and used in new ways. The two Donatello statues that had been sited in the outside, semi-public spaces of the palace were transferred to the Palazzo della Signoria, the seat of the highest official bodies, and the now unchallenged authority in the city. The bronze *David* which had been set up in the middle of the courtyard in the Medici Palace, was positioned in a similar situation in the Palazzo Vecchio, on its original, elegantly decorated pedestal. The existing marble harpies accompanied by 'very pleasing tendril ornament in bronze' were now supplemented by four Florentine coats-of-arms as a sign of the statue's new ownership. Donatello's *Judith*, which had been been placed over a fountain basin in the garden of the Medici Palace, was now to be seen as a monument to the overthrow of a tyrant and the reclamation of civic liberty. It was erected, immediately after its seizure, in front of the main portal of the palace, facing the public, and with the

10   Cosimo commissioned this statue of *Judith* from Donatello (*c.* 1456–7). It was originally displayed in a secluded part of the palace, with a Latin couplet, attributed to Piero, which may have been designed to forestall criticisms against Cosimo for the sin of *luxuria* (arrogance and vainglory).

> *Regna cadunt luxu, surgunt virtutibus urbes*
> *Caesa vides humili colla superba manu.*
> (Kingdoms fall through licence: cities rise through virtue.
> See the proud neck struck by a humble hand.)

After the overthrow of the Medici, the statue was redisplayed in front of the palace, labelled with a new inscription:

> *Exemplum salutis publicae civis posuere.*
> (A healthy example to put before the public of the city.)

new inscription 'Exemplum salutis publicae civis posuere' (A healthy example to put before the public of the city) (Wackernagel, 1981: 63).

The period from approximately 1454–94 had been a period of relative peace and prosperity in Italy. In the sixteenth century it was looked back on as a 'golden age' (Burke, 1974: 324). A large part of this 'golden age' was constructed around the myth of the Medici, a myth which was begun by Giorgio Vasari, who represented the early Medici in a series of frescoes, and through his writing, as the creators of the arts and the golden age. Vasari's *Lives*, published in 1550, is dedicated to the ruling Medici Duke, Cosimo I, with the words: 'It can be said that in your state, even in your own most blessed house, the arts have been reborn' (Gombrich, 1985a: 30). This mode of address became established and further series of adulatory frescoes were produced later, during the seventeenth and eighteenth centuries.

Gombrich traces the references to the Medici as creators of a 'golden age' right back to the time of Cosimo *Pater Patriae* himself, and asks why he, a city banker and merchant, was addressed in such lavish terms as 'He cherished the sacred poets, gave us back the golden age of Augustus Caesar' and 'Now to me, now, Medici, under your guardianship, returns the benign golden age of old Saturn' (Gombrich, 1985a: 32). The answer suggested is that the conventional themes that were offered to the powerful at the time were those of the warrior with great deeds in battle, or those of the fame of ancestors. In the case of Cosimo de Medici, neither of these was appropriate. Gombrich suggests that it is the illegitimate ruler who needs the most metaphysical props for his power and propaganda, and in Cosimo's case, with neither glorious ancestors, nor warlike deeds to write about, poets were forced into new and rather extraordinary claims. Vasari, working directly for the later generations of the Medici when they were reinstalled in Florence, had every reason to extol the virtues of the earlier generation. He did his work well (Rinehart, 1981: 275). That this work continued and still continues we have already seen (Taylor, 1948: 69).

The effect of the animation of the theme of the 'golden age' of art was to endow those artefacts produced for the palace, but physically detached from it at the time of the rupture, with specific qualities of desire. At the break-up of the early Medici dynasty, the objects from the house were dispersed and many of them came on the market. This in itself created one of the conditions for the emergence of a specific type of collector. During the sixteenth century the process of commissioning specific things for specific spaces was felt by the newly rich to be too slow and cumbersome. In addition, artists were no longer content to follow the whims of patrons, and began to produce to sell in the marketplace as opposed to working from within the artist/patron relationship. The wealthy began to buy ready-made items for their houses, creating both a market for these artefacts as commodities, and the possibility of the development of collections of paintings, sculptures, and other portable pieces.

However, this was not so in the second half of the fifteenth century. The 'first museum of Europe' was constituted for the sole benefit of the family who owned it. New relations of advantage/disadvantage and new subject positions emerged which succeeded for a long time in maintaining the Medici as rulers of Florence.

4 | *The irrational cabinet*

First, the collecting of a most perfect and general library, wherein whosoever the wit of man hath heretofore committed to books of worth ... may be made contributory to your wisdom. Next, a spacious, wonderful garden, wherein whatsoever plant the sun of divers climate, or the earth out of divers moulds, either wild or by the culture of man brought forth, may be ... set and cherished: this garden to be built about with rooms to stable in all rare beasts and to cage in all rare birds; with two lakes adjoining, the one of fresh water the other of salt, for like variety of fishes. And so you have in small compass a model of the universal nature made private. The third, a goodly huge cabinet, wherein whatsoever the hand of man by exquisite art or engine has made rare in stuff, form or motion; whatsoever singularity, chance, and the shuffle of things hath produced; whatsoever Nature has wrought in things that want life and may be kept; shall be sorted and included. The fourth such a still-house, so furnished with mills, instruments, furnaces, and vessels as may be a palace fit for a philosopher's stone.

Francis Bacon, *Gesta Grayorum* (1594) (quoted in Impey and MacGregor, 1985: 1)

By the end of the sixteenth century, collections and 'museums' had become fairly commonplace in Europe. Although these were often substantially different in practice, all had a single objective, that of producing a 'cabinet', a model of 'universal nature made private'. These 'museums' were organised in a variety of ways but, in each, spaces and individual subjects had the function of bringing together a number of material things and arranging them in such a way as to represent or recall either an entire or a partial world picture. These representational systems, these 'museums', emerged over a period of less than a century across a wide geographical and social field. The nature and identity of each system came about through the relationships and interactions of the various constitutive elements.

This chapter will discuss the general epistemic elements that formed the context for the emergence of these cabinets or 'museums'. In particular, one specific external element, 'the art of memory', will be discussed. We shall see that the representational systems, the 'museums', had a very close relationship to the art of memory.

Museum histories have, until very recently, presented the 'cabinet' as a stereotype. The archetypal 'cabinet of curiosity' is the German *Wunderkammer*, which is understood as a disordered jumble of unconnected objects, many of which were fraudulent in character. It has been pointed out that, in 1685, for example, a wolf was killed, stuffed, clothed, bearded, and masked to resemble a burgomaster whose reincarnation the wolf was supposed to be. This was then placed in a local cabinet of curiosities as a memorial and as visual proof of the existence of werewolves (Evans, 1987: 195).

The material contents, the collections, of the *Wunderkammer* have been correctly identified in some detail for a considerable time, but the rationality that underpinned the relationships of these collections has not been understood. Thus the forms of knowledge shaped by these cabinets has gone unrecognised. The 'museum movement' was 'intensely personal and haphazard in plan' writes one writer of the 'museums' of this period (Alexander, 1979: 9). 'These cabinets were unsystematic and idiosyncratic in composition and were filled to the point of overflowing' (Ames, 1983: 94); and the 'magpiety' of the *Wunderkammer* demonstrates the disorder and confusion of the German prince (Taylor, 1948: 122). 'The strange, the wonderful, the curious, the rare, were more and more welcomed by the credulous with each passing day' (ibid.: 125). The German *Wunderkammer* is seen as the product of a saturnine disordered mind, where superstition and magic combine with 'pre-scientific stirrings' (Van Holst, 1967: 103).

In traditional museum histories, the target of cataloguing the world is acknowledged as one of the functions of the cabinet of curiosities, but this itself is seen as a ludicrous idea. The very presence in the cabinet of items with a magical or transcendental significance leads to the dismissal of the idea of picturing of the world as totally irrational and incomprehensible. Nonetheless, in traditional histories, these cabinets are acknowledged as important and have not been ignored, but sometimes their discussion is treated with a certain degree of contempt.

It is necessary to mention briefly the German *Kunstkammer* (cabinet of curiosities), an expression that conjures up the image of a 'Faustian' universality in collections, something peculiar to that sombrely reflective age, the late sixteenth century. At the time when Shakespeare was writing *Hamlet* , his contemporaries were assembling all kinds of objects in a 'Theatrum Mundi'. Here there were early scientific and pre-scientific stirrings ... The *Kunstkammer* also served as an arsenal of alchemy and housed materials with magical powers ... the teeth of fossilized sharks, used to detect poisons; and the 'unicorn', whose origin from the walrus was still unknown and which was supposed to have the power of transmuting harmful materials. In these surroundings the belief in the magic power of precious stones, which had come down from late antiquity, was still alive. One of the Habsburgs saw in his crystals revelations of the power of the Almighty, even the reflection of Godhead itself.

(Van Holst, 1967: 104)

In the last ten years there have been attempts to re-evaluate the historical documents relating to the cabinets, although the most interesting work has been carried out outside England. Researchers in Italy, Germany, and the United States have been more willing to suspend the mind-set of the twentieth century and to try to question the original documents to dis-cover what they have to reveal (Foucault, 1974: 6). Much of this work remains untranslated and therefore relatively inaccessible in England.

Some such work has been collated in Impey and MacGregor's *The Origin of Museums* (1985). Here, however, although the individual articles retain the enquiry into the identity and difference of each specific localised manifestation, the editors are searching for unifying factors, weak forms of continuity, that appear to establish a 'tradition' (Foucault, 1974: 229). Thus, following the remarks from Bacon that are quoted at the beginning of this chapter, with which they introduce their collection, the authors comment, 'With due allowance for the passage of years, no difficulty will be found in recognizing that, in terms of function, little has changed' (Impey and MacGregor, 1985: 1). The implication is that museums are doing much the same now as they were during the period of the Renais-sance *episteme*. This 'sameness' is characterised as 'keeping and sorting the products of Man and Nature and ... promoting their significance ... in a programme whose aim was nothing less than universality' (ibid.: 1). The absolutely crucial question of what this 'universality' might be now, or might have been during the late Renaissance, is never raised. 'Uni-versality' is not addressed as a concept, still less as a problematic concept which has temporal and spatial variations.

It is quite clear from the existing histories that the cabinets were con-stituted with the aim of representing a picture of the world. There are many references to '*theatrum mundi*' (Van Holst, 1967: 103); 'the

11 *Kunstkammer* by Frans Franken the Younger (panel early seventeenth century). The German *Kunstkammern* have been seen by some twentieth-century museum historians as 'arsenals of alchemy', the scenes of 'scientific and pre-scientific stirrings'. The compilation of objects to present a world-picture was in itself felt to be irrational.

macrocosm, the all-embracing universe' (Taylor, 1948: 125); '*mundus symbolicus*' (Bazin, 1967: 56); and 'universality' (Impey and MacGregor, 1985: 1). This is, however, in all cases, taken as given and is not questioned or explained.

Heidegger points out that when the world is pictured, the world exists as a view (Heidegger, 1951: 10). The existent as a whole is positioned as that with respect to which man orients himself. The existent understood as a view is then only understood as existent in so far as and when it is held at bay as a view by the person who represents and establishes it. This is, in fact, a mark of modern times and was not possible in the Middle Ages, when, in direct contrast to the world view, the world was that which was created by the Creator-God. Being in medieval times meant belonging to a definite level in the order of created things, and thus made to correspond to the cause of creation. But the world was not objectified and brought as a representation before the gaze as something which was susceptible to knowledge and control. In modern times, the character of the world is sought and found in representations, and these representations present the world as something that can properly be known, manipulated, assessed, and improved.

Modern representation, *representatio*, means to bring that which is present before one as something confronting oneself, to relate it to oneself, and to force it back into this relation to oneself as the normative area. *Representatio* entails the assembling of the world and the presentation of it to the assembler, such that the character of the existent is graspable and controllable. Thus man puts himself into the setting of the world picture, the site from which the view of the world must be objectively constituted. In the same process that constructs the world as a view, man is constructed as subject (Heidegger, 1951: 12).

The cabinet, in so far as it had the function of a '*theatrum mundi*', was one of the earliest and most comprehensive attempts in this constitution of the world as a view. The functions of these 'cabinets of the world' were twofold: firstly, to bring objects together within a setting and a discourse where the material things (made meaningful) could act to represent all the different parts of the existent; and secondly, having assembled a representative collection of meaningful objects, to display, or present, this assemblage in such a way that the ordering of the material both represented and demonstrated the knowing of the world. In addition to this, both the collecting together of the material things, and their ordering, positioned the ordering subject within that system of order.

This form of ordering was not 'scientific', however, in that it was not based on mathematical procedures (Heidegger, 1951: 3). In the 'cabinet

12 This credence vessel, from the Emperor's *Kunstkammer* in Prague is made from silver and fossilised sharks' teeth.

of the world', the epistemic ordering is drawn from the Renaissance *episteme*. Systems of correspondences formed the basis for both the collection and the exposition of material things and also for the constitution of the ordering subject as both subject and object.

A major epistemological rupture occurs in the position of man within the world picture. Where, in the earlier period, man is subsumed within the hierarchised cosmology, and the world, the existent, is understood as an expression of the Creator-God, in the later period the subject is struggling to find a way to represent the world as his own creation, part of which struggle represents the emergence of the subject him/herself. Magic, erudition, and the classical past are repositioned at a time when new attention to nature and experimental science is emerging, and when the journeys of discovery are forcing the expansion of the medieval interpretation of the world. Foucault's Renaissance *episteme* is, in fact, positioned at the moment of total expansion of the old medieval cosmological world before its collapse into the flat tables of difference of his classical age. The 'cabinet of the world' emerged from within this general epistemic structure. The world picture that the subject assembled and represented was that informed by the Renaissance *episteme*. Although Heidegger suggests that the attempt to form the world as a view was characteristic of the modern world, the world that was so pictured at the end of the sixteenth and beginning of the seventeenth century was a world that was expanded from medieval epistemic structures and thus was pre-modern.

It is likely that the physical organisation of this material Renaissance world picture was dependent on a contemporary cognitive method, the art of memory. The art of memory was a method used to recall and orally present a picture of the world. It is explicitly referred to by many of the more recent papers on the 'cabinets' of the late sixteenth century that have been collected by Impey and MacGregor (1985) (for example, Bostrom, 1985: 100; Seelig, 1985: 87; Olmi, 1985: 7; Laurencich-Minelli, 1985: 19; Hunt, 1985: 198; and Scheicher, 1985: 32). Most of these are passing references only, although many of them refer to Italian sources that appear to explore the subject further. Kaufmann (1978) discusses the idea in rather more detail, with explicit reference to the idea of *representatio*, and his work will be discussed later.

What is the art of memory and how did it relate to the 'cabinet of the world'? This chapter and the next will suggest that the picture of the world presented by the 'cabinet of the world' was constituted through the articulations of the rules of the Renaissance *episteme*, using techniques that related to the techniques of the art of memory. A specific regime of truth was constituted that has since been characterised as irrational, following both the fading away of the Renaissance *episteme*, and the deliberate denial of some of its aspects.

In the investigation of this idea, certain problems are anticipated. Firstly, the Renaissance *episteme* in the late sixteenth century depended on similitudes which could be endlessly rewritten. It is likely, therefore, that in the search for the similitudes that linked the collections, only the most common and the most obvious, or those that are specifically spelt out, will be visible. Many others will remain invisible.

Secondly, one feature of the art of memory is that it empowers the unique vision of the individual to contruct his/her own memory images. If the material ordering of things in the cabinets are indeed memory images, again, many of their references will now be invisible. Combined with both of these aspects is the further deliberate obfuscation caused by the need to hide 'secret' knowledge.

Thirdly, in the discussion of the Medici Palace it became clear that the interpretation of documents varied according to the specific interest of the interpreter. Foucault suggests that in the period following the Renaissance, there were stringent attempts to separate 'truth' from 'falsehood'. The knowledge of the sixteenth century was seen as disordered and confused (Foucault, 1970: 51). It has been pointed out that the rationality of the sixteenth century is still, in some instances, perceived in exactly this way (Taylor, 1948: 122; Ames, 1983: 94). Much of the evidence for the constitution of the 'cabinet of the world' as a rational structure of knowledge will therefore have been lost, stripped away in the effort to find a form of 'truth' that could be recognised and legitimated.

The first case-study was constituted with a very narrow focus and represented a very limited localisation: the Medici Palace was a single event during the latter part of the fifteenth century in Florence, one assemblage of spaces, subjects, and things. The second case-study is constituted with a broader field of vision and extends into a much larger field of localisation, both geographically and in terms of volume.

The first case-study discussed an articulation of practices that had certain specific features and which was described as the first European museum (Taylor, 1948: 69; Alexander, 1979: 20) The second case-study has been selected partly because the features are different, but partly also because this, too, is often characterised as 'the direct ancestor' of the present-day museum (Cannon-Brookes, 1984: 115; Taylor, 1987: 202).

One important function that developed for the Medici Palace was the creation and maintenance of a network of advantage/disadvantage given the rupture of older forms of enforcement. This remains an important aspect of functionality in the second case-study, but new forms emerge. A greater variety of relations of advantage/disadvantage in the dispersed subject positions can be identified. In addition, new functions emerge. The most important of these is the attempt to 'objectify' knowledge, to use the specific articulated moments to picture the world.

In the first case-study, collecting practices were examined in relation to one family and one site. The process of collecting itself emerged as a new practice, created through the articulations of the various elements that together shaped the Medici Palace. Collecting as an activity barely existed before this, and became radically changed as the Medici Palace itself shifted and changed. By the end of the sixteenth century, collecting practices are beginning to be well established. Differential modes and scales of collecting operate and there is no essential 'collector', but there are many differentially positioned collecting subjects operating in specific and linked networks.

The articulations that were discussed in the analysis of the first case-study effected the shift from defensive to expository space as part of the relations of advantage/disadvantage. The second case-study will demonstrate how other uses of expository space emerged, while at the same time the power of propaganda through display remained.

The first case-study showed how new subject positions came about, one of which was that of the subjected gazer, where to see meant to adopt a particular subject position within a network of powers. The second case-study elaborates on the manipulation of the gaze, either in relation to the position of the viewing subject, or in relation to the question of who is granted access to see what. The relationship between seeing and knowing becomes stronger and more complex as seeing emerges as the strongest and the most judgemental sense (Lowe, 1982: 6).

The 'cabinet' – some meanings outlined

The use of the word 'cabinet' seems to stem mainly from the period under discussion and it has several contradictory meanings.

During the late Renaissance, 'cabinet' referred to the container, generally a cupboard with shelves and drawers, which was used to hold a collection of small things. Amerbach, for example, taking over his father's collection in Basle, in 1562, builds a new space, a 'vaulted chamber', and has new 'cabinets' to his exact specifications made to hold the collections. A large cabinet can be seen in the Historisches Museum at Basle, together with

13 The Dutch merchant Philip Hainhofer supervised the making of this *Kunstschrank* (1625–31) which was bought by Gustavus Adolphus. This very large piece of furniture was a 'cabinet of the world' in miniature, designed to contain objects that represented the animal, vegetable, and mineral kingdoms; the four continents; every period of historical time; tools for every variety of work, and pleasure; and the traditional allegories of the four seasons, the five senses, the virtues, time, and place.

a smaller one which was intended primarily for coins but which incorporates on one side three arcades in which stood three bronze statuettes (Ackermann, 1985: 63). The cabinets were often made to hold specific items and were constructed accordingly. Philip Hainhofer in Uppsala in the early seventeenth century built several *Kunstschränke*, intended to be *Kunstkammern* in miniature (Bostrom, 1985: 92).

In the English context it is suggested that the term was used from the early seventeenth century onwards to refer to 'a closet beyond the principal bedchamber where the owner's collection of curiosities, pictures and other small works of art could be displayed for the delectation of close friends and important guests' (Hill, 1986: 150). By about 1750 the bedchamber had moved to the first floor, but the cabinet remained apart as a small gallery. Plans for châteaux in France at this time show the 'cabinet' as a smallish room contrasting with the 'salon' used for grander occasions.

In documents from this period, the word 'cabinet' may be used to refer both to the cupboards or containers of the collections, including the room spaces, and to the entire collection: thus Ackermann discussing the collection of Amerbach uses the words 'collection' and 'cabinet' interchangeably: 'After the death of Basilius Amerbach, the collection passed to the Iselin family ... the cabinet was in danger of being sold abroad ... the Basle Council decided to buy the cabinet ... in this way originated the first collection to be bought by a city' (Ackermann, 1985: 64).

This loose use of words is common to other writers and it is difficult, therefore, to gauge the size or scope of any collection. The Pomeranian *Kunstschrank*, for example, one of those made by Hainhofer, did not contain collections of natural and man-made artefacts, as did the others which were intended to be miniature complete *Kunstkammern*, but instead held a collection of tools for virtually every human occupation (Bostrom, 1985: 92). Bostrom suggests that this is because this particular 'cabinet' was only meant to form part of the ducal collection at Settin.

Clearly, any evaluation of the aims and intentions of collectors at this time will be difficult if it is not known whether the available evidence is a part or a whole.

'Cabinet' is sometimes used metaphorically. Thus John Evelyn, discussing his visit to Rome, refers to the city as 'the Worlds sole Cabinet' (Hunt, 1985: 195).' Cabinet' was not the only term used to describe collections, and in some cases it is not used at all. In Italy during the sixteenth century the main terms used are '*studio*', '*studiolo*', '*guardaroba*', '*museo*' (Laurencich-Minelli, 1985: 23), and slightly later, '*galleria*'. In the Schloss

Ambras the different rooms were called *Kunstkammer*, *Turkenkammer*, *Antiquarium*, *Heldenrust-kammer* (Scheicher, 1985: 29, 30), names which indicate the contents of the rooms. Thus *Schatzkammer* (treasury), is commonly found (Distelberger, 1985: 40) as is *Anatomie-kammer* (Menzhausen, 1985). When discussing the collections that relate most to 'museums', the discussion generally centres around the *Kunstkammer* (Neverov, 1985; Fucikova, 1985; Menzhausen, 1985; Distelberger, 1985). Quiccheberg, in 1565, refers to the *Kunstkammer* at Munich as *theatrum*, or *theatrum sapientiae* (Seelig, 1985: 76). Other expression are used for other spaces. Borromeo constructed a *nymphaeum*, for example: a monumental fountain with eighteen rooms, where he displayed his collections (Aimi *et al.*, 1985: 25).

The word 'museum' is very rarely used during this period, and when it is, it is used in Latin, loosely meaning a specific place where the muses may be studied. Often this is a room to read in. In the sixth edition of Edward Phillips's *New World of Words: Or, Universal English Dictionary* (1706) 'museum' is defined as a 'Study or Library; also a College, of Publick Place for the Resort of Learned Men' (Hunter, 1985: 168).

General epistemic elements

Foucault's Renaissance *episteme* was considered in relation to the first case-study, where it was found that elements of the medieval *episteme* still had a strong directing role in the constitution of knowledge. The oral-chirographic culture of the Middle Ages ordered by the epistemic rules of anagogy meant that the signs that made up the world were interpreted with reference to the existence of the Creator-God. Transcendent being created and sustained immanent becoming. Knowing was in relation to God and the supernatural. Life was led under the aegis of powerful forces from a hierarchised universe. Space and time were more heterogeneous than they would become later. Reality was more intense and fluid, less exact and discriminating (Lowe, 1982: 12), although within this an evaluative and calculating gaze was emerging. The general character of the age consisted of a mixture drawn from the older medieval elements and the newer Renaissance elements (Burke, 1974: 245).

The second case-study is chronologically placed at exactly the moment on which Foucault focuses, the last decade of the sixteenth century and the first three decades of the seventeenth century. Foucault's analysis of the Renaissance *episteme* revealed a world that was more centripetal, and more immanently preoccupied than the Middle Ages. Renaissance similitude created a converging, centripetal world of order where the macrocosm resembles the microcosm, and man occupies a privileged point in the universe (Foucault, 1970: 22). Magic and erudition are accepted by the sixteenth century as being on the same level, as knowledge was constituted by the meticulous accumulations of confirmations of the interpretations of visible signatures (Foucault, 1970: 32). Marks, words, and signs formed (for those who could read it), one vast single text, which Foucault describes as a 'treasure-hoard of the second degree', one that refers to the notations of nature which, in their turn, obscurely denote the pure gold of the things themselves (Foucault, 1970: 34). Knowledge consisted in relating one form of language to another form of language: in making everything speak.

The 'cabinet of the world' was a form of language, with a complex relationship to the other languages of the world. The encyclopedic project that Foucault identifies in the last few years of the sixteenth century tried to spatialise material knowledge according to cosmological structures, to reconstitute the order of the universe by the way in which words and texts were linked together and arranged in space (Foucault, 1970: 38). In a similar way, the 'cabinet of the world' ordered its material images and similitudes to reveal the order of the world.

The observation of the natural phenomena of the world which had begun in the Middle Ages (Bronowski and Mazlish, 1970: 135) took a more energetic and empirically based form as the enquiry into the workings of the universe emerged. Journeys of discovery enlarged mental horizons. At the same time, the cosmology of the late Renaissance revived and occultised medieval magical knowledge. The world was divided into the macrocosm (that which represented God, whose products were understood as Nature) and the microcosm man, whose products were now understood as art. The world of art and the world of nature were in constant oscillation, either in competition or in partnership. In one sense, frequently used by the occult philosophers among others, art was the 'Ape of Nature', and it is represented thus in cosmological maps (Godwyn, 1979: 76, 88). The division of art and nature, representing the microcosm and the macrocosm, is found in the new categories *artificialia* and *naturalia*.

The mutual interrelationship of things that were placed in either of these categories mirrored or referred to the interrelationships of God and man, the macrocosm and the microcosm. In this, an elaborate system of correpondences was constructed, and this system was frequently deliberately obscure, often to protect 'secret' knowlege from profane eyes (Bernheimer, 1956: 228). The object of occult striving to penetrate beyond the world of appearances was not only to describe the forces of nature, but also to control them (Evans, 1973: 197). Although this was a magical pursuit, and it was constantly placed by its exponents within 'natural' rather than 'black' magic, this was dangerous knowledge which often brought its followers into conflict with the established church.

The ancient art of memory

Many of the researchers working within the history of the 'museum' at this period refer to the use of the art of memory although these references remain undeveloped. The art of memory was a mnemotechnic skill used to train and extend the memory. As such it acted as a tool for knowing. Originally emerging during classical times as an oratorial aid, the rules for the practice of this art were still known in the medieval monasteries. These old mechanical directions for memorising important texts as an aid to both devotion and oration were transformed during the fifteenth and sixteenth centuries into vast abstract theoretical edifices that tried to explain all the variable and mutable structures of the world.

During classical times, the art of memory consisted of a technique of rhetoric, with the aid of which an orator could deliver long speeches without failure of memory. The mnemonic of places and images (*loci* and *imagines*) formed the basic structure. A *locus* is a place easily grasped by the memory, a house, an intercolumnar space, an arch. Images (*imagines*) are forms, marks, simulacra of that which is to be memorised.

The art of memory is described as being like inner writing. Those who know the alphabet can write down what is dictated to them and read it out. Those who have learnt mnemonics can set in places what they have heard and later deliver it again from memory. 'For the places are very much like wax tablets or papyrus, the images like the letters, the arrangement and disposition of the images like the script, and the delivery is like the reading' (*Ad Herennium*, quoted in Yates, 1966: 6).

The basic task was to imprint on the memory a series of *loci* or places. The most common type of mnemonic place system was the architectural type, although fields, gardens, and journeys could also be used. The building to be remembered was recommended to be spacious and varied, and each of its spaces should be imagined in detail, including the decorations. The images by which the speech was to be remembered should then be placed in the imagination on the spaces. The images should be drawn from the themes that the speech addressed; a weapon would be appropriate for the theme of warfare, or an anchor for naval matters. When the memory is required, all of the spaces are visited in turn and the deposits (the images) demanded of their custodians. The ancient orator would move mentally through the building as he progressed through his speech, so that the ordering of the images presented him with the sequence that his speech required. Cicero emphasised that the invention of mnemotechnics rested on two things: firstly, the notion that order was important for memory, and secondly, the discovery that the sense of sight was the strongest sense (Yates, 1966: 4).

Yates (1966) emphasises the piercing and intense inner vision that was necessary in order to practise this art. In the absence of paper, and with no resources for discourse other than speech aided crucially by memory, an inner gaze with a selecting, ordering, synthesising, and recall function was developed, a gaze that 'worked' through an intimate knowledge of architecture and artefacts, places and objects.

The rules of place of the art of memory are specific in relation to suitable locations. It is better to form the *loci* of the memory in some deserted place as too many people are distracting. Memory *loci* should not be too like each other as the resemblance will be confusing. They should not be too big as the images will seem too vague, nor too small or the images will be overcrowded. The *loci* must not be too bright or the images placed on them will glitter and dazzle, nor too dim or the shadows will obscure the images. The intervals between the *loci* should be of moderate extent, perhaps of 30 feet, 'for like the external eye, so the inner eye of thought is less powerful when you have moved the object of sight too near or too far away' (Yates, 1966: 8).

These are precise rules in relation to spaces, with an acute visual emphasis on not only the regulation of space but also the regulation of light, the control of people, and the regulation of the distance between subject and object.

In the choosing of images to remember with, the student of rhetoric is advised to choose those things that will be easiest to remember, that is, those things that are the most striking or unusual, beautiful or hideous, comic or obscene.

> Now nature herself teaches us what we should do. When we see in everyday life things that are petty, ordinary, and banal, we generally fail to remember them, because the mind is not being stirred by anything novel or marvellous. But if we see or hear something exceptionally base, dishonourable, unusual, great, unbelievable or ridiculous, that we are likely to remember for a long time ... nature shows that she is not aroused by the common ordinary event, but is moved by a new or striking occurrence. Let art, then, imitate nature, find what she desires, and follow as she directs ... We ought then to

14 In the 'Abbey memory system' devised by Johannes Romberch in his *Congestorium Artificiose Memorie*, 1533, the Abbey acts as the building to contain the images representing parts of the speech (or sections of the material to be remembered). Abbeys would have been familiar to many of those who wished to remember large quantities of material, as most scholars would have been monks at this time.

set up images of a kind that can adhere longest in memory. And we shall do so if we establish similitudes as striking as possible.

(Ad Herennium quoted in Yates, 1966: 10)

An example is offered that would be useful to the counsel for the defence in a specific law-suit which involves the poisoning of a man, the motive of which was to gain an inheritance. There were many witnesses and accessories to the act. The example consists of an image of a sick man lying in bed, with the defendant at the bedside, holding in his right hand a cup, in his left, tablets, and on the fourth finger, a ram's testicles. The cup would remind the counsel for the defence of the poisoning, the tablets of the will or the inheritance, and the testicles of the ram, through the verbal similarity of the word 'testes' - of the witnesses. In the following *loci* details of the rest of the case would be placed.

It is clear from this one example that the art of memory is an articulatory practice and that the meanings of the articulations of bodies and things are likely to be extremely puzzling. Without the explanation that is given, the scene described above would be quite meaningless, and would be interpreted today as a miscellaneous jumble of things that could have no possible connection. The images that are chosen for the memory images are clearly those that have a personal association, although verbal and other similitudes might have been commonly employed by many memorisers.

Yates traces the knowledge of the art of memory through the Dark Ages to the Middle Ages. During the Middle Ages the art of memory moves from rhetoric to ethics (Yates, 1966: 57). It is treated along with definitions of the four cardinal virtues and their parts. Memory is employed to remember heaven and hell. During the later Middle Ages the art of memory moved out of the context of the church.

Artists are likely to have known of the rules of the art of memory. The place rules of the memory theories are particularly striking in their sense of space, depth, and lighting. It has been suggested that Giotto's frescoes, depicting the virtues and the vices in the Arena Cappella in Padua (probably painted about 1306), were produced with a knowledge and understanding of the art of memory. Much care is taken to make sure that the physical conditions do not obscure the images that are to be placed in the *loci*. Giotto's images are regularly placed on the walls, not irregularly as classical directions advise, and the artist has interpreted the directions about variety in *loci* in his own way by making all the painted backgrounds of the pictures different from one another. He is perhaps here following the advice for making memorable images (Yates, 1966: 93).

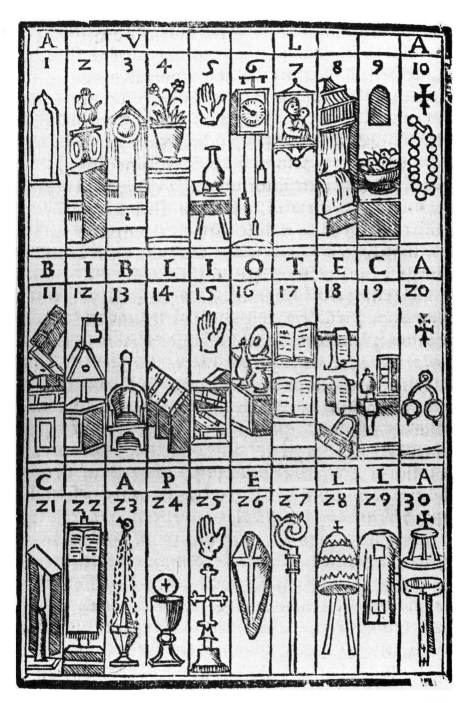

15 Many of the images to be used in the Abbey memory system devised by Johannes Romberch (1533) are religious artefacts. A hand marks the fifth, fifteenth, and twenty-fifth image. This hand was used like the other images and would have helped the user of the system keep his place.

It is likely that many paintings and illustrations in manuscripts produced at this time were aids to memory. Certainly there is documentation for the placing of memory images, that is imaginative 'pictures', on texts to remind the scholar of the commentary he wishes to make (Yates, 1966: 99). An Italian manuscript of the early fourteenth century, for example, shows representations of the three theological and the four cardinal virtues seated in a row together with the figures of the seven liberal arts. It has been suggested that someone has been using these figure to memorise the parts of the virtues as defined in the *Summa Theologiae*. The parts of the virtues are written on the images and their attributes accompany them, all an elaboration to hold together a mass of complicated material (ibid.: 100).

The art of memory was likely to have been used at this time to try to recall the entire ordering of the universe. It is possible that figures expressive of the whole medieval encyclopedia of knowledge (the liberal arts, for example), ranged in order, and having written on them the material relating to them, might be the foundation of a phenomenal memory. Other memory techniques used the order of the images of the zodiac, with additional information inscribed on them, or the familiar ordering of images in a building, so that a metaphorical walk through such a space would enable the recall of the entire order of knowledge (Yates, 1966: 101).

It would seem that by the Middle Ages the techniques for memorising had both an inner and an outer expression. While the classical inner mental ordering was still practised, a new form of use of the inner images is indicated by their appearance in paintings or in the drawn notations on the manuscripts of the monks.

The art of memory was originally practised to aid the memory of the known world. In ancient times it served the orators and was discussed as a part of rhetoric. In medieval times it was called upon by the schoolmen as a devotional exercise and as part of the morality of the soul. With the progress of the sixteenth century, these arts began to look to some scholars more and more like childish games. With the advent of the printed book, it was no longer necessary to remember and be able to articulate all the parts of a complicated *summa*. The conditions that had led to the emergence of fantastic memories were changing. Age-old memory habits were being destroyed. To Erasmus and the humanists, the art of memory was medieval and barbarous, associated with the antiquated methods of the schoolmen, and to be swept away.

However the art of memory did not wane, but entered upon a new and strange lease of life. It was taken up by the main philosophical movement of the Renaissance, the neoplatonic movement, which, with its hermetic core, transformed many of its elements into a hermetic or occult art, and in this form it continued to take a central place in the thought structures of the time. The older techniques of the art of memory, occultised and made infinitely more complex, were still called upon to represent the entire order of the universe although the universe of the Renaissance is infinitely more magical and less static than that of the schoolmen. Sixteenth-century learning combined new empirical knowledge with notions derived both from magical practices and from the ancient classical heritage (Foucault, 1970: 32). During the late Renaissance the art of memory was adapted to become a method of description, discovery, and synthesis of this complex world. The older abstract elements were transformed into an active concrete mode to be of use in a newly secular and active scientific society. The emphases on the use of individual corporeal similitudes, and rare and unusual images, arranged in a personal order to aid the memory, and remembered in an appropriate space, remained from the older forms.

The 'Memory Theatre'

> He calls this theatre of his by many names, saying now that it is a built or constructed mind and soul, and now that it is a windowed one. He pretends that all things that the human mind can conceive and which we cannot see with the corporeal eye, after being collected together by diligent meditation may be expressed by certain corporeal signs in such a way that the beholder may at once perceive with his eyes everything that is otherwise hidden in the depths of the human mind. And it is because of this corporeal looking that he calls it a theatre.
> (Viglius Zuichemus writing to Erasmus: quoted in Yates, 1966: 132)

Giulio Camillo, born around 1480, was one of the most famous men of the time, although largely forgotten today. His fame rested on his occult and magic Memory Theatre. In 1559 a guidebook to the collections of the villas near Milan (Yates, 1966: 134) mentions among the excellent 'pitture', the 'lofty and incomparable fabric of the marvellous Theatre of the most excellent Giulio Camillo', which is described above.

During the early sixteenth century the characteristics of the art of memory had begun to change. In the past, memory spaces and images had been abstract and found in the imagination. Now, these spaces and images began to take on material forms, and began to appear in the real concrete world. A concrete 'memory theatre' emerged which acted as a cognitive tool. In a single glance, the 'memory theatre' could reveal the secret of the universe which could then be apprehended, understood, synthesised, and memorised. Knowing was to be facilitated through real things which demonstrated through their individidual characteristics the specific parts of knowledge, and through their places in space, the interrelationships of these parts.

The term 'theatre' was frequently used in the documents of the time to indicate a complete treatment or compilation of a particular theme. On the whole, these 'theatres' referred to abstractions. Camillo's Theatre was unique in that it actually existed, constructed at the court of Francis I in France (Bernheimer, 1956: 225). Interestingly, although the term 'theatre' during the Renaissance generally referred to a 'compilation' or 'compendium', among the meanings of the word in the Middle Ages were those of a place of assembly or of a marketplace where merchandise was laid out, or organised in ranks. An alternative early definition of the word '*theatrum*' defines it as a complete exhibition of a certain kind of specimen (Bernheimer, 1956: 230). It would appear that both the contemporary and the older meanings of the term are recalled in the memory theatre.

The 'memory theatre' was described by a contemporary: it consisted of a space that was at least big enough to hold two people, was made of wood, marked with many images, and full of little boxes (Yates, 1966: 132). Possibly it was larger, on an architectural scale, as it seems to have been designed to walk into rather than merely look at (Bernheimer, 1956: 227).

The Theatre, which was probably semicircular, rose in seven grades or steps which were divided by seven gangways representing the seven planets. These levels were accessible through seven doors. The mystical significance of the number seven is related to the seven times of seven words in the Lord's prayer. Within these divisions a whole cosmology was inscribed in decorated images which were enriched by the addition of a great number of boxes and coffers. Papers containing explanatory texts hung from the walls. It was also possible that codices dealing with all aspects of the world were incorporated into the theatre. From this point of view, the theatre had the features of a medieval *Summa* (Bernheimer, 1956: 231). Interestingly, words and objects are inextricably mixed, both to be gazed upon, read, and interpreted.

The spectator stood where the stage in a standard model of the theatre would be and looked out to this vast memory machine (Yates, 1966: 139) where the structure of the world was displayed as it appeared to most thinkers in Camillo's time; orderly, rational, and stratified. Every level or bench became a simile for a level in the divine plan (Bernheimer, 1956: 227). Camillo did not lose sight of the fact that his Theatre was based on the principles of the old art of memory, but his use of memory was to represent the eternal order of truth, which was to be remembered through an organic association of all its parts with their underlying eternal order. The art of memory was still using places and images according to the old rules, but a radical change had come over the philosophy and psychology behind it, which was now no longer scholastic, but neoplatonic (Yates, 1966: 145). The Theatre was a system of memory places using the basic images of the planetary gods. As one went up the Theatre by the gangways of the seven planets, the whole of creation would fall into an ordered representation (ibid.: 141).

The seven levels represented the seven archetypes of creation: the seven planets; the simple elements of matter; the elements in a state of mixture; man's inner being; the juncture in him of body and soul; the varieties of his work; and finally the arts, which were last in the order of creation, and therefore of precedent, and so occupied the top bench (Bernheimer, 1956: 227). In order to put this scheme into a visual form, the primary concepts were set forth as images painted over the doors, with subordinate concepts represented underneath. Every metaphysical group thereby formed an architectural whole. The benches presumably held the boxes, and the explanatory scrolls hung from the walls.

The method of presentation was allegorical, using the symbols of classical mythology, although in a very abstruse way. For example, the simple elements on the second bench were symbolised by the 'banquets', referring to Oceanus, who in Homer had given a banquet to the other gods. The next level contained a scene interpreted as a simile of things derived from a mixture of elements. Caves, again reminiscent of Homer, recalled the grotto on the coast of Ithaca where nymphs had woven fabrics and wild bees had stored their honey. Man's inner world was symbolised by the three Gorgons who shared one eye, just as the three souls of man had to rely on only one divine ray. Pasiphae, who loved the bull, symbolised the juncture of man's body with his soul, and the mantle of Mercury was linked to human work, both giving realisation to the will of the gods. Finally, Prometheus was represented as patron of the arts.

This sequence of painted images was broken at one point. Instead of an image of Apollo, a three-dimensional pyramid appeared in the centre of the theatre, which represented 'the breadth of all things' with God at the highest point 'unrelated and in human relation'. A dynastic interpretation supplemented the philosophical and theological one, turning the edifice into a 'royal theatre'. Francis I, for whom it was built, was represented within it (symbolised by the triangle) as God on earth (Bernheimer, 1956: 228).

The 'Theatre' was a vision of the world and of the nature of things seen from a height, from the stars themselves, or from the supercelestial founts of wisdom behind the sky. Camillo's exposure to the occult philosophy, embodied in the writings that were rediscoverd by Marsilio Ficino, and which were believed to be the work of the ancient Egyptian sage, Hermes Trismegistus, was reflected in his memory system.

The creation of man was in two stages in the 'Theatre'. First there was the appearance of the 'interior man', the most noble of God's creatures and made in his image, on the grade of the Gorgon Sisters. Then on the grade of Pasiphae and the bull, man takes on a body the parts of which are under the domination of the zodiac. The 'interior man', the *mens*, is created divine and has the power of the star rulers; on falling into the body, the *mens* comes under the domination of the stars. Man can escape this domination through the hermetic religious experience of ascent through the spheres to regain his divinity. This notion was behind Camillo's claim that the whole universe could be remembered by looking down on it from above (Yates, 1966: 147). In this atmosphere, the relationship between man (the microcosm) and the world (the macrocosm) took on a new significance. The microcosm could fully understand and fully remember the macrocosm, and was able to hold it within his divine *mens*, or memory. The memory became a mystical tool for grasping the relationships of the world and reuniting man with God.

Camillo's magic system worked in part through the use of the memory images as inner talismans. A talisman was an object imprinted with an image that rendered it magical through having been made in accordance with certain laws. The inner use of talismanic imagery gave the memory which was constructed the power to unify the contents of the mind (Yates, 1966: 155).

The complexities with which the cognitive structure of the 'Theatre' was constructed meant that the ideas had to be 'explained' or 'demonstrated' by the constructor, who was regarded as a very powerful, not to say dangerous, philosopher. The knowledge that the 'Theatre' made available became (if the system was believed in) immensely wonderful and precious, and therefore something to be guarded closely. Occult links to the secret orderings of the universe, revealed through the signatures and correspondences of the talismanic imagery, made the 'Theatre' a privileged apparatus articulating knowledge and powers on many levels, including celestial/terrestrial, magical/material, sovereign/subject. One of the reasons that the 'Theatre' was built at the court of Francis I was that it would make all those secrets unknown to the ordinary subject available to the monarch. This would, of course, give him fantastic powers.

The Theatre presents a remarkable transformation of the art of memory.

The rules of the art are clearly discernible in it, with a building divided into memory places, on which memory images are placed. The emotionally striking images of classical memory, transformed into the 'corporeal similitudes' of the devout Middle Ages are transformed again into magically powerful images at the end of the sixteenth century (Yates, 1966: 157). The religious intensity of the medieval memory has been transformed into a divine memory with powers to grasp the highest reality through a magically activated imagination.

Camillo's Theatre represents a new Renaissance plan of the psyche, a new mental map, a change that has happened within memory, and from which outside changes derived their impetus. Where the medieval mind used memory to help any weakness, the Renaissance mind believed that through the divine magic power of the memory it could grasp the nature of the world. The magic of celestial proportion flowed from this world memory into the magical words of poetry and into the perfect proportions of art and architecture (Yates, 1966: 172). In the vast, magical, polyvalent space of the universe, man stands as a privileged point (Foucault, 1970: 22). It now became possible to represent the world through the magical synthesising power of the *mens*, which was the central core of the subject to whom the existent as such is related (Heidegger, 1951: 10).

To Erasmus and his circle of humanists, the art of memory was no longer of interest, rendered both archaic and unnecessary by the printed book. It appeared both too close to the practices of the schoolmen, and too close to secret and suspicious knowledge. There is no doubt that the art of memory, with its capacity for both revelation and concealment, was particularly sought by those Renaissance philosophers that were drawn to the occult. In the late sixteenth century, competing interpretations of the world included a variety of occult versions. Foucault's Renaissance *episteme* acknowledges fully the possibility and indeed the necessity of magical explanations within a structure of knowing that was grounded in interpretation and resemblance. Humanist explanations of events, both in the sixteenth century and in subsequent centuries, have consistently played down or denied both the existence and the power of occult explanations (Yates, 1967). The art of memory with its occult connotations was ignored.

The 'cabinet of the world' – the 'memory-cabinet'

Foucault describes an encyclopedic project that appeared at the end of the sixteenth century, or in the first few years of the seventeenth century, which aimed to reconstruct the order of the universe by the way in which words were linked together and arranged in space. The form and structure of language was seen to be analogous to the form and structure of the world that it represented, but in its totality rather than in each individual word. Thus all the languages of the world, taken together, in their interlacing and in their positioning in space, made up the truth of the world by analogy (Foucault, 1970: 37). Foucault cites de Savigny, who contrived to spatialise acquired knowledge in the form of a circle, and the project of La Croix du Main, who envisaged a space that would be at once an encyclopedia and a library, and would permit the arrangement of written texts according to the forms of adjacency, kinship, analogy, and subordination (Foucault, 1970: 25). *Convenientia, aemulatio, analogy,* and *sympathy* indicate how the world must fold in upon itself, duplicate itself, reflect itself, or form a chain so that things can resemble one another. This underlying structure of the world, once understood, was to be used as the organising principle of the texts that were the concrete manifestation of accumulated knowledge.

The 'cabinet of the world' was a further example of this encyclopedic project, an example that encompassed both the space of the library and the space of the theatre. The 'cabinet of the world' was Camillo's Memory Theatre made material, existing in physical form. The 'cabinet of the world' presented physical things whose identities, links, and connections would be articulated and interpreted according to their visible surface signatures (which in some cases would be imprinted with talismanic images), and which in their totality would represent a world view, a cosmological explanation, which included within it the position of the subject for whom the view was constituted. The arrangement and meaning of the material things in the physically existing memory theatre (the 'cabinet of the world') would be made according to *convenientia, aemulatio, analogy,* and *sympathy.*

Three important elements combined to allow a variety of 'cabinets of the world' to emerge. These elements are epistemological (the Renaissance *episteme*), organisational (mnemonic techniques drawn from the art of memory), and programmatical (Camillo's Memory Theatre). Many different 'cabinets of the world' did in fact emerge, all rather different according to who the major owner/collector was (prince, scholar, or merchant), what kinds of powers the collector had (financial, intellectual, political, magical), and which world view was upheld by the individual collector (the prince at the centre of a political arena, the scholar at the centre of intellectual links, the merchant at the centre of a trading network).

South of the Alps, the 'cabinet of the world' often consisted of both inside and outside spaces. In this relatively mild climate, architecture blurred the distinction between indoors and out, and a palace-garden could be built that would become a '*theatrum mundi*' (Hunt, 1985: 198). Universal harmony, understood as a unity between the microcosm and the macrocosm, art and nature, was represented by fantastic concoctions, beasts, fountains, grottoes, and caves, where inside became outside, water became rock, and other inversions constituted a physical manifestation of a philosophical schema.

The princely *Wunderkammern* and *Kunstkammern*, which were mainly to be found north of the Alps in Germany, Bavaria, and Austria, demonstrate a different form of 'cabinet of the world'. The macrocosm and the microcosm were similarly represented, although in a way rather different from that of the palace-garden. The elements of creation generally took the form of different types of material, including gold, silver, and other precious metals and minerals; but these minerals now were shaped into forms that related to the power and identity of the subject to whom they belonged. The fantastic animals, the elaborate carvings, were less likely now to refer to the world of nature, as would be appropriate in a garden setting, but were more likely to refer to the powers and wealth of the prince (Kaufmann, 1978). The representation of the microcosm was, in this articulation, much more specific, and took the form of direct references to the prince. Thus, in the *Kunstkammer* of Rudolf II, the paintings of Arcimboldo (considered for a long time as totally irrational), with their heads made up of plants, branches, leaves, and vegetables, contained direct pictorial emblematic references to the house of Habsburg. As harmony existed between the elements and the seasons, so harmony existed under the rule of the Habsburgs (ibid.: 26).

The *Kunstkammer* took its place within the body politic. Spaces were used as part of Habsburg diplomatic negotiations; visitors of state were taken through the rooms, and it was customary to bring a gift intended for the collection (Seelig, 1985). The relational sequences of the discourse of the *Kunstkammer* articulated various positions of the subject. Thus the visiting subject became incorporated within the articulated network by occupying a subjected position not only through the exercise of the gaze, as in the earlier case study, but also through the symbolic depositing of material things. In colluding and assisting in the accumulation of material that represented not only the world, but also the place within it of the prince, so the subject colluded and concurred with the power the prince laid claim to. This, in turn, partly constituted the subject position of prince.

In this way, these *Kunstkammern* operated more directly as technologies of power than did the garden-palaces. Viewing the assemblages as a 'tourist', as John Evelyn and other English visitors did, and deciphering and interpreting their complex messages was, at one level, a personal experience. Donating to the assemblage as part of the mechanism of international state and dynastic diplomacy was on a more public, less personal level, and was more overtly coercive.

Both the palace-garden and the *Kunstkammer* operated on a large scale, in terms of space, wealth, and volume. The idea of the 'cabinet of the world' is also to be found on a small scale. One of the meanings of 'cabinet' is 'cupboard'. Many collectors at all social levels had collections that were limited to the contents of a cupboard. The *Kunstschränke* made by Hainhofer were constructed as miniature *Kunstkammern* with the features of the '*theatrum mundi*' represented on a miniature scale. The 'cabinet' on the scale of a single piece of furniture also operated as a memory theatre, as a cognitive technique to picture the world.

The palace-garden, the *Kunstkammern*, the *Kunstschränke*, and the scholarly collections were different variations of the 'cabinet of the world'. Each articulated the epistemic rules of Foucault's Renaissance *episteme*, the cognitive tool of the memory theatre, and used Camillo's Memory Theatre as a programme. If the existing histories of museum are reread using the techniques of 'effective' history and taking account of Foucault's *epistemes*, it is revealed not only that the 'cabinets of curiosity' are far more than the mere miscellaneous products of disordered minds, but also that these 'direct ancestors' of modern museums were constituted from within a quite different frame of reference.

The 'cabinet of the world'

5

Networks and prototypes

During the 1570s in Florence a prototype for the 'cabinet of the world' emerged. Although this particular cabinet existed for approximately twenty years only (Olmi, 1985: 10), it seems to have had the status of exemplar (Bostrom, 1985: 99; Scheicher, 1985: 31; Olmi, 1985: 7; Kaufmann, 1978: 24). The *studiolo* of Francesco I (1541–87) was an attempt to gather together artefacts that represented the order of the world, to constitute a secret site in and from which the prince could position himself symbolically as ruler of that world. It further operated as a microcosm of art and nature, articulating their relationships to the elements, the humours, and the seasons as presented in mythology, literature, history, and contemporary technology (Rinehart, 1981: 276). The room itself was secret. It is never referred to in the sixteenth-century inventories of the palace (ibid.: 278).

The elaborate scheme of decoration is explained by Vincenzo Borghini in his correspondence with Giorgio Vasari. It was drawn up in about 1572 by various members of the Accademia del Disegno and consisted of a design whereby all matter within the hierarchy of the cosmos and all works of art formed of this material complemented each other in a harmonious unity. The *studiolo* bears a striking conceptual resemblance to the Memory Theatre of Camillo (Yates, 1966: 139). References to the Theatre of Camillo have recently been suggested (Olmi, 1985: 7) but details have not been published in English.

The *studiolo* was a small room without windows, resembling closely the interior of a large cupboard (Scheicher, 1985: 31). Camillo's Theatre was 'at least big enough for two people'. Windows are not mentioned in connection with this space, which seems to have been erected as an internal space within a room. Within the *studiolo* were cupboards, with the contents of each cupboard shown in their appointed place within the universal system by means of painting and sculpture. Borghini describes it: 'E' invenzione delle decorazioni dovene servire come per un segno et quasi inventario da ritrovar le cose.' The decorations on the cupboards were symbolic of their contents, and although they would have acted to help find and identify the objects inside them, as Scheicher suggests, they would also have worked as a symbolic recall of the contents in their positions within the cosmic hierarchy. The painted images would have offered a compendium of structured, hierarchised knowledge at a glance.

The cupboards within the *studiolo* were kept closed; the material collection existed in its cosmic order, but was not visible. Kept in a closed, windowless room, in closed dark cupboards, the objects themselves, although actually present in their materiality, in effect acted as though they were an abstract experience. Their presence, and their meaning, was indicated through the symbolic images painted on the cupboard doors. This is very close to the closed boxes and the painted images of the Memory Theatre of Camillo, where the painted scenes are references to specific concepts that relate to each other within the magical cosmological system.

Paintings in the *studiolo* were originally planned and hung in matched vertical pairs with matched subjects that were chosen to represent the elements (fire and water, earth and air) (Rinehart, 1981: 280). The paired paintings were hung with the rectangular paintings above, related to statuary niches in the fixed form of the room and the oval paintings below (ibid.: 276). An artist was commissioned to draw up schemes of paintings representing the correspondences that structured the world, which were then submitted to the prince for his approval. The world represented was that recognised and permitted by the prince.

The spectator in Camillo's Theatre would stand where the stage in a modern theatre would be and would gaze out into the 'auditorium' (Yates, 1966: 137). The prince in the *studiolo* symbolically claimed dominion over a world that he had represented to himself, with himself positioned at its centre (Heidegger, 1951: 10). Positioned at the centre of the represented world, the prince as man himself represented a privileged point saturated with analogies (Foucault, 1970: 22). This representation of the world (that world picture sanctioned by the prince), together with the fact that the room was secret, combined to constitute a specific subject position, a position that reserved to the prince not only the knowledge of the world constituting his supremacy, but the possibility of knowing itself. This secret knowledge gave the prince specific powers and advantages.

Approximately fourteen years after its establishment, the secret nocturnal *studiolo* was dismantled and the objects were given new meanings in new

16 View of the east wall of the *Studiolo* of the Grand Duke Francesco I. Paintings hang in matched pairs, with allegorical subjects representing the elements; rectangular paintings above and oval paintings below.

spaces. In 1584 an open, light, and airy gallery was created in a part of the palace that was then opened up for the people of Florence as a public space. The political climate demanded a shift in the relations of spaces, material things, bodies, visibility, and accessibility. The play of powers required that this suite of relations modulated from open to closed, from light to dark, from private to public.

This 'museum', in its early closed form, is often invoked as a prototype (Bostrom, 1985: 99). It may have been an interim structure, midway between the partially materialised magical Memory Theatre of Camillo, and the more completely physical manifestations of later examples. In its material form, the link to Camillo is strong, but in the absence of further information about either the design scheme or the contents of the cupboards, only speculation can suggest the strength of epistemological links between the *studiolo* and the Theatre.

It is known, however, that the Memory Theatre was used as one element in the planning and organisation of encyclopedic collections. Here again the evidence is sparse in English, although there is a fairly substantial bibliography in German and Italian. A small quarto had been published in Munich in 1565 by Samuel Quiccheberg, (or Quicchelberg) (Hajos, 1958: 151), the Bavarian Duke Albrecht V's Flemish adviser on artistic matters. In this treatise, Quiccheberg referred to the magical memory system (Seelig, 1985: 87). Quiccheberg explicitly states that he is not using the word *theatrum* metaphorically, as other writers have done, but is referring to the physically existing theatre of Camillo (Kaufmann, 1978: 25).

Quiccheberg offers guidelines for the setting-up of an all-embracing collection, which is in accordance with the encyclopedic project. One of his aims was to promote their founding and their enlargement, according to the different means of different collectors (Seelig, 1985: 86). His writings contain a detailed classification system and many practical instructions on establishing a collection in both large and small spaces (Hajos, 1958: 152). He also refers specifically to the Munich *Kunstkammer*, referring to it as the '*Theatrum*' or '*Theatrum Sapientiae*' (Seelig, 1985: 86) and comments favourably on its use of space: describing 'a formation of cloister-like ambulatories, which, with four wings comprising several floors, surround a courtyard' (ibid.: 77). From the centre of the courtyard the entire structure could be apprehended.

Quiccheberg's classification system consists of five classes, with ten or eleven 'inscriptions' in each, which indicate further subdivisions or specifications about the items to be included. Each class appears to comprise a number of separate but related collections. The classes and major subdivisions are described by Hajos as follows: first class – religious art, and pictorial material related to general or regional history; second class – sculpture, numismatics, the applied arts; third class – the approximation of a museum of natural history, with original specimens and artefacts; fourth class – science and mechanics, material relating to games, sports and pastimes, arms and armour, costume; fifth class – paintings and engravings, genealogy, portraits, heraldry, textiles, fittings and furnishings (Hajos, 1958: 152). Clearly, the use of 'numismatics' is an anachronism, as are the expressions 'the applied arts' and 'a museum of natural history'. The selection and translation of terms here makes this description difficult to use in searching for an 'effective' history of this specific example.

It would seem that Quiccheberg intended to 'juxtapose original specimens and related artefacts'. This may refer to Camillo's boxes and images with their explanatory texts, or may be a reference to the display of '*naturalia*' and '*artificialia*'. Quiccheberg makes explicit reference to the use of images to aid the memory, and contrasts the power of looking over the power of reading (Hajos, 1958: 155).

Quiccheberg was writing during the 1560s and using the ideas of Camillo, whose 'Theatre' was being talked about thirty years earlier, at the beginning of the sixteenth century (Yates, 66: 130). Quiccheberg's work, with its attempt to present a schema, was to act as a guide in the assemblage and display of collections. Thus Camillo's ideas were to be indirectly influential for a long period.

At the beginning of the seventeenth century, the Memory Theatre emerged in a new form in England. English occult philosophers, particularly the Oxford doctor, Robert Fludd, developed magico-religious theories of the universe which looked back to the early Renaissance and to ideas of the macrocosm and the microcosm. The link to the ideas of Camillo, in Italy nearly eighty years before, is strong (Yates, 1966: 322). Also like Camillo, Fludd's memory system takes the form of a theatre. It is possible that he had heard of the work of Camillo while travelling in France, or that he knew the later, and infinitely more complex, more magical, and more secretive system of Giordano Bruno (ibid.: 336). It is also possible that he had come across a work published in England in 1618, the year before he published his work in Germany written by John Willis, in which a memory system of sets of identical theatres or memory rooms as *loci* are suggested. Willis referred to these memory rooms as 'theatres' but also as 'repositories' (ibid.: 33). Bruno's system also made use of memory rooms.

Both Fludd's and Bruno's memory rooms were to be affiliated to the round heavens by being metaphorically placed in the zodiac through a highly occult system of macrocosm–microcosm correspondence (Yates, 1966: 331). Both Bruno and Fludd used elements from the medieval art of memory, utilising lists of names or things in alphabetical order. These included the names of the most important mythological figures and lists of vices and virtues, often referred to by a visual alphabet (ibid.: 334).

The 'Ptolemaic Universe' devised by Fludd was conceived as 'The Mirror of the Whole of Nature and the Image of Art' (Godwyn, 1979: 22). The sublunary world contains the elements of fire and air, which move upwards to the skies, and earth and water, which are pulled downwards to the world. Under the aegis of these elements are the three realms of nature: *animal*, which includes people, animals, insects, and fish; *vegetable*, including plants, roots; and *mineral*, including metals, ores, and minerals, each ruled by the appropriate planet.

This reflecting universe (Godwyn, 1979) includes four circles of the arts: the liberal arts (engineering, time-keeping, cosmography, astronomy, geomancy, arithmetic, music, geometry, perspective-drawing, painting, and fortification); art supplanting nature in the animal realm (apiculture, silkworms, egg-hatching, medicine); art assisting nature in the vegetable realm (tree-grafting, cultivation of the soil); art correcting nature in the mineral realm (distillation with alembic and retort).

Fludd produced many diagrams and illustrations which picture his theories, using specific images that represent a specific part of his cosmology. In his drawing of the 'mirror' of the two worlds, described above, a drawing of an eagle is part of his animal realm, and a drawing of several trees is a part of the vegetable realm. Equally, the elements are pictured, with their symbols linked to parts of the zodiac by dotted lines. Nature herself is also pictured, as a beautiful virgin, with symbols that demonstrate her power. Art is pictured as a monkey, 'the Ape of Nature'.

It is a short step from the picturing of the world as a figured diagram to the picturing of the world through the relationships of meaningful things. Quiccheberg adapted the earlier Memory Theatre of Camillo into a written scheme with which to structure a comprehensive encyclopedic collection, or series of collections, into a coherent unity that represented the entirety of the world. Fludd further offered a two-dimensional illustrated cosmology that represented the world through symbolic and magic images. In the various manifestations of the 'cabinet of the world', both of these cosmological representations will be found used as sources.

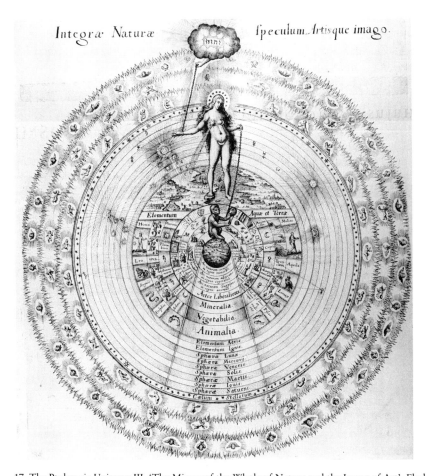

17 The Ptolemaic Universe III, 'The Mirror of the Whole of Nature and the Image of Art'. Fludd's elaborate cosmic schemata gives us some idea of the way in which the world was pictured. God has carved the universe out of the clouds of nothingness, and the outside circle represents the incorporeal, metaphysical realms inhabited by the nine orders of angels. The *Caelum Stellatum* is the heaven of the fixed stars, with the sphere of the zodiac and the seven Chaldean planets. The sublunary region is compounded of the four elements: fire, air, water, and earth.

The elements of fire and air are represented as circles around the elements of water and earth, which are shown as a realistic landscape. Here stands Nature, depicted as a beautiful virgin, with the sun on her breast and the moon on her belly; her heart gives light to the stars and planets. Her right foot stands on earth, her left in water, signifying the conjunction of sulphur and mercury without which nothing can be created. The helper of Nature is Art, the 'Ape of Nature'. He bears the same relation to Nature as she does to God, this being represented by the chain of being. The three realms of Nature are *animal* (containing pictures of dolphin, snake, lion, man, woman, eagle, snail, and fish); *vegetable* (trees, grapes, wheat, flowers, and roots); and *mineral* (talc, antimony, lead, gold, silver, copper, orpiment, and sal ammoniac).

The arts, man's opportunity of making the earth a happy and beautiful place, are represented by four circles: *liberal arts* (engineering, timekeeping, cosmography, astronomy, geomancy, arithmetic, music, geometry, perspective drawing, painting, and fortification): *Art supplanting Nature in the animal realm* (apiculture, silkworms, egg-hatching, medicine): *Art assisting Nature in the vegetable realm* (tree-grafting, cultivation of the soil): *Art correcting nature in the mineral realm* (distillation with alembic and retort).
Many of the objects in the collections of the 'cabinets of the world' would have represented some of these features.

The *Kunstkammern* – the 'cabinets of the world' on a political level.

The *Kunstkammern* form a quite specific series of 'cabinets of the world'. Three particular 'museums' are examples, all palaces and collections belonging to members of the house of Habsburg: the *Kunstkammer* of Duke Albrecht V of Bavaria in Munich; that of his brother, Ferdinand II (1529–95) at Castle Ambras; and the *Kunstkammer* of their nephew, Rudolf II in Prague (1552–1612). There are many connections between the three different 'museums', not least that Rudolf bought Ferdinand's collection on his death.

The evidence is scanty in the case of the first two of these instances, but they introduce important aspects. The third example presents a more complete picture.

The *Kunstkammer* of Albrecht V Duke of Bavaria in Munich was the earliest of the three specific instances under discussion, slightly preceding the establishment of princely *Kunstkammern* at Ambras and Prague. A new building, Munich's first Renaissance building, was begun in 1563. This was only one space in a series of spaces concerned with the collections, which were progressively constructed during the 1560s and 1570s. Other parts of the building contained specific parts of the collection. The *Antiquarium*, for example, begun in 1568, housed antique and other sculpture on the ground floor, and a library on the top floor. In the early years the collection was open to ambassadors, princes, artists, and academics (Seelig, 1985: 78)

Quiccheberg worked for the Duke of Bavaria, and is credited with an active part in the foundation and organisation of the library, and the reorganisation of the *Kunstkammer* (Hajos, 1958: 151). It is likely therefore that the scheme on which this collection was based was in accordance with his scheme which drew on the work of Camillo. There are hints of this: a distinction is drawn between the *Wunderkammer*, Quiccheberg's 'miraculosarum rerum promptuarium', and the *Kunstkammer*, Quiccheberg's 'artificiosarum rerum conclave' (Seelig, 1985: 84).

The second 'museum' is the collection of Ferdinand II, who was appointed Governor of the Tyrol in 1564 and started an extensive rebuilding programme at Schloss Ambras. In 1573, following the completion of this, a new building enterprise was begun in the Lower Castle, in order to create new spaces to contain the collections. The collections were arranged in the four large interconnected buildings which made up the additions to the Lower Castle at Ambras. The spaces enabled the division of objects into sets. Three buildings contained the collection of arms and armour,

18 The ground floor of the 'Antiquarium' of the Wittelsbach Residenz in Munich by Jacopo da Strada (1568; alterations 1586–1600), built to hold sculpture, demonstrates how the sculpture was incorporated into a complex scheme of allegory and symbol. This was only one of the spaces constructed to hold artefacts, the divisions of which may have been based on Quiccheberg's ideas for classifications of collections.

and the fourth contained the *Kunstkammer*, which therefore represented a fairly small part of the entire collection. The first hall of armour contained the equipment for tournaments, the library, and an antiquarium. A further room, the *Turkenkammer*, contained trophies from the Turkish wars. All of these spaces had to be traversed before reaching the *Kunstkammer*, which must therefore have represented an internal space, although not a dark one.

The space that contained the *Kunstkammer* was large with windows on both sides, and without any decoration. The objects articulated with the space. In the middle of the hall eighteen cupboards were placed back to back down the centre of the room. In front of them stood two transverse cupboards. The walls between the windows were covered with pictures from floor to ceiling. In the middle of the room there were various chests partly filled with portraits and used to store items that were being studied (Scheicher, 1985: 30).

There is a strong similarity between the Schloss Ambras *Kunstkammer* and the *studiolo* of Francesco I in Florence (Scheicher, 1985). Both collections were partly constituted and arranged through the rules for the art of memory. The basis of the arrangement was primarily the raw material of the artefacts, with works of the same material grouped together in the same cupboards. The cupboards in the *Kunstkammer* are all painted in plain colours so that the objects could be clearly seen against a background, as in the rules of place in the art of memory. Blue was used for cupboards containing gold, and green for those containing silver. The row of cupboards was also assured of the best possible light being placed in the middle of the room in front of the windows. The importance of correctly modulated lighting, it will be recalled, is emphasised in the rules of place.

Scheicher cites the universal scale of Robert Fludd. Nature is represented in the *Kunstkammer* by plants, animals, bones, horns, and minerals. The realms of animal, vegetable, and mineral are thereby all represented.

One item is described that would appear to be a sign of *similitude*. This is a pair of antlers, 'enveloped within a growing tree'. Resemblance as a form of *similitude* imposes adjacencies that in their turn guarantee further resemblances (Foucault, 1970: 18). 'Place and similitude become entangled: we see mosses growing on the outside of shells, and plants on the antlers of stags, a sort of grass on the faces of men.' All these are signs of *convenientia*, and it is likely that the antlers entangled in the living tree are an example of the play of resemblances between things. Probably also, there are other resemblances hidden in the arrangements and juxtapositions of other material things. An example of *convenientia* can be cited, because this has been cited as an example of a typical 'curiosity'. Other examples of specific forms of similitude, *aemulatio*, *analogy*, or the play of *sympathies* could perhaps be discovered in the original inventories.

The Schloss Ambras *Kunstkammer* contained a large collection of natural material that had been worked by man. These included corals that had been carved into mythological beasts or figures and mounted in cases which were partly gilded and populated with small animals of glass or bronze. The carved corals were imported from Italy and later mounted in southern Germany or South Tyrol in nacre, glass, bronze, and gold. The corals became meaningful objects through the articulation of natural materials with the skills of men, which together represented the unity of all things. This was an important element of the 'cabinet of the world'. Borghini, designer of Franceso's *studiolo*, had also thought that all things could be linked with both art and nature. Bacon had suggested that cabinets should contain 'whatsoever the hand of man by exquisite art or engine has made rare in stuff, form or motion' (Impey and Mac-Gregor, 1985: 1). In addition, coral had magical connotations, which produced a further layer of meaning.

Other aspects of the *Kunstkammer* can be noted. One of the cupboards, painted flesh-coloured, contained automatons and scientific instruments, such as clocks, watches, astrolabes, and compasses, that signified man's power to dominate nature (Scheicher, 1985: 34). These also signified as meaningful objects within the 'museum', as examples of the latest developments in technology.

This 'cabinet of the world' contained those things that revealed the extremes of nature's powers: the particularly large, the particularly small, the misshapen, the monstrous. Ferdinand owned the largest-known bowl of wood, playing cards for giants and for dwarfs, and portraits of the crippled and the deformed. There is possibly a link here with the instructions in the art of memory to choose the most striking images.

The cupboards were filled with things according to the nature of the material, so that each might contain both worked and unworked items in the same raw material. In the cupboard marked 'bones', for example, were placed turned objects of ivory and also the arm bone of Duke Herman, an ancestor.

In terms of its identity, this specific 'museum' related closely to the previous one, that of Albrecht, Duke of Bavaria. The collections were united by the same overall aim of encyclopedic representation, and many of the collected items themselves had either originated from the same geographical source, or had been acquired by the same agents (Scheicher, 1985: 38).

The third 'museum' to be discussed is the most complete example. The *Kunstkammer* of Rudolf II at Prague Castle was reassessed in 1966 following the discovery of a previously unknown inventory. The researcher asserted that the collection was not a cabinet of curiosities, but that 'it represented a consistently systematic collection of various objects from the different realms of nature, human arts and human knowledge, founded on an encyclopedic principle' (Fucikova, 1985: 51). Another writer goes further in saying 'It had a carefully organized content based on the system of correspondences,' and also that 'we may consider Rudolf's possession of the world in microcosm in his *Kunstkammer* an expression of his symbolic mastery of the greater world.' (Kaufmann, 1978: 27). The research on the *Kunstkammer* of Rudolf II in Prague carried out by Kaufmann is the most useful for our purposes. Kaufmann presents the *Kunstkammer* as a form of *representatio* and suggests that it is an expression of imperial magnificence and a symbol of the Emperor Rudolf's claim to power (ibid.: 22).

This cabinet, like the *studiolo* of Francesco I or the *Kunstkammer* of Ferdinand in Ambras, or of Albrecht in Munich, was designed to be encyclopedic in scope. Rudolf's *Kunstkammer* was larger, but the same divisions according to material can be identified (Kaufmann, 1978: 24). The collection of objects contained examples of all that was to be found in nature or made by man. It was a complete representation which, as Foucault reminds us, was posited as a form of repetition: the theatre of life or the mirror of nature (Foucault, 1970: 17).

Kaufmann suggests that Rudolf's *Kunstkammer* followed the principles of Camillo's magical Memory Theatre and that possibly the emperor regarded the objects in his *Kunstkammer* as magical talismans to strengthen his power. It is probable that the links to the idea of magical memory systems are, in fact, stronger, and that the *Kunstkammer* may have been the inspiration for the memory system of Giordano Bruno (Yates, 1972: 28). Bruno's ambitious metaphysical edifice embodied a universal reform of knowledge based on hermetic, cabalist, and Lullist doctrine. He was understood during the sixteenth century by some as a mage, or occult philosopher, communicating to those deemed fit to hear the secret traditions of the world of spiritual powers (Evans, 1973: 229). The interest of the court at Prague in the occult arts is well documented (ibid.: ch. 6) and there are strong links with Bruno. The orientation of the 'art' of Rudolphine Prague was towards a revelation of mystery, whether through the medium of canvas, the manipulation of stones, or the alchemical or cabalistic arts (ibid.: 162). The passion for 'glyptics' (the cutting and

19 *Spring*, one of the figures from the base of the fountain by Wenzel Jamnitzer which stood in the *Kunstkammer* of Rudolf II.

engraving of gems) in Prague articulated a love of rare and exotic material with an opportunity for a conscious display of skill and a belief in talismans and the astral powers of stones.

Heidegger suggests that the picturing of the world includes the structuring of the subject as part of that world view (Heidegger, 1951: 9). Many of the artefacts in the collection represented the world ruled in harmony by the emperor. The fountain by Wenzel Jamnitzer, which stood 10 feet high in the *Kunstkammer*, represented the cosmos in the form of an imperial crown. Four gods representing the four seasons made up the base. Above them came gods and creatures representing the four elements. Above them in the heavenly sphere were four winds and four archangels, then the four eagles that represented the house of Austria. At the summit was the figure of Jupiter, representing the emperor, astride an eagle. Here in one object, a universal scale is represented, with nature represented through the four seasons and the four elements, and the celestial world referred to by the winds and the angels. The emperor is symbolised as the controller of the universe. As the French king was mirrored in the memory system of Camillo as God on earth (Bernheimer, 1956: 228), so the emperor is structured into the universal cosmos through this artefact, and as this was part of the collection, through the *Kunstkammer*. These references to the centripetal world of similitudes with the emperor as a fixed, privileged, analogical point are also to be found in other objects within the collection, as we have already seen in the case of the paintings of Arcimboldo (Kaufmann, 1978: 26).

The *Kunstkammer* of Rudolf II was a carefully organised 'museum', articulated through an understanding of the world with a greater than usual emphasis on the magical aspects of the world. Its contents were organised to exhibit a world picture, with objects that symbolised all aspects of nature and art, as conceptualised by the occult philosophers, such as Robert Fludd and Giordano Bruno. This organisation depended on the concept of resemblance, where the objects and their proximities suggested macrocosmic/microcosmic links. Within this mesh of correspondences the subject, in this case the emperor (the prince) occupied a relation of both interiority and exteriority: an interior relation in that he is part of the world, and in fact the world is generated by him; exterior, in that he controls this world, and is thereby both singular and transcendent in relation to it (Foucault, 1979: 7).

The *Kunstkammer* had a quite specific diplomatic function. Ambassadors were customarily taken to visit it on the eve of their departure, and a visit was sometimes used as mark of special favour (Kaufmann, 1978: 22). Rudolf seems to have spoken in and through his *Kunstkammer*.

20 Portrait of Rudolf II as *Vertumnus*, the god of the seasons (*c*. 1590). This was the culmination of a series of paintings representing the seasons and the elements, painted by Arcimboldo, which were based on the system of correspondences of microcosm to macrocosm and in turn to the body politic. The paintings suggested that just as the various objects which were depicted (e.g. cannons and wicks in *Fire*), existed in harmony, and as the individual heads hung together in harmony, so the world existed in harmony under the rule of the emperor. The combination of the fruits and flowers from all seasons seen in this portrait suggests the return of the golden age with the rule of Rudolf.

Gifts were exchanged with other collectors, the quality of the object expressing the worth or *virtu* of the collector. Rudolf exhibited his magnificence in his collections (ibid.: 23). The collection was a form of imperial display: as he was first among emperors, Holy Roman Emperor, so he was first among collectors.

The *Kunstschränke* – the 'cabinet of the world' in miniature

The *Kunstkammern* were large-scale evocations of the compendium of the world, with a wide focus. Similar compendiums of universality can be identified on a smaller scale elsewhere. Lower in the social hierarchy the world picture was drawn with a smaller, finer brush.

One example can be found in the early seventeenth century in Holland. The merchant Philip Hainhofer of Augsburg was the owner of a small cabinet. His *Kunstkammer* contained objects that were not there on a permanent basis, but which might, if the need arose, be exchanged or sold. The collection of this very small 'museum', therefore, was very much a part of Hainhofer's commercial activities (Bostrom, 1985: 91). Hainhofer acted as an agent for wealthier clients in the collection of objects, and also supervised the making of three great *Kunstschränke*, very large pieces of free-standing furniture designed to hold collections: 'cabinets of the world' in miniature. For at least two of these *Kunstschränke*, Hainhofer chose the objects that they would contain from his own collections. The cabinets were made at the merchant's expense and later purchasers were found for them by sending written descriptions of them to princes all over Europe via business contacts. One of the *Kunstschränke* was sold to Archduke Leopold V of Austria (d.1662) who presented it to his wife's nephew, Grand Duke Ferdinand of Tuscany.

One of the main characteristics of the *Kunstschränke* was as a small-scale version of the princely *Kunstkammern* (Bostrom, 1985: 95). The contents of two of Hainhofer's *Kunstschränke* are known from an inventory. They are divided into *naturalia* and *artificialia* (natural products worked by hand, such as carved precious stones, rosaries, and a knife, fork, and spoon of amber are included in the *naturalia*). Within these two main divisions, the objects are grouped by material and function. In one of the cabinets (the one ultimately bought by Gustavus Aldolphus, and thus known as the 'Uppsala *Kunstschrank*'), the animal, plant, and mineral kingdoms are represented, as are the four continents known at that time, and every historical period from classical times up to Hainhofer's own period. Instruments designed for every variety of work were exhibited alongside those needed for pastimes and aesthetic pleasure. These divisions relate to the organisation of a memory theatre.

The Uppsala *Kunstschrank* expressed universality through its pictorial images. These images formed a comprehensive catalogue which represented two themes: that of the triumph of art and science over nature, and that of 'a compendium of all Holy Scripture'. Also represented are the traditional allegories of the four elements, the five senses, of virtues, and of time and place. In the central section of the *Kunstschrank*, wooden intarsias depict Augsburg at the outbreak of the Thirty Years War, that is at the time of the production of the furniture. These images relate closely to the totality of contents required for a memory theatre, which includes the positioning of the pictured world within a contemporary context.

Many of these objects contained in the *Kunstschränke* seem strange but become meaningful if understood through the similitudes of the Renaissance *episteme*. Four allegories of the seasons are painted in a manner akin to Arcimboldo, as heads made from fruits, flowers, and branches. It has been shown that Arcimboldo's paintings of the seasons and the elements in the *Kunstkammer* of Rudolf II, long regarded as jokes which expressed the disorder and confusion both of Rudolf and his collections, were in fact made meaningful through the system of correspondences of microcosm to macrocosm and in turn articulated with the body politic (Kaufmann, 1978: 26). It is highly likely that these images in the *Kunstschränke* were meaningful in a similar way, although as they were presumably not painted for a specific person, the political and personal references would be more general.

Other images have a similar potential in relation to meaning constituted through similitude: beautiful heads, which turned upside down are seen to represent skulls; a head is made up of the heads of two men, a horse, and a ram (Bostrom, 1985: 98). This concern for metamorphosis pervades much of the pictorial imagery of the *Kunstschränke*. Hainhofer particularly admired 'landscape stones' with, as he put it 'self-made landscapes and buildings'. Clearly, he subscribed to the doctrine of signatures and read and interpreted the language of material things. The visible surfaces of the things which he specifically selected to go into the drawers of the *Kunstschränke* are marks from which the invisible analogies can be found (Foucault, 1970: 26).

Many of the items had a magical significance, either in their form or their material. These include a ewer of coco-de-mer standing on a mountain of coral. The Seychelles nut was thought to be an antidote against poison, and apotropaic properties, particularly against the evil eye, were attributed to coral. Some of the coral twigs were carved in shapes that were thought to avert all sorts of evil. Further objects were thought to have medicinal or prophylactic properties, or were effective as aphrodisiacs:

bezoars (stones from the stomachs of camels); a musk pouch; a bowl of *terra sigillata* (Bostrom, 1985: 97). One of the elements represented by this small-scale 'cabinet of the world' was magic, which through its articulations with other elements (medicine, gesture, sexuality) placed some of the objects in meaningful relational sequences.

This small 'museum' emerged in relation to other earlier and contemporary 'museums'. Hainhofer had had many opportunities to observe other examples. He was given the opportunity to see Francesco I's *studiolo* in Florence as a young man, and had later seen some of the elaborate gardens, including those of the Medici villa at Pratolino, which he describes in a diary of a visit to Italy (Bostrom, 1985: 99). Here he would have seen the palace-garden used as a memory theatre, with different schemes representing the unity of art and nature, and the harmony of the world. He knew about the cultural circles in the Bohemian capital, Prague (R. J. W. Evans, 1973: 181). Hainhofer was also interested in the occult arts and had connections with the Rosicrucian movement. Robert Fludd's book *Utriusque Cosmi Historia* was published at the time that Hainhofer was making his cabinets and appears to have influenced their form and content (Bostrom, 1985: 100).

It is highly likely that the *Kunstschrank* of Gustavus Adolphus was intended to serve as a miniature *Kunstkammer*, a '*theatrum memoriae*', a 'museum' articulating ideas drawn from both Camillo and Fludd, with innumerable pictures and objects in meaningful relational sequences in compartments and drawers, which operated through their interaction and complex polysemic meanings to enable the subject to picture the world.

In addition, the *Kunstschkrank* as a specific example of the 'cabinet of the world' constitutes a new subject position, that of the cultural agent who produces and procures cultural goods which are then sold in the marketplace. This separation of producer and consumer entails further separations and new practices. The secret correspondences of the *Kunstschkrank* had to be 'demonstrated' to the new owner. The second *Kunstschrank*, for example, was presented to Gustavus Adolphus at the end of the Thirty Years War, and was 'demonstrated' to the king by Hainhofer at the presentation ceremony (Bostrom, 1985: 94). Presumably Hainhofer explained the various links in the world picture articulated through the various material things with their specific meaningful and multiple signatures. This need for expertise and explanation of the objects and their relationships marks the beginning of the emergence of the cultural agent or 'museum' maker as 'expert', or 'connoisseur'.

The world pictured by scholars

In Florence, in the late sixteenth and early seventeenth centuries, the combination of medicine, empirical study, and the exploration of the natural world prompted the collection and display of meaningful objects. In these cabinets, the occult aspects of the Renaissance world view were less emphasised than in the *Kunstkammern*, but nonetheless magic was undoubtedly one among the many elements that characterised scholarly 'museums'.

Physicians and university teachers in Italy at the end of the sixteenth century made their own specific collections. A close network of scholar–collectors, who visited each other's collections, exchanged items, and wrote lists for each other, was established. Much of the impetus for these collections came from the study of medicine (Whitehead, 1970: 51) which involved the empirical study of plants, herbs, roots, and minerals. Although these experiments did not at this time lead to the improvement of medical techniques, the accumulation of knowledge of the natural world was to be instrumental in the establishment of herbariums, natural history collections, and gardens during the seventeenth century (Foucault, 1970: 131).

The collections of these physicians have been linked to the idea of the Memory Theatre. Connections have been suggested, for example, between the museums of Aldrovandi and Giganti and the art of memory (Laurencich-Minelli, 1985). Aldrovandi, however, stated that he found books on the art of memory useless in his 'museum' (Olmi, 1985: 7), but he thereby indicated that memory systems were indeed consulted as the basis for classification.

Giganti's 'museum' at Bologna contained an encyclopedic collection, with paintings, books, antiquities, natural things, instruments, and things from the New World. He conceived his collection as constituting a unity (Laurencich-Minelli, 1985: 19). The interactions of the spaces and the collections expressed the sameness rather than the differences of the things of the world. In a short poem dedicated to Aldrovandi's 'museum', Giganti described the 'museum' as the place for the simultaneous evocation of art and nature (ibid.: 19).

In Giganti's 'museum' the books and other things were mixed, so that 'library' and 'museum' were abstract concepts rather than divisions of space and material as we would understand them today. The ceiling of the space containing the bookshelves was used to hang material things, and tables for books were placed in the room where most of the material was displayed. In the physical arrangement of the objects, there was no distinction between natural and man-made things. Every space was filled and a visual harmony was achieved. It is very likely that relationships of resemblance were represented in the way in which the things were placed together.

Two systems of symmetry have been detected in the ordering of the collections (Laurencich-Minelli, 1985). The first concerned the individual items, which were arranged according to 'alternate microsymmetry'. Similar items were never displayed together, but were always interspersed with other dissimilar objects. The second system, 'repeating macro-symmetry', consisted of objects grouped according to themes. The alternating components involved in the microsymmetrical arrangements frequently form two series each with internal homogeneity. One of the series is invariably of natural material. The example given describes a horizontal row of things which combines starfish and portraits on a repeating basis, which is crossed by a vertical row of repeating torpedo fish and starfish.

The rules of place and image seem to be in operation here, articulating the relations of *resemblance* and *sympathy* that are characteristic of the Renaissance *episteme*. The stars are reflected in the faces of men through analogy (Foucault, 1970: 22), and portraits and starfish possibly evoke this relationship, while also reminding the viewer of the universal '*convenientia*' that there are as many stars in the sky as there are fish in the sea (ibid.: 18). Giganti's 'museum' may well be shaped by some of the structures of knowing of the Renaissance.

In Aldrovandi's 'museum', an examination of the index of the natural objects shows that the collection was not ordered according to comparative or functionalist principles. Related items are rarely catalogued together, and where they are, they have irregular rather than consecutive numbering, as though they had been displayed according to the idea of alternate microsymmetry, as in Giganti's 'museum'. It is likely that principles of correspondences have been used to order things within visible relational sequences that both demonstrate and constitute the meanings of these things.

In an engraving dated 1622, showing the interior of Calceolari's 'museum', it is interesting to note the variety and arrangement of objects. Cupboards with shelves surround the room on three sides; at the base of the cupboards are open shelves with vases and other vessels that are interspersed with shells and fish. The arrangements appear to echo those in Giganti's 'museum' (see Plate 1).

Books are placed on the shelves, neatly stacked at one end. Above are narrow drawers pulled out to show the contents, many small oval-shaped boxes, all identical in shape and size, with similar decorations on the lids; above the drawers, five more shelves nearly fill the space to the ceiling. They have shells of many sorts displayed upon them, interspersed with small vessels. In the middle of each side a classical statue stands, and at the end of the room above the shelves of books are two boxes with small sculptures of riders on horseback. In the space above the shelves many birds are standing, some in lifelike postures, with their beaks open, and one has its head turned and its wings partly outstretched. A few sea creatures, such as shells and starfish, are positioned among them. Hanging from the ceiling is a wonderful array of odd beasts, many different kinds of fish, some in fragments, and a human head is hanging from its hair.

In many of these 'museums' there is a concentration on objects from the natural world. In some cases these are linked to man-made objects; *naturalia* and *artificialia* articulating the unity of creation.

In other 'museums' the cataloguing of the natural world seems to be an important aspect in itself. An engraving of Imperato's 'museum' in Naples, dated 1599, shows an arrangement of various things, books, vases, and pots, with animals (exclusively water animals, including an enormous crocodile) attached to the ceiling. Shelves below contain books on one side of the room and small pots and vessels on the other side. Birds stand on some shelves. Clearly to be seen on the ceiling is a two-tailed lizard, presumably a 'monster'.

The approach of the medieval bestiaries, which emphasised the connections and the ancient friendships between man and beast by concentrating on the study of the living creature, its character and its intelligence, was familiar to and accepted by these physicians/naturalists. These bestiaries were based on the book about beasts by the anonymous author known as Physiologus, and in his book could be found the legends and fables of the unicorn and the mermaid which would be known to sixteenth-century collectors (Whitehead, 1970: 52). The compilation of legends, fables, quotations, and indeed anything that was known about the creatures that were being studied, was a basic structure of knowing during the Renaissance, when no distinction was made between observation (that which one had seen for oneself), documentation (that which had been seen and commented on by others), and fable (that which had been imagined by oneself or others) (Foucault, 1970: 39–40).

The collection and classification of animals was often related to both their living or imagined behaviour (Foucault, 1970: 129). For example, in the engraving of Imperato's 'museum', high up on the right can be seen a stuffed pelican, in the act of opening its breast with its beak in order to resuscitate its dead young with its own blood. This is a material representation of the symbol of man's redemption through Christ's blood, taken straight from the pages of the Physiologus (Olmi, 1985: 10). Language and things are interwoven, in a common space, but the primacy of language is indicated in that the corporeal thing (the bird) is displayed as the material representation of the fable.

It is likely that the collections were seen as material forms of writing. The original, abstract art of memory, was like 'inner writing' (Yates, 1966: 6), with the placing, the ordering, and the representation of ideas through images and spaces compared to the act of writing. 'For the places are very much like wax tablets or papyrus, the images like the letters, the arrangement and disposition of the images like the script and the delivery is like the reading' (*Ad Herennium*, quoted in Yates, 1966: 6). The gathering together of meaningful objects, organised and arranged in specific sequences in a special space, produced a 'script' to be 'read'.

The 'script', the 'universal' or 'encyclopedic' aim, varied in each of these cabinets according to the position of the collecting and representing subject. Where the prince wishes to represent to himself the world of imperial and political power through material things that constructed the entirety of the world-that-may-be-dominated, the scholar/physician wished to represent to himself the world-that-may-be-known: in Aldrovandi's case 'le cose sotterranee et le altre sopraterrannee' (Hunt, 1985: 193). In each case, these representations also constituted specific subject positions, in that the scholar/physician made the cabinet, but equally the cabinet made the scholar/physician.

The palace-gardens – the world indoors and outdoors

One of the meanings of the word 'cabinet' in sixteenth-century England was that of a 'summerhouse or bower in a garden'. It was used thus at least until 1737 (Hunt, 1985: 193). In 1671 John Evelyn noted that the 'whole house and garden' of Sir Thomas Browne was a 'paradise and cabinet of rarities, and that of the best collection, especially medals, books, plants, and natural things'. This close relationship of house and garden, which was so admired in England in the later seventeenth century, first made its appearance as part of the 'cabinet of the world' in Renaissance Europe, and especially in Italy.

The garden was a potent metaphor in Renaissance Italy. Charles VIII, on conquering Italy after the fall of the Medici, had this to say of the gardens that he saw in Naples: 'Vous ne pourriez croire les beaulx jardins que j'ay vu en ceste ville, car, sur ma foy, il semble qu'il n'y faille que Adam

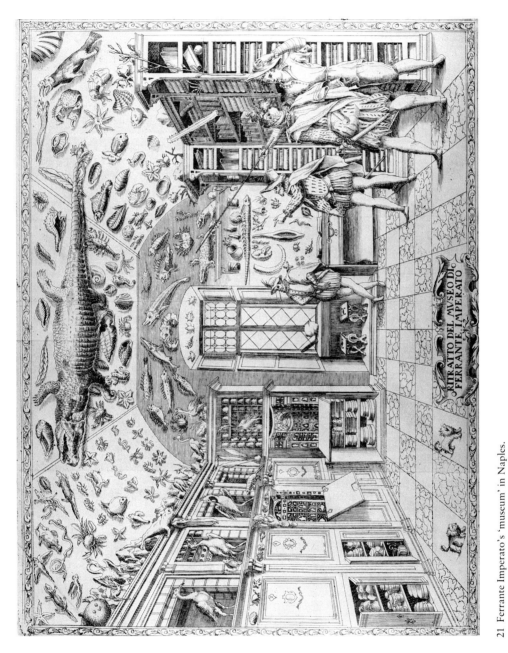

RITRATTO DEL MVSEO DI FERRANTE IMPERATO

21 Ferrante Imperato's 'museum' in Naples.

et Eve pour en faire ung paradis terrestre tant ilz sont beaulx et plains de toutes bonnes et singulieres choses' ('You could not believe the beautiful gardens which I saw in that town for, on my faith, it seems that the only thing missing was Adam amd Eve to make it an earthly paradise, they were so beautiful and full of good and remarkable things') (Comito, 1971: 483).

Tales from earlier times spoke of the southern garden as walled round by air from all enmity or impurity of the elements, and full of powerful talismanic images. The golden age created around the early Medici later in the Renaissance characterised the period as a time when Italy was 'cultivated no less in the mountains and sterile places than in the fertile regions and plains' (Comito, 1971: 486). Images of fecundity, nurture, and a lost magical paradise align with peace and prosperity under a great and good ruler within the space of the garden.

During the sixteenth century the garden came to signify a new sense of the possibilities inherent in a leisured and cultivated existence, life lived with a sense of style. The harmonies of nature were evoked in new plans for gardens which embodied a change from closed to open planning. The encircling walls of the garden were opened and turned outward to the landscape rather than inward to the courtyard (Comito, 1971: 487). At the same time, the closed walls of the castle were turned inside out and, perforated by windows and loggias, brought into relation with the gardens that surrounded it and the prospect beyond it.

Gardens with classical antiquities were created where the statues acted as memory images of the classical past, and plants and animals were used to recall the complete lost world of the Garden of Eden that was still recoverable with human skill (Hunt, 1985: 198). The images and proportions of the friezes on the façades of villas, which were derived from the architecture of ancient temples, measured and constituted a present greatness (Comito, 1971: 488). The past and the present were brought into a relationship with the cosmos through the ordering of the images, the spaces, light, and density.

Following the Palazzo Medici in the fifteenth century, many palaces in the sixteenth century displayed sculpture in the gardens or courtyards. The physical and functional unity of internal and external spaces was emphasised. Loggias blurred the division between inside and outside. Sculptures were embedded in the walls of both the house and the garden. In the Orti Oricellari, the garden of Lorenzo de Medici's brother-in-law Bernardo Rucellai, classical sculpture was displayed alongside every plant mentioned in classical literature (Hunt, 1985: 196). Botanical gardens incorporated buildings to display natural rarities and curiosities

22 *View of the Gardens and the Cortile of the Belvedere in Rome* by Hendrick van Cleeve. This painting, dated 1589 but based on a drawing made in Rome in about 1550, shows how the Renaissance popes placed their antique statues in the gardens of the Belvedere, a pleasure villa built at some distance from the old Vatican palace, to which it was connected by two long galleries.

(Hunt, 1985: 193). Lorenzo de Medici had earlier displayed peacocks, parrots, apes, and a giraffe among other exotic beasts in his garden at Poggio a Cajano (Comito, 1971: 489). Rare plants and rare pictures were equally valued.

Animals, plants, and flowers were represented in stone, shell, and precious materials. Grottoes and waterworks emphasised the congruence of the world, with artificial animals given real horns and tusks; natural rock and sometimes precious stones carved into illusionist caves. The elements were interchanged and mixed, water seemed carved like stone, stone seemed to flow like water, statues moved as hydraulic machinery brought the stones to life.

The Villa Aldobrandini at Frascati was regarded by many travellers in the seventeenth century as the paradigm of these rare and curious experiences (Hunt, 1985: 198). A natural hillside and rustic fountains were discovered behind a formal theatre; the art collections within the house were echoed by natural materials in the alcoves of the exedra; a cabinet built into one end of the terraced hillside manifested rain, birdsong, music, and rainbows through the ingenious use of machinery.

In these gardens and palaces an emphasis on unity, harmony, and completeness can be identified, an attempt to find both symbolic and physical links between different material elements and different spheres of creation. The unity of art and nature is articulated.

The example of the palace-garden was followed in Elizabethan England at Theobalds. Burghley, Elizabeth's Lord Treasurer, planned a 'conspectus of the universe, the nations, of England and her governers, considered as a setting for England's queen' (Comito, 1971: 498). The presence chamber of the house was described as a grotto, with water streaming out of a rock, the zodiac with sun and moon on the ceiling, and on the wall, six trees hung with the heraldic shields of England's nobility. The regal pretensions of Theobalds were embodied in its transformations of the natural world, which were presented as a perfected cosmos that encapsulates all the greatness of history.

The Renaissance world, with its centripetal universe folded in upon itself (Foucault, 1970: 17) was pictured and represented as a view which simultaneously included and represented the subject.

Conclusions

This chapter has suggested that the 'confused and disordered' 'cabinets of curiosity' can be better understood as 'cabinets of the world', and a number of different manifestations of the 'cabinet of the world' have been discussed. The rationality that explains the structure of knowledge that informed the 'cabinet of the world' can be understood, at least in part, through a combination of several elements. These include the epistemological practices of the Renaissance *episteme* (interpretation, resemblance, esoteric knowledge); mnemonic techniques (places and images); and models of the world presented through two-dimensional (Fludd) and three-dimensional (Camillo) exemplars. The proper target of the 'cabinets of the world' will vary according to the subject position of the 'collector' (prince, scholar, merchant).

In all of the instances that have been discussed above, some strong (though necessarily partial) links have been identified that confirm this thesis. In many cases the evidence is slight, ambiguous, or incomplete. The problem of working with texts that have been written from within other philosophical frameworks has been noticeable throughout.

The understanding of the significance of the 'universal museum', as it is commonly called, is illuminated by Foucault's exposition of the Renaissance *episteme*. In outlining the system of *resemblances* and the play of *sympathies*, and in underlining the importance of the unity of the world, an insight is offered into a totally different form of organisation of the world that is extremely difficult to grasp from the standpoint of the late twentieth century.

Many of the present-day comments on the encyclopedic project are so firmly entrenched in the modern *episteme* as to make their explanations virtually meaningless. In fact, much of the work remains at the level of description. An explanation of the articulations of the collections of the late sixteenth century can only begin to be worthwhile if it acknowledges the immense epistemological rupture that exists between now and then. The neutral stance of Foucault's methodology makes some sort of a reconstruction possible because it does not accord value to practices and programmes that have been judged to be nonsensical and irrational. Similarly, Yates's analysis of the practices of the art of memory recognises that the occult is a rational way of knowing, and as such she offers evidence that can be used in 'effective' history.

The 'cabinet of the world' has been analysed from existing accounts based on archival work that has not been informed by the work of either Foucault or Yates. These museum histories have also, in the main, been written from a position that accepts contemporary definitions of 'fine art'. In discussing the encyclopedic project as expressed in the collections of these princes, for example, one of the basic problems is that previous research has been premised on this specific view of 'art'. Much of the work has been limited to a discussion of only one aspect of the entire collection, that of the contents of the *Kunstkammer*, on the grounds that it is these objects that later form the 'art collections'. Most of the research does not question the constitution of the category 'art', even though it is clear that this category does not explain the aim, content, or original organisation of the collections. Thus Hajos, for example, refers to Quiccheberg's work with the collection of the Duke of Bavaria as 'the reorganization of the art collections' (Hajos, 1958: 151).

A double selectivity has therefore been in operation in the museum histories of this period: an exclusion of material that is not seen to be relevant to the history of 'art', and an exclusion of material that cannot be accommodated within contemporary notions of 'truth'. Work on documents and collections using the methodologies of effective history would provide a more usable past.

The Repository of the Royal Society

6

During the Renaissance, writing was the privileged epistemological structure. Objects had marks written upon them, signatures, messages, that demanded reading and interpretation. Natural and artificial things were thought of in much the same way as manuscripts and texts. An accumulation of objects and an accumulation of texts signified in the same way, and were displayed mixed together in the same spaces. In the Memory Theatre of Camillo, for example, images carried the same messages as words, sometimes words were used, sometimes pictures. In Giganti's 'museum' in Bologna, the objects and the texts together represented the unity of the world. In Imperato's 'museum' in Naples, what we would now call objects and what we would now call books said the same thing: the stuffed and mounted pelican told the same story as the words in the Physiologus. Knowing consisted of 'relating one form of language to another form of language; in restoring the great unbroken plain of words and things; in making everything speak' (Foucault, 1970: 40).

The classical *episteme*

Shortly after the beginning of the seventeenth century this profound relationship of language with the world was dissolved. From then on, words and things would become separated. Henceforward the eye was destined to see and only to see, the ear to hear and only to hear. Thus an enormous reorganisation of culture came about (Foucault, 1970: 43)

Up to and during the sixteenth century, the empirical domain of things was perceived as a complex of kinships, resemblances, and affinities that were endlessly interwoven; and the interweaving of language and things in a space common to both presupposed a privilege on the part of writing (Foucault, 1970: 3). Knowledge meant knowing and relating all the dense layer of signs with which a thing may have been covered, in making everything speak. The proper function of knowledge was interpretation.

The arrangement of signs was ternary and fluid, but during the shift in culture that was to herald the classical age, signs would become binary (Foucault, 1970: 42) and this would render them stable. Language ceased to be the material writing of things and became simply the way of organising the representation of signs. Man clarified, through language, the creation of God (Dreyfus and Rabinow, 1982: 20). Thus, in the sixteenth century, one asked how was it possible to know that a sign did designate what it signified; but from the seventeeth century one asked how was a sign linked to what it signified.

Resemblance as a primary function of empirical knowledge was now perceived to be muddled, confused, and disordered. Experience must be analysed in terms of order, identity, difference, and measurement (Foucault, 1970: 52). Thus there occurred some fundamental modifications to the Renaissance *episteme*. Analysis was substituted for the hierarchy of analogies. Previously an analogous correspondence had been posited between earth and sky, planets and faces, the microcosm and the macrocosm. Now, comparison was used in order to discover identity and difference through measurement against a common unit, or by position in an order. Where previously the interplay of similitudes was endless, and it was always possible to discover new ones, now a complete enumeration became possible. Comparison could aim at perfect certainty, the old system of similitudes could not. Complete enumeration and the assignment of each point in relation to the next permitted an absolutely certain knowledge of identity and difference, although this also has its own relativity, in that things could be classified in more than one way. Knowledge, however, now had the possibility of finite boundaries.

The activity of mind would no longer consist of drawing things together by setting out a secret kinship, or attraction, but in discriminating, that is, establishing identity on the basis of difference. To know was therefore to discriminate and, as a consequence of this, history and science become separate: history was to consist of the perusal of written works and opinions; science would be constituted by the confident judgements that could be established through measurement and experiment.

The fundamental element of the classical *episteme* is the link with the mathesis. Relations between things were to be conceived in the form of order and measurement, although it was always possible to reduce problems of measurement to problems of order. The relation of all knowledge to the mathesis was posited as the possibility of establishing an ordered succession, even between things that were not measurable. Thus analysis became a universal method (Foucault, 1970: 57)

Knowledge was not thereby absorbed into mathematics, nor was mathematics the foundation of all knowledge, but, in correlation with the quest for the mathesis, a certain number of empirical fields emerged that were formed for the first time and that were founded on a possible science of order. These new fields were coextensive with the classical age. They took the form, not of the algebraic method, but of a system of signs. These fields were general grammar, natural history, and the analysis of wealth, all of which are sciences of order in the domain of words, being, and needs. None of these could have been founded without the relation that the entire *episteme* of western culture maintained at that time with a universal science of order. Order is to the classical age what interpretation was to the Renaissance.

There were two forms of comparison; measurement and order. In the case of measurement, the whole was considered and divided up into parts, resulting in a number of units, which were measured according to mathematical relations of equality and inequality. Measurement enabled an analysis of like things according to the calculable form of identity and difference. It could be seen that comparison by measurement required a division to begin with, followed by the application of a common unit. Order was established without reference to an exterior unit, by relating hierarchies of complexity between things. Comparison by order was a simple act that enabled the passing from one thing to the other by means of an absolutely uninterrupted movement. In this way a series was established, which could be intuited independently of anything else. Order established elements, the simplest that could be found, and arranged differences according to the smallest possible degrees. Difference was defined by visible morphological features, rather than by the interpretation of hidden resemblances. The seeing of things was now privileged over the reading of things. To see was to know.

Knowing consisted of measuring the visible and then reducing all measurement to a serial arrangement which, beginning from the simplest, showed differences as degrees of complexity.

Interpretation was a knowledge based on similitude. The ordering of things by means of signs constituted a knowledge based upon identity and difference. The endless and closed world of resemblances now found itself split down the middle; on the one side, signs had become tools of analysis, marks of identity and difference, principles whereby things could be reduced to an order, keys for a taxonomy; and on the other hand, the empirical nature of things furnished the infinite raw material for the analysis of divisions and distributions. On the one hand, the general theory of signs and classifications, and on the other, nature and immediate resemblances. And between the two, the new forms of knowledge that occupied the area opened up by this split, occupied it by making links between the two sides, between theory and nature, between being and knowing.

And how was this representation made? What counted as a valid relationship? Signs were defined by three different aspects of their relationship to things: the certainty of the relation (constant or probable), the type of relation (belonging to the whole or separate), and the origin of the relation (natural or conventional).

In discussing the relation of the sign to what it signified, Foucault points out that similitude in the sixteenth century triumphed over space and time, by drawing together disparate things. In Foucault's classical age (the seventeenth and eighteenth centuries), the sign, in order to be a sign, had to be presented as an object of knowledge at the same time as that which it signifies. The constitution of the sign also implied analysis, in recognising that it indicated this and not that. It became an instrument for analysis. The sign enabled things to become distinct, to preserve themselves within their own identities.

In the case of the origin of the relation, during the Renaissance, the man-made sign had primacy over the natural sign; it indicated the difference between man and animal, and instinct and rational knowledge. However, in the classical age the use of signs was an attempt to discover the arbitary language that would authorise the deployment of nature within its space, the final terms of its analysis and the laws of its composition, not, as before, the rediscovery of signs beneath the primitive text of a discourse sustained and retained for ever. It was no longer the task of knowledge to dig out the ancient and pre-existing word from unknown places where it might have been hidden; the task of knowledge now was to fabricate a language, that as an instrument of analysis and combination, would really be the language of calculation and of clarification. Language as a medium of representation was seen as reliable, uncomplicated, and transparent, which by its nature made representation possible (Dreyfus and Rabinow, 1982: 20).

A new gaze

Up to the end of the sixteenth century all that existed were histories. Belon wrote a *History of the Nature of Birds* and Aldrovandi wrote a *History of Serpents and Dragons*. History consisted of the complete and unitary fabric of all things visible and invisible, and to write the history of a plant was to include all that was known about it (Foucault, 1970: 129). The division into observation, document, and fable did not exist before the seventeenth century. Signs during the sixteenth century were part of the things themselves, whereas later they became modes of representation. During the classical age, signs became binary and language ceased to be the material writing of things and became a way of organising things (Foucault, 1970: 42). During the seventeenth century, history became natural (ibid.: 128).

The documents of this new history were not other words, or texts, but unencumbered spaces in which things were juxtaposed; herbaria, collections, gardens. The place of history was a non-temporal rectangle in which, stripped of all commentary, of all enveloping language, creatures presented themselves one beside the other, their surfaces visible, grouped according to their common features, and thus already virtually analysed, bearers of nothing but their own individual names (Foucault, 1970: 131).

The seventeenth century saw the proliferation of collections, botanical gardens, and menageries among the nobility and the aspirant bourgeois intellectuals in Europe (Ornstein, 1938: 5; Simpson, 1984: 187; MacGregor, 1983: 90). Societies and institutions also began to assemble artefacts and specimens, often for the purposes of teaching (MacGregor, 1983: 84). These institutional and the private collections were frequently short-lived, dispersed on the death of their compiler, or at a change in institutional fortunes, or (as was the case of the collection of Rudolf II) in times of war (MacGregor, 1983: 91). Where the play of dominations was not subject to abrupt reversals, collections remained intact and were augmented and reorganised throughout the classical period. One example of such an accumulation is the princely collection at Dresden which remained intact for many decades, not to be disturbed until the looting forays of Napoleon (Menzhausen, 1970).

On the whole there was a great mobility of collections and occasionally entire cabinets changed hands. Methods of acquisition included personal contact with ambassadors and travellers, written requests to travellers, or foreign travel on the part of the collector him/herself. Missionaries were prominent in importing foreign goods into Europe. Shops sprang up to cater for the increasing appetite for 'rarities', such as one in Paris called 'Noahs-Arke, where are to be had for money all the Curiosities naturall or artificial imaginable, Indian or European, for luxury or Use, as Cabinets, Shells, Ivorys, Purselan, Dried fishes, rare Insects, Birds, Pictures, and a thousand exotic extravagances' (MacGregor, 1983: 91).

The classical age operated in a classified time, and in a squared and spatialised development, where the establishment of records, of filing systems for them, the drawing up of catalogues, indexes, and inventories, worked as a way of introducing an order between all things. The classical age stripped away much of the contextualising material that had accrued to things and ideas during the Renaissance. In part, this was achieved through methods resembling those of botanists.

Foucault describes natural history as nothing more than the nomination of the visible. Hence its apparently simple and obvious naïve appearance. It may appear that the early naturalists were suddenly, through looking harder and more closely, able to see that which had not been seen before; but this was not, in fact, the case. The classical age used its ingenuity to see as little as possible and to restrict its area of experience. Observation from the seventeenth century onwards was a knowledge based on perception, furnished with a series of systematically negative conditions. Hearsay was excluded, as were taste and smell, because of their lack of certainty and the difficulty of rendering exact expressions in words; the sense of touch was very narrowly employed in the designation of a few fairly self-evident distinctions; which left sight with an almost exclusive privilege, being the sense by which proof was to be both perceived and established. And even then, not all the elements that presented themselves to be seen were utilisable; colours in particular were difficult to use for comparative purposes. Observation therefore assumed its powers through a visibility freed from all other sensory burdens and restricted to black and white (Foucault, 1970: 133).

To observe was to be content with seeing, and with seeing only a limited number of things in a very systematic way. There was a deliberate restriction and exclusion in the aspects of things that were to be perceived. Linnaeus pointed out that every annotation in relation to specimens should be a product of number, of form, of proportion, of situation. This enumeration would be sufficient, but it was indispensable. Limitation set the conditions for comparison. By seeing that which could be recognised and analysed and compared, it was possible to give a name that could be accepted by all. Thus the magical, confused, various, and haphazard nature of things could be tamed, named, and displayed on a table to constitute a firm base of knowledge. 'Snakestones', previously prized for their efficacy against snake bite, would become fossil-types known as 'ammonites', and 'devils' toe-nails' would be reclassified as 'gryphites' (Skeat, 1912).

Analysis of the structure of the visible in relation to natural history showed the mechanism by which the whole teeming area of the visible was reduced to a system of variables, all of whose values could be designated, and which would enable the great proliferation of beings that occupied the surface of the earth to enter into the sequence of a descriptive language and into the field of the mathesis. Having set up an order based on measurement and series that was considered the correct way in which to describe and understand animals and plants, this order, through the establishment of words, was transposed and redeveloped within the same frame of reference, for the classification of the social world (Foucault, 1970: 76). Thus doctors botanised in the pathological garden (Foucault, 1976: 7, 89) and in the reorganisation of prisons a Linnaean classification of human crimes and punishments was constructed (Foucault, 1982b: 99). The same classificatory methods were employed to order the products of nature and the products of the social. As a result, the complex social, political, economic, and cultural elements that shape people, their actions, and their material products and possessions, were reduced to mono-dimensional taxonomies.

At the institutional level, the correlatives of the visible patterning of the natural world were the botanical gardens and natural history collections. Their importance for classical culture was to be found not in what they allowed to be seen but in what they hid and in what, in this process of obliteration, they allowed to emerge. In terms of natural history, they screened off anatomy, and function, and concealed the organism, in order 'to raise up before the eyes of those who await the truth the visible relief of forms, with their elements, their mode of distribution, and their measurements' (Foucault, 1970: 137). These collections were books furnished with structures, spaces in which characteristics combined and in which classifications were physically displayed through the ordering of things, three-dimensional catalogues which in their physical existence confirm a being, a knowing, and a truth.

The establishment of herbaria, botanical gardens, and zoological collections in the classical age has been described as indicating a new curiosity about exotic plants and animals. Foucault suggests that this curiosity had existed for some time, but that what had changed was the space in which these things could be seen and described. During the Renaissance, the strangeness of animals was a spectacle, to be featured in fairs and tournaments, which took the form of a moving circular procession or show. 'The natural history room and the garden, as created in the classical period, replaced the circular procession of the "show" by the arrangement of things in a "table"' (Foucault, 1970: 131).

But neither collections nor gardens were new in the classical age. Although not as prevalent or as elaborate as the spectacles that were the major expository form, and which were used with specifically political purposes (Strong, 1973), gardens, museums, studios, and collections had been established during the fifteenth and particularly the sixteenth centuries.

What was new in the classical age was the form of arrangement and the ordering of material. During the Renaissance, collections, both indoors and out, had been articulated to present a circular, harmonious representation of the world. The *studiolo* of Francesco I de Medici was constituted as a place from the centre of which the prince could symbolically reclaim dominion over the entire natural and artificial world (Olmi, 1985: 5). The museums of Giganti and Calceolari were constituted through circulating harmonies that related both natural and artificial signs to the plays of resemblance and similitude. The gardens and grottoes of Renaissance Italy provided a circulating experience where both inside and outside spaces, water and land, could together present a '*theatrum mundi*'. Their collections of antiquities constituted a memory theatre of the classical past, while natural history collections of animals and plants were a memory theatre of that complete world lost with the Garden of Eden but recoverable by human skill. Evelyn gives the garden the task 'to comprehend the principal and most useful plants, and to be as a rich and noble Compendium of what the Globe of the Earth has flourishing upon her boosome' (Hunt, 1985: 198). Cabinet and garden were articulated to link both art and nature. The circular, polysemic spaces of the Renaissance collections both constituted and were constituted by the fluidity and multiplicity of meaning that the Renaissance *episteme* permitted.

Between the age of the theatre and the classical age, that Foucault refers to as 'the age of the catalogue', a new way of seeing and saying, a new way of connecting things both to the eye and to discourse, came into being. A new way of making history (Foucault, 1970: 131). The circular relationships of resemblance, infinitely variable, and often personal, are replaced by a tabulated, documented, limited canon of order. The dynamic potential of relationships between things and of new ways of interpreting things would vanish in the two-dimensional epistemological space of the 'museum', along with the words that had formerly contextualised material things. Things which had been displayed together to demonstrate the variety and richness of the world would now be displayed apart, linked not to something dissimilar through hidden resemblances, but to something that had the same morphological features, that looked the same, and could be classed in the same family or species.

The development and display of series of similar things became a priority. Specialised collections developed, and along with them, specialised institutions. The late seventeenth century sees the separation of gardens from cabinets in England, for example, with the two institutions of botanical garden and 'museum' able to concentrate on their own special material things more effectively when physically separated (Hunt, 1985: 202).

Other separations and other series came into being. The gaze, which distinguished and formed series on the basis of external form, reorganised and regrouped material things. During the sixteenth century, pictures had formed part of a mixed group of objects, linked through hidden resemblances. In the Medici Palace, for example, paintings and tiles together formed wall decorations; in the Theatre of Camillo, paintings and inscriptions were offered together for the interpretation of secret messages; in Giganti's museum, paintings are displayed together with starfish. Now, at the end of the seventeenth century, pictures were seen as part of a series, and fitting into a decorative scheme. They were not yet considered as individual objects (Van Holst, 1967: 162) but were grouped with others of the same broad type. The combined display of fish and portraits would no longer be seen as either possible or rational.

Series were used to form two-dimensional decorative schemes. A painting by Johann Bretschneider shows the picture gallery of the Habsburgs in Prague. The paintings cover the wall from floor to ceiling, and are arranged symmetrically by size and by topic. One contemporary writer says that the walls 'were not to be hung with anything save paintings, so that one painting should touch the frame of the other' (Van Holst, 1967: 161). Larger paintings occupy the central wall space, while smaller ones are arranged round them in a decorative fashion, portraits and flower paintings being arranged symmetrically according to topic, rather than by artist, country, or date. The arrangement was decided according to the visible features of the works rather than the symbolic meanings and their correspondences as in, for example, Francesco's *studiolo*. The horizons of the paintings were considered so that those with different horizons did not hang too near each other. Large and small frames were not combined (ibid.: 163). Old and modern paintings hung together.

Paintings were 'formatised' by being cut down, or extended to fit into the space that was available (Bazin, 1967: 89). Oval pictures were produced from rectangular ones. Half-length portraits were produced from full-length. In the Vienna Stallburg, about 40 per cent of the paintings had been 'formatised', and in the Mittelsbach collection then housed in the Palace of Schleissheim near Munich, about a third of the paintings were 'reformed' (Van Holst, 1967: 162).

Matching series, which had previously been constituted on the basis of their deep connections or their connections through the mystical power of numbers, such as the balance between the twelve apostles and the twelve ancient Roman emperors (Van Holst, 1967: 91), were now put together on the basis of morphological features. In the Medici Palace, Piero might have had a series of images of ancient heroes, which formed a series through the materials that were represented. These would have included gold, silver, and bronze, probably in the form of coins; precious stones, perhaps in the form of rings and gems; and marble, in the form of a sculpted bust. Thus the catalogue of materials, which linked to the Renaissance classification of the world, would have been of prime importance in forming a series.

In the classical age, new priorities emerged for the constitutions of series. Coins and sculptures, for example, would be separated. New orderings were suggested for things according to their form and series of sculptures were formed according to their shape. In 1762, for example, J. D. Koehler in his book *Suggestions for Travelling Students* advised would-be collectors to be systematic, and to divide statues into 'upright standing', 'seated', 'nudes', and 'clothed' (Wittlin, 1949: 85). The resulting series would privilege a visual similarity and harmony. Thus in the classical age, those priorities of the Renaissance, the classifications of the world described by the art of memory, were not important. Neither were the priorities which were to emerge with the modern age: the place of origin of the sculpture, the identity of artist, and the date of production.

In the same way that paintings were seen as series, as elements making up part of a whole, fragments were not acceptable, and sculptures and other objects were completed (Bazin, 1967: 89), often not very competently. Replicas and small, scale copies of well-known works were used to form complete representations (ibid.: 52, 73). It was not until the beginning of the eighteenth century that the question of distinguishing the 'true' from the 'false', the 'real' from the 'copy' would arise (ibid.: 116). During the seventeenth century the concept of authenticity was not important. The idea of a complete series was more valued.

Drawings lost their individual identity by being stuck together into large volumes, unified and presented as a series through being framed with delicately coloured matching edges (Van Holst, 1967: 162). Copies or 'views' of entire collections were produced as the idea of collecting became fashionable across Europe. Engravings and gouache copies of individual paintings, or of a group painted together, were sold and acted as proto-catalogues (Bazin, 1967: 160, 244, 324).

Collections emerged in new geographical areas that had been slow to move out of the Middle Ages and had been cut off from the cultural centres of Europe, such as England and Denmark. The spaces containing collections began to separate, entailing divisions both in the material objects and in new 'research' areas; archives were established as the tabulations of material things demanded registers and filing cabinets; specific individuals were appointed to organise collections. Objects and subjects were constituted as meaningful in new ways. New practices and new technologies began to emerge, but in a haphazard and fragmented way.

23 *The Imperial Gallery in Prague*, by Johann Bretschneider, 1714. The paintings are arranged according to the visual and decorative effect.

At the beginning of the eighteenth century, treatises to guide amateur collectors began to appear (Bazin, 1967: 115). In 1727, for example, Caspar Neickel, a dealer from Hamburg, produced *Museographica*, written in Latin for distribution across Europe. This offered guidance on locations for acquisition of material suitable for collections, problems of classification, and techniques of caring for things in what would now be known as a controlled environment. Neickel discusses 'old curio cabinets' as well as 'cabinets of art'. In relation to display, he suggests a table in the middle of each space where things brought from the repository could be studied. Things are divided into groups of *naturalia*, *curiosa*, and *artificialia*. The two older divisions of *naturalia* and *artificialia* which are drawn from much earlier ways of dividing the world, are now supplemented by a new classification, *curiosa*.

Familiar problems appear in the rereading of these histories. Bazin, in his discussion of this work, concentrates on the classification of 'paintings' and '*objets d'art*', which he discovers in the division devoted to *artificialia*. Although he points out that the things which he wishes to select and call 'art' are not treated from an aesthetic point of view in these earlier collections, or by Neickel (Bazin, 1967: 115), nonetheless he seems unaware that he is in fact violating the earlier categories, and imposing later forms of classification. An inability to accept the earlier forms of division as rational or sensible is evident. These earlier divisions are regarded as so meaningless and irrational as to be totally irrelevant, and, as the material things are made meaningful in new divisions and new classifications, the earlier truth is ignored and cast aside.

The formation of the category of 'art' had not emerged at this time in the classical age (Kristeller, 1951: 497). However, both Bazin (1967) and Van Holst (1967), major sources for this and earlier periods, read the historical documents as though 'fine art' as a classification had existed as an absolute for ever. It is clear that the seventeenth-century documents are used as inert material to confirm the 'memory' of the twentieth-century researcher (Foucault, 1974: 7).

The gaze of the age of the catalogue searched for difference, based on measurable surface features. Old confusing elaborations were cut away to reveal individual singularities. Many of the collections that emerged during the seventeenth and eighteenth centuries were established with the aim of tabulating knowledge in accordance with the mutation of culture that Foucault describes. But these aims often coexisted uneasily with other intentions which were not epistemological, but which had their own forms and targets. Many articulations of elements are contradictory, within a dispersed and fragmented field that has little unity.

The Repository of the Royal Society

The third case-study, the Repository of the Royal Society in England, came into being at a time when values and practices in England were at a point of rupture and discontinuity (Thomas, 1973: 512). The effects of the Civil War had been deeply unsettling and had led to an intellectual ferment that enabled the overthrow of ideas in a way that had proved impossible in the older intellectual centres in Europe (Bronowski and Mazlish, 1970: 152). New sources of authority and opinion were sought (Hunter, 1981: 26). The concern for the reform of knowledge that was to be demonstrated in the Repository of the Royal Society was only one instance of the general interest in a major epistemological reorganisation (ibid.: 118).

The Repository of the Royal Society was constituted in part by a shift in collecting practices from private to public (which in itself implied a shift into permanence), which combined with an intended complete reform of knowledge. This reform of knowledge was seen as an instrument to create a new 'truth', a cutting tool appropriate for a new *episteme*. A new rational language was to be created that would enable the new rational ordering of things. A universal language, able to be used by merchants, divines, and scientists, would be used to classify objectively ideas and data about natural phenomena in what might 'prove the shortest and plainest way for the attainment of real knowledge, that hath been yet offered to the World' (quoted in Hunter, 1981: 118). Representation of the empirical world was to be effected by language which bore a transparent relationship to things. At this time, words, rather than representing thought, were understood to represent material things. Thus it was thought that it would be possible to form a 'universal' collection of material things that would be identical in classification to the 'universal' language. Language and things would represent the same divisions of the world. This universal language was a self-consciously new linguistic discourse set up with new aims in a deliberate attempt to construct a new regime of truth (Foucault, 1977: 14). The Repository, the 'museum' of the Society, was an integral part of these ambitions.

The Royal Society was founded in 1660 by a group of men who had initially met at Gresham College as an experimental science club (Bronowski and Mazlish, 1970: 214). This informal group was re-formed as a self-consciously public institution. The imperatives for the emergence of collective institutions included both the economic and the ideological. Experimental science entailed a complex articulation of equipment, space, and subjects that was beyond the resources of individuals, and thus led to the joint provision of a laboratory (Ornstein, 1938: 67) and a 'keeper' or 'curator' to set up experiments and look after the instruments.

'Science', that is, the pursuit of knowledge (Hunter, 1981: 8) was regarded, following Baconian ideals, as a communal activity, with groups of scientists working together for the collective good (Bronowski and Mazlish, 1970: 220).

Other scientific societies had emerged in Europe, notably the 'Accademia del Cimento' in Florence and the 'Académie des Sciences' in Paris. One of the forerunners of the Italian society was the 'Accademia dei Lincei' in Rome (1600–30), whose symbol, a lynx tearing at a Cerberus, represented the struggle of scientific truth with ignorance and falsehood (Ornstein, 1938: 74). This society was part of a scheme that took an earlier form of communal life as its model. A plan had been devised to establish common, scientific, non-clerical monasteries in the four corners of the globe, working towards scientific co-operation. The proper study of 'science' was to be furthered by the establishment of a museum, library, printing office, botanical gardens, and laboratories in each house. A form of non-religious brotherhood was envisaged (ibid.: 75).

There is some evidence that the early plans for the Royal Society followed this model. Evelyn proposed purchasing an existing building outside London and establishing apartments or cells for members, 'somewhat after the manner of the Carthusians'. In addition:

> There should be an elaboratory for rarities and things of nature, an aviary, dove house, physick garden ... Every person of the society shall render public account of his studies weekly if thought fit, and especially shall be recommended the promotion of experimental knowledge as the principal end of the institution.
>
> (Ornstein, 1938: 99)

In the event, the idea of this austere, controlled, medieval institution, inspired by the monastery, was replaced by the idea of a 'college'. 'Institutionalisation' was seen as a more productive way of pursuing scientific enterprise (Hunter, 1981: 35).

The Royal Society was established 'for the promotion of Experimental Philosophy' towards a 'design of founding a Colledge for the Promoting of Physico-Mathematical, Experimental Learning' (Purver and Bowen, 1960: 5). This public society represented a new form of group endeavour, with a formal constitution; membership by subscription; rules and regulations; and elected officers and members. This acted as a model from which stemmed many other derivative societies (Hunter, 1982: 12). The original ambitions for the Society intended it to be structured as a national research institute, a 'college' with a specific, purpose-built building providing a permanent base with facilities for lectures (Hunter, 1981: 41), and a large-scale financial endowment such that perpetuity was ensured (ibid.: 35, 38, 39).

The aims of the Royal Society were comprehensive: 'according to our opportunities to make inquisitive experiments ... that out of a sufficient number of sure experiments the way of nature in workeing may be discovered' (Purver and Bowen, 1960: 6). In part as a reaction to the apparently irrational, uncontrolled, and proliferating links between things that were accepted during the Renaissance, the scientists of the Royal Society were determined to accept as 'true' only that which they could prove through replicable experiment. No existing hypotheses were to be entertained 'till by mature debate and clear arguments, chiefly such as are deduced from legitimate experiments, the truth of such experiments be demonstrated invincibly' (Ornstein, 1938: 109). The Fellows were urged in their reports to be succinct; 'to return back to the primitive purity, and shortness when men delivered so many *things* almost in an equal number of *words*' (Bronowski and Mazlish, 1970: 226).

A second aim was to begin a comprehensive collection: 'In order to the compiling of a complete system of solid philosophy for explicating all phenomena produced by nature or art, and recording a rational account of the causes of things' (Ornstein, 1938: 109). The collection of material things would become significant through order and comparison, the new rationality. The collection would be called the 'Repository' in the minutes of the Society, with 'museum' being seen as the Latin equivalent of this (Hunter, 1985: 163). The main task of the Repository would be to make it easy 'to find likenesse and unlikenesse of things upon a suddaine' (Hunter, 1981: 65). This one Repository was seen, to a certain extent, as part of a larger scheme. The private collections which were rapidly emerging, and which were regarded rather scornfully by some members of the Royal Society, nevertheless would, the first secretary to the Society suggested, 'at length make up such a Store-house, as our Society designeth for a Universal History of Nature' (ibid.: 65).

Bacon had advocated the inductive method in science, which led to the need for a collection of material as a store of data (Hunter, 1981: 13, 18) on which to base observations and hypotheses. Part of the work of the Society was to be the 'viewing and discoursing of curiosities of nature and art' (Ornstein, 1938: 109). The Society had begun to accumulate experimental equipment and unusual natural specimens from its earliest years (Hunter, 1985: 162) as 'a General collection of all the Effects of Arts, and the Common or Monstrous Works of Nature' was 'one of the Principal Intentions' of the Society (Sprat, 1667: 251).

The process of acquisition of the collections presupposed an interrelationship of epistemological aims with social aims. Gifts from benefactors were solicited (Hunter, 1981: 67) with the intention that the collection itself would become a valuable tool for the reform of knowledge (Hunter, 1985: 163). Although largely founded upon the purchase of the cabinet of one Robert Hubert, it was hoped that the Repository of the Society would be more effective than the private cabinets, which were regarded as haphazard, and that it would 'be employed for considerable Philosophical and Usefull purposes' (ibid.: 163). It was hoped that the corporate life of the Society as an institution would entail some measure of permanence for the collections, unlike the private collections which were vulnerable to dispersal on the death of their owner. This was used as an inducement in the solicitation of gifts (Hunter, 1981: 67), which were not long in arriving (Weld, 1975: 189). 'In short time it [the collection] has increased so fast, by a contribution from all Parts ... that they have already drawn together into one room, the greatest part of all the several kinds of things, that are scattered throughout the Universe' (Sprat, 1667: 251).

The aims of the Royal Society in relation to the collection were ambitious. The founders aspired to a 'complete' collection, one that would enable the construction of a universal taxonomy which would accurately mirror the order of nature (Hunter, 1985: 164). 'Complete' is here understood as the compilation of a series with linking units. In 1669 the botanical collector Thomas Willisel was employed by the Society to travel throughout the British Isles to obtain 'such natural things, as may be had in England, and were yet wanting in the society's repository' (ibid.: 164). It was intended that a complete series of specific types of specimen would be collected: 'a full and compleat a Collection ... of Fossile-Shells', for example. These series were for study rather than for fun: 'for the most serious and diligent study of the most able Proficient in Natural Philosophy' rather than for 'Divertisement, and Wonder, and Gazing, and like Pictures for Children to admire and be pleased with' (Torrens, 1985: 211).

Universal language schemes

Several Fellows of the Royal Society were involved with the philosophical base, the structure, and the development of a universal 'rational' language (Hunter, 1985: 164). The perceived need for this language arose through a combination of several factors. Firstly, there was a concern that whereas in earlier times, Latin had in effect acted as a universal language, the increasing use of the vernacular had led to scientists from different countries being cut off from each other's work (Knowlson, 1975: 7). This was the reason for the publication of some works in Latin, as for example

Neickel's *Museographica* (Bazin, 1967: 115). A universal language would enable scholars from all over the world to communicate, and once established, would also enable communication with non-Europeans, a need that was becoming more vital as voyages of discovery revealed the languages of the Far East or West (Knowlson, 1975: 8).

The search for the original language of the world which had occupied sixteenth-century scholars was linked to this. The belief that there had once been a *lingua humana* from which all other languages had descended, and which had provided an insight into natural secrets and supernatural truths, lay behind the investigations of ancient languages carried out by the cabalists and the Rosicrucians (Knowlson, 1975: 13; Foucault, 1970: 36). Many of the mnemotechnical schemes of the sixteenth century had worked with the structures of ancient languages and letter forms to provide ways and means of discovering similitudes (Thomas, 1973: 265; Foucault, 1970: 33). That part of the Lullian art that had the function of an art of memory used letter notations to represent concepts, arranged on concentric wheels, which when revolving produced new combinations of these concepts (Yates, 1966: 174–6) and transformed the classical art into a newly investigative art (ibid.: 185). In the seventeenth century, the art of memory was discussed by writers like Robert Fludd (who was still enmeshed in Renaissance epistemic structures), but was also of interest to thinkers whose ideas were more strongly related to the classical age, such as Bacon, Descartes, and Leibniz (ibid.: 368). During the seventeenth century the art of memory was transformed from a method of memorising the encyclopedia of knowledge and of reflecting the world in memory, to an aid for investigating the encyclopedia with the object of discovering new knowledge.

The Baconian use of the art of memory replaces places and images by 'prenotations' and 'emblems':

> This art of memory is but built upon two intentions; the one prenotation, the other emblem. Prenotation dischargeth the indefinite seeking of what we would remember, and directeth us to seek in a narrow compass, that is, something that hath congruity with our place of memory. Emblem reduceth conceits intellectual to images sensible, which strike the memory more; out of which axioms may be drawn better practique that in use...

Places are further defined as:

> order or distribution of Common Places in the artificial memory, which may be either Places in the proper sense of the word, as a door, a corner, a window, and the like; or familiar and well-known persons;

or anything we choose (provided they are arranged in a certain order), as animals, herbs; also words, letters, characters, historical personages.
(Yates, 1966: 371)

There is evidence that the architectural spaces of Bacon's house articulated with the practices of 'local memory'. One of the galleries in his house, Gorhambury, had painted glass windows, and John Aubrey tells us, 'every pane with severall figures of beast, bird and flower: perhaps his Lordship might use them as topiques for local use' (Yates, 1966: 370).

Bacon used an art of memory with strong links to the ancient classical art, but proposed to transform it for use in scientific enquiry. The memorising of matters in order to identify and order them better, for drawing out the particulars of natural history, and for exercising the judgement, transformed the art into an investigative tool for natural science, with the principles of order and classification being adapted to tools for classification (Yates, 1966: 372).

The connection between linguistic schemes and the art of memory has not yet been fully investigated (Cohen, 1977: 147, n. 43) and the link to the use of repositories and collections in these schemes is barely hinted at in the literature. That the art of memory did have conceptual links with universal language schemes is shown in John Willis's book *The Art of Memory* (1621), where he states that an idea is 'a visible representation, bestowed by the imagination in one of the places of a Repositorie, by the remembrance whereof we call to mind that which was thereby signified'. All the language systems of the mid-seventeenth century were based on the notion that ideas can be visually represented by drawings, pictograms, or any agreed-upon marks (Cohen, 1977: 14).

A further impetus motivated many scholars in the construction of universal language schemes, and this was the idea that a new rational language could be more direct, simple, and regular, and thus prove useful as an educational tool (Cohen, 1977: xxiii). The new language would clarify, once and for all, the relationships and qualities of the natural world. The actual composition of the 'words' used – the lines, shapes, and dots – would provide an accurate description of the thing it referred to (Knowlson, 1975: 15). Language would not merely enable knowledge, it would in itself *be* knowledge, as the visual perception of the 'word' and its 'real character' would demonstrate the thing itself (Knowlson, 1975: 8). Both speech and knowledge would emerge from that which could be seen (Cohen, 1977: 7). The pure gaze would become the pure language: a speaking eye (Foucault, 1976: 114).

The philosophical grounding of this idea is that all that is visible is

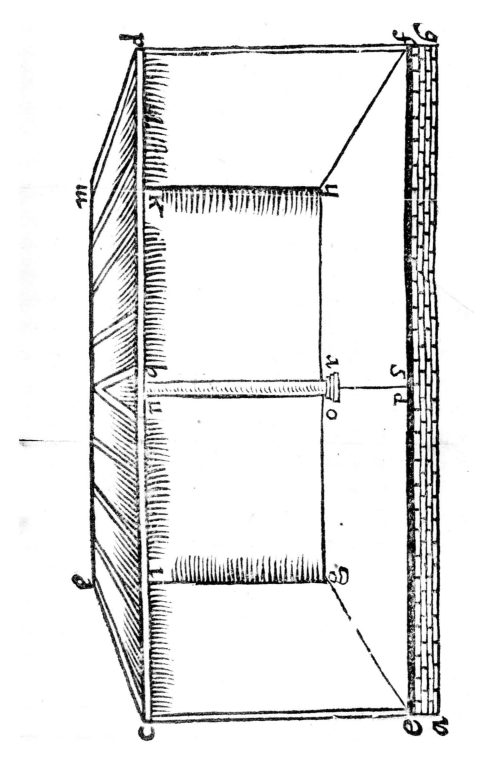

24 *Memory Theatre or Repository* from J. Willis, *Mnemonica*, 1618. Letters representing ideas or things are placed in the corners of the repository in the same way as images were placed in the abbey in the system devised by Johannes Romberch.

expressible, and that it is wholly visible because it is expressible (Foucault, 1976: 115). It was thought that perceptions and ideas were constituted in the same way from one person to another. The same concepts resulted from the perceptions of things through the senses. Differences in ideas must therefore come about through the use of different words to describe these concepts (Knowlson, 1975: 16). A universal language, where agreed notations were attached to these universal concepts, would therefore provide the basis for universal harmony.

Universal language schemes and the Repository

John Wilkins's work, 'An Essay Towards a Real Character, and a Philosophical Language' (1668) was the most significant of the universal language schemes in England. He states one of his basic principles thus:

> As men do generally agree in the same Principle of Reason, so do they likewise agree in the same *Internal Notion* or *Apprehension of things* ... So that, if men should generally consent upon the same way or manner of *Expression*, as they do in the same *Notion*, we should then be freed from that Curse in the Confusion of Tongues, with all the unhappy consequences of it.
>
> (Knowlson, 1975: 17)

The 'Universal Language' would be a language able to be spoken by all the peoples of the world, which would enable universal harmony, and which was to be written with newly designed symbols.

Wilkins aimed to provide a grammar of things and his first priority was to fix the lexicon. He organised all existing things and all ideas into a series of classified tables according to his 'method', which separates on the basis of identity and difference (Cohen, 1977: 31). Wilkins had primarily compiled an exhaustive classification of notions from all spheres of thought, rather like an embryonic thesaurus. He had then divided the notions into forty genuses, or 'heads of things', such as World, Manners, Beast, each of which had a generic character. Each genus had a set of differences: 'Beast' for example being divided into whole-footed or cloven-footed. Each difference had its several species: with 'cloven-footed' divided into kine, sheep, and goat. Each genus had its own written visual symbol, with difference and species identified by attached marks. Further attached symbols indicated the grammatical nature of the word (adverb, for example) (Hartley, 1960: 55).

Wilkins spelt out his philosophical principles in his book. The most important of these was that our mental concepts are a faithful reflection

Tranfcend. {	General	—ᴧ—	Animals {	Exanguious	—ⵏ—	Action {	Spiritual
	Rel. mixed	—ᴠ—		Fifh	⊥		Corporeal
	Rel. of Action	—ᴖ—		Bird	⊥		Motion
	Difcourfe	—ᴜ—		Beaſt	⊤		Operation
	God	—	Parts {	Peculiar	⊤		
	World	—⊦—		General	+	Relation {	Oecon.
	Element	⊥	Quantity {	Magnitude	⊥		Poſſeſ.
	Stone	⊤		Space	⊤		Proviſ
	Metal	⅄		Meaſure	⊦		Civil
Herb confid. accord. to the {	Leaf	ᴧ	Quality {	Power Nat.	⊥		Judicial
	Flower	⋏		Habit	ᴨ		Military
	Seed-veſſel	—ᴧ—		Manners	ᴔ		Naval
	Shrub	⊤		Quality fenfible	ᴛ		Eccleſ.
	Tree	⊥		Diſeaſe	θ		

The Differences are to be affixed unto that end which is on the left fide of the Character, according to this order;

1   2   3   4   5   6   7   8   9
ᴠ— ᴗ— ᴧ— ᴦ— ᴦ— ᴧ— ᴦ— ᴧ— ᴠ—

The Species fhould be affixed at the other end of the Character according to the like order.

1   2   3   4   5   6   7   8   9
—ᴧ —ᴗ —ᴧ —ᴧ —ᴝ —ᴦ —ᴧ —ᴧ —ᴧ

And whereas feveral of the Species of Vegetables and Animals, do according to this prefent conſtitution, amount to more than Nine, in fuch cafes the number of them is to be diſtributed into two or three Nines, which may be diſtinguiſhed from one another by doubling the ſtroke in fome one or more parts of the Character ; as fuppofe after this manner, —ᴧ— —ᴧ—. If the firſt and moſt fimple Character be made ufe of, the Species that are affixed to it, will belong to the firſt combination of *Nine* ; if the other, they will belong according to the order of them, unto the fecond Combination.

Thofe Radicals which are paired to others uppon account of *Oppofition*, may be expreſſed by a Loop, or ⟨o⟩ at the left end of the Character, after this manner, ᴑ—

Thofe that are paired upon the account of *Affinity*, are to be expreſſed by the like Mark at the other end of the Character, thus, —ᴑ

The double Oppofites of *Exceſs* or *Defect*, are to be defcribed by the Tranfcendental points, denoting *Exceſs* or *Defect*, to be placed over the Character, as fhall be fhewed after.

Adje-

25 'Description of the real character', p. 387 from *Essay towards a Real Character and a Philosophical Language* by John Wilkins, 1668. The precise shape of the notation represented a precise idea or thing.

of the phenomena of nature, and since words stand for concepts, language is, or can be, a similar reflection (Slaughter, 1982: 161). If there exists one real world for all, it is knowable to all; all that is required is a thorough cataloguing of all the 'things' of the world. In the cataloguing of the 'things' of the world, Wilkins had the collaboration of the botanist John Ray, who had drawn up what was to be the most comprehensive classification of plants before Linnaeus (Hunter, 1981: 12). Classified tables of natural phenomena were provided, which were intended to enable the language at the same time to describe and to define the components of the natural world, thereby serving an important taxonomic function as well as a linguistic one (Hunter, 1985: 164).

At the same time, Hooke, as 'curator' of the Royal Society, was arranging its collections 'under its several heads, according to the exact Method of the Ranks of all the Species of nature, which has been compos'd by Dr. Wilkins and will shortly be published in his Universall Language' (Sprat, 1667: 251; Slaughter, 1982: 159). The meaning given to objects in the 'museum' was derived from the universal language scheme. Catalogues of the museum were begun in the 1660s by Robert Hooke, and by John Aubrey in the 1670s, according to the system of classification of Wilkins's 'Essay', but very regrettably neither has survived (Hunter, 1985: 164).

Hooke had, however, his own contribution to make to the theories of the classification of words and things. In his 'General Scheme or Idea of the present state of Natural Philosophy' (1666) he developed the notion of a repository of things and their related information, similar both to the collections of the Royal Society and to Wilkins's universal language. Hooke's scheme was to set out an 'algebra' or method of scientific enquiry which would present a new theoretical method. This was grounded in the empirically collected information about things and phenomena. This information, these collections, and this 'matter of philosophical history' were all to be stored in an information bank or repository, and from this data new axioms or theories could be derived. It was to be the repository that connected empirical things with the taxonomic tables of the philosophical language (Slaughter, 1982: 159). The repository was understood as identical with a data-bank, with words and things accorded the same philosophical importance. What Hooke proposed was that for more efficacious storage and/or memory, information was to be distributed to 'heads of inquiry' which did not need to be 'very nice or curious, they being in them laid up only in Heaps as it were, as in a Granary or Storehouse; from then afterwards to be transcribed, fitted, rang'd and Tabled' (ibid.: 159).

Hooke's taxonomic table divided into the major categories of artificial and natural things. The visible world was then divided into the celestial

Scheme 3.

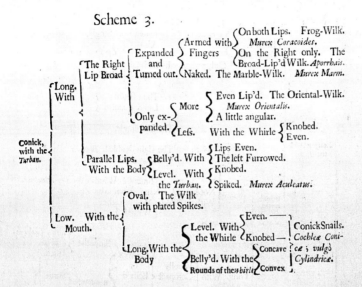

Conick,
with the
Turban.

- Long. With
  - The Right Lip Broad
    - Expanded and Turned out.
      - Armed with Fingers
        - On both Lips. Frog-Wilk. *Murex Coracoides.*
        - On the Right only. The Broad-Lip'd Wilk. *Aporrhais.*
      - Naked. The Marble-Wilk. *Murex Marm.*
    - Only expanded.
      - More
        - Even Lip'd. The Oriental-Wilk. *Murex Orientalis.*
        - A little angular.
      - Lefs. With the Whirle
        - Knobed.
        - Even.
  - Parallel Lips. With the Body
    - Belly'd. With
      - Lips Even.
      - The left Furrowed.
    - Level. With the *Turban.*
      - Knobed.
      - Spiked. *Murex Aculeatus.*
- Low. With the Mouth.
  - Oval. The Wilk with plated Spikes.
  - Long. With the Body
    - Level. With the Whirle
      - Even. ──── ConickSnails.
      - Knobed ── Cochleæ Conicæ ; vulgò
    - Belly'd. With the Rounds of the *whirle*
      - Concave ? Cylindricæ.
      - Convex

Scheme 4.

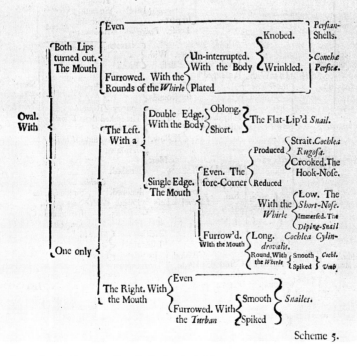

Oval. With

- Both Lips turned out. The Mouth
  - Even ──────────── Perfian-Shells.
  - Un-interrupted. With the Body
    - Knobed.
    - Wrinkled.
  - Conchæ Perficæ.
  - Furrowed. With the Rounds of the *Whirle* Plated ──────────
- One only
  - The Left. With a
    - Double Edge. With the Body
      - Oblong.
      - Short.
    - The Flat-Lip'd *Snail.*
    - Single Edge. The Mouth
      - Even. The fore-Corner
        - Produced
          - Strait. *Cochlea Rugofa.*
          - Crooked. The Hook-Nofe.
        - Reduced
          - With the Whirle
            - Low. The *Short-Nofe.*
            - Immerfed. The *Diping-Snail*
      - Furrow'd. With the Mouth
        - Long. *Cochlea Cylindrovalis.*
        - Round, With the *Whirle*
          - Smooth *Cochl.*
          - Spiked *Umb.*
  - The Right. With the Mouth
    - Even ────────────
    - Furrowed. With the *Turban*
      - Smooth
      - Spiked
    - *Snailes.*

Scheme 5.

26　Page from Grew's *Musaeum Regalis Societatis* (1681).

and the terrestrial, and then into further subdivisions. These taxonomic 'heads of inquiry' provided the individual subjects or topics about which 'histories' were to be written. The histories were to consist of either a description of the things themselves, or a philosophical discussion of their nature. These histories were to be transcribed in symbols, thus being linked to the idea of the universal language (ibid.: 160).

A further catalogue was compiled by the botanist Nehemiah Grew in the late 1670s and was published in 1681 as *Musaeum Regalis Societatis, or a Catalogue & Description of the Natural and Artificial Rarities Belonging to the Royal Society and Preserved at Gresham Colledge*. This followed a more up-to-date classification scheme than that of Hooke's or Wilkins's essay; nevertheless the taxonomy relates well to the classifications that Foucault describes as typical of the work of the classical *episteme*. In classifying shells, they are distinguished according to their structural and decorative surface features (Hunter, 1985: 164) with the separate aspects of the specimens itemised in great detail. Distinctions are made between the varieties of mouth, lips, and body, which may be even, angular, spiked, knobbed, on one or both sides, furrowed, and smooth.

Monsters had been seen by Bacon as part of the phenomena that would need to be included in a complete inventory (Houghton, 1942: 195). In the preface to the catalogue, however, Grew aspires to 'an Inventory of Nature' which would include 'not only Things strange and rare, but the most known and common amongst us' (Hunter, 1985: 164). Grew condemned the cult of rarities that was often to be found as part of the collections of many of the seventeenth-century '*virtuosi*'. He also advocated a full but precise description in catalogues, and condemned the existing obscurantism of many existing catalogues. In his own, he used the 'museum' specimens to convict other writers of inaccuracy and misidentification (ibid.: 165).

These schemes for the ordering of words and things represented a new articulation of the material world with language, knowledge, and memory. Experience was to be ordered in terms of order, hierarchy, and difference (Foucault, 1970: 52). A complete enumeration was looked for, as this was now seen to be possible (ibid.: 55). These aims accorded perfectly with the fundamental change in western culture identified by Foucault. The empirical domain which had been seen in the sixteenth century as the complex web of kinships, resemblances, and affinities in which language and things were endlessly interwoven, was now reorganised in a new configuration (ibid.: 54). The link to the mathesis is suggested by the new 'algebraic' theories of Hooke, which propose the possibility of establishing an ordered succession in words, material things, and 'matters of philosophical history'. The universal language, partly constituted through the ordering of a universal collection, becomes part of the universal method of analysis (ibid.: 57).

The task of knowledge in the classical age was to fabricate a language that acted as an instrument of calculation and clarification. Language, in so far as it was reliable and transparent, made representation possible (Dreyfus and Rabinow, 1982: 20). The work of Hooke and Wilkins depended on the view that the relationship between words and things is immediate, transparent, uncomplicated, and direct. In the Repository of the Royal Society, the representation of the world was to be effected through the classifying and ordering of the empirical world, which separated and differentiated as it named and exposed.

The seventeenth century worked with the concept that languages were basically lexical. Linguists sought to establish an isomorphic relationship between language and nature, words and things. The order of words was thought to be exactly approximate to the order of things. However, as a philosophical endeavour, this was short-lived. At the end of the seventeenth century a discontinuity has been identified that, in effect, consisted of a massive cultural mutation, hitherto unremarked upon. In the eighteenth century, linguistic schemes emphasised the syntactical rather than the lexical, and assumed that language reflected the structure of the mind rather than the structure of things (Cohen, 1977: xxiv). It was now to be understood, as we ourselves 'know', that words represented thoughts rather than things. In this case, it was no longer rational to attempt to put together a visual grammar of material things. It was recognised that the attempt to match exactly an order of objects with an order of words was 'irrational'.

The limitations of the tabular taxonomy based on the visual grammar of nature, which had after all excluded from the table of knowledge some aspects of material things (colour, texture, and smell, for example) and most aspects of non-material things (thoughts, beliefs, values) (Cohen, 1977: 32), had serious implications for the future of the Repository. The interest in constructing a table of words and things waned and the Royal Society turned its scientific attentions to other things. The Repository, which had had neither permanent officers nor a permanent building, became a burden of unwanted material rather than the sharp, epistemological cutting tool it was intended to be.

The failure of the Repository

The characteristics of the third case-study, the Repository of the Royal Society, were partly drawn from the articulations of an ordered tabulation of knowledge, where identity and difference interacted with the observation, measurement, and comparison of visible features. The legends and fables of the past were cut away as a separation was made between documentation, fable, and observation. The knowledge that shaped this 'museum' was not the drawing together of things in the setting out of a kinship or secretly shared attraction, but rather the discrimination between things (Foucault, 1970: 55). The ordering of the specimens demanded the inclusion of both the commonplace and the monstrous, in a joint taxonomy, which not only identified the specimens in their individuality, their order, their difference, but also related this discrimination to the language which described these things. A new relationship between the expressible and the visible was constructed.

> To describe is to follow the ordering of the manifestations, but it is also to follow the intelligible sequence of their genesis; it is to see and to know at the same time, because by saying what one sees, one integrates it spontaneously into knowledge; it is also to learn to see, because it means giving the key of a language that masters the visible.
>
> (Foucault, 1976: 114)

The third case-study can be seen as an attempt to construct a new rationality on the basis of a new ordering of the concrete domain. This attempt failed. The failure can be perceived in comparing the catalogue of the initial collection that was acquired by the Royal Society, that of Robert Hubert, with Grew's *Musaeum Regalis Societatis*. Although by 1681 the collection was two or three times larger than Hubert's, mainly because of gifts received, it retained the same basic features, with an emphasis on rare and exotic specimens rather than the commonplace. The animals represented included crocodiles, chameleons, armadillos, and the fragments of a tiger. Throughout, material from overseas dominated at the expense of domestic material, in spite of the efforts of Thomas Willisel. The idea of compiling a complete taxonomy was impossible. Grew noted in exasperation in his catalogue that a 'perfect' classification was not feasible 'because as yet the Collection itself is not perfect' (Hunter, 1985: 166).

The failure of the programme of the Repository can be discussed in relation to the idea of the development of appropriate technologies (Gordon, 1980: 250). A programmatic schema fulfils its vocation only in so far as it is complemented by the elaboration of a technology. In the case of the Repository, the technologies were insufficiently developed to allow the programme to be put into effect.

Foucault asserts that unsuccessful programmes generate their own 'successes' in another field. The 'failure' of prisons to fulfil their planned function as reformatories, far from precipitating their breakdown, acted as an impulse for the perpetual effort to reform the prison, which continually reinvokes the original model of its original aborted programme (Gordon, 1980: 250). The failure of the Repository led to the creation of a 'museum' that, although it did not act as a scientific databank for infomation, did act as a compilation and repository of the values of rarity, pleasure, and curiosity. As such it related to other contemporary elements that included personal cabinets, ostentatious display, and social gain through the possession of unusual things. These relationships shaped the Repository as a discourse that had stronger social than scientific characteristics.

What were the areas in which technologies had not been developed? How did the elements articulate to constitute a social rather than a scientific discourse?

A crucial factor was the lack of a large-scale endowment (Hunter, 1985: 166). The organisers of the Society were well aware of the limitations this imposed on their efforts, and were envious of the Académie des Sciences established by Louis XIV and Colbert, with salaries for research workers and lavish facilities. John Evelyn put it: 'We see how greedily the French, and other Strangers embrace and cultivate the design: what sumptious Buildings, well furnished Observatories, ample Appointements, Salries, and Accomodations they have erected to carry on the Work; whilst we live Precariously, and spin the Web out of our own bowels' (Hunter, 1981: 40). This lack of funding and support partly led to the institutional weakness of the Society, which remained an amateur body, dependent on subscriptions and on voluntary effort to sustain the research for which it had been established (Hunter, 1982: 13; Bronowski and Mazlish, 1970: 224).

Funding had its effects on spaces and subject positions. The Society had limited funds at its disposal, which meant problems with spaces and staffing in the Repository. The 'operators' of the Society looked after the Repository in addition to their other duties. Hooke, for example, as 'curator' to the Society had to run the weekly business meetings and prepare the equipment for the experimental work, in addition to caring for the collection (Ornstein, 1938: 110). This proliferation of duties led to a history of neglect in respect of the Repository (Hunter, 1985: 166).

A new specialised subject position, limited to the care of the Repository and its collections, did not emerge.

Other factors compounded these problems. A basic mismatch can be perceived between the stated aim to make a 'perfect' or 'complete' collection and the soliciting of gifts with which to make up the collection. It is clear that although the Repository was part of a larger aim to classify the products of nature, this was not fully developed and fully thought through in relation to the accumulation of material things. The gifts that the Society received made up a collection that was not based on the desired taxonomic principles (Ornstein, 1938: 111, 115). These donations included, for example, 'Stones taken out of Lord Belcarre's heart in a silver box, a bottle full of stag's tears, a petrified fish and a petrified foetus' (Weld, 1975: 190) and in the main consisted of 'casual Presents, which either strangers, or any of their own members bestow'd upon them' (Sprat, 1667: 251). Donation was, in fact, the main form of collection. This, as a form of passive collecting, results in the accumulation of things that, in general, bear no relation to each other unless there is a very clearly stated collecting policy, and refusals are made. This haphazard accumulation of material can be contrasted with the rigorous selection of material in the *studiolo* of Francesco I in Florence. A rigorous grid of inclusion/exclusion was operated, such that the contents of the *studiolo* made up a complete and rational structure, within its own epistemic framework (Rinehart, 1981). The Repository of the Royal Society failed to implement a rigorous selection grid.

It is no doubt also useful to contrast the fact that Francesco I operated as a single autonomous powerful subject, and that the Repository was operated through a group of disparate subjects, each with their own specific subjectivities, and without sufficient corporate funds or a unified identity. It was necessary in this case to attempt to create, firstly, the conditions that would ensure the social acceptability of the Royal Society itself as an institution, and thereby its continuation, and only secondly would it have been possible to develop instrumental technologies to achieve the epistemological aims.

The collection of things by donation meant that items were presented that seemed appropriate from the point of view of the donor. The gifts that were accepted by the Society reflected the interests (Ornstein, 1938: 130) and practices of the *virtuosi* who formed the bulk of the membership and who made the donations. The friendship groups that constituted the members of the Society also formed the network of donors to the Repository. The membership was typical of the general leisured culture of London: well-informed, cultivated dilettantes with a wide range of social interests (Hunter, 1981: 71), of which the Royal Society and its

Repository was only one. Donation to the Repository had a social cachet, and was used by the donor as a sign of honours received (Ornstein, 1938: 130). The items that were given related to the needs of the donor rather than to the needs of the receiving institution as expressed in a fully developed systematic collecting policy.

The values of the *virtuosi* tended to be antipathetic to the serious study of science. The *virtuoso* stopped at the point where the genuine scientist began (Houghton, 1942: 194). Bacon had pointed out their tendency to trivial curiosity and their stress on the social esteem of knowledge (Hunter, 1981: 65). It was easy and pleasant to accumulate material, but much harder to systematise it: 'Mere compiling will content me' were the words of one *virtuoso* (ibid.: 68).

Bacon's emphasis on the inclusion of monsters, and 'everything ... in nature that is new, rare, and unusual' appeared to support a predilection for the odd and the peculiar, which was again supported in other ways. Natural philosophy was the study of the second book of God and the proper reaction was one of wonder. From this emerged a tendency to stress the unfamiliar, either in the sense of the uncommon, found rarely and in distant parts of the globe, or in the sense of the unknown, the unexplained, unrecognised by people without special apparatuses or training (Houghton, 1942: 195). Thus golden rod, the best herb for the stopping of blood, was a rarity when it came from 'beyond the seas' but ceased to be one when it was found growing in Hampstead (ibid.: 194).

The passion for contemporary 'engines', trick mirrors, and mechanical toys which were often found in the cabinets of the *virtuosi*, together with the shells and plants from across the seas, may be explained in relation to the admiration for the ingenuity of God. Ingenuity and skill were valued, as was the production of 'conceits', not only as part of literature, but in relation to artefacts too. A pot, a drinking-glass, and Evelyn's chair were all 'conceited' (ibid.: 198). In part, this enthusiasm is an element that persists from the late Renaissance, where automata, fountains, artificial storms, and strange animals were displayed in gardens to celebrate the links between art and nature and the skill of man as the reflection of God on earth.

A further element with its roots in the distant past also had a bearing on the enthusiasm for the rare. Mystery and magic were still of overriding interest (Houghton, 1942: 199). The cult of the rare and the marvellous was furthered through the desire for reputation and for maintaining or creating a social position. The 'curious' cultivates 'all things opposite to the vulgar sort, intricate and rare, or else they are nothing worth'. It is dishonourable to meddle with mechanical things, which are tainted with vulgarity, unless 'they be such as may be thought secrets, rarities, and special subtilties'. This can be related back to a tradition of magic and secret knowledge that was revealed only to the 'magi' and was kept secret from the vulgar person. Porta, for example, refused to make his rarities available to the public because 'there are many most excellent Things fit for the Worthiest nobles, which should ignorant men (that were never bred up in the sacred Principles of Philosophy) come to know, they would grow contemptible, and be undervalued' (ibid.: 204–5).

Thus the cult of the rare was constituted through many facets that together overruled the intentions of the scientists among the members. The most 'scientific' members were in any case likely to be equally interested in the rare, the magical, the wonderful, and the unusual. John Wilkins, for example, had a collection at home of 'magical curiosities', among which was 'a hollow statue, which gave a voice and uttered words by a long concealed pipe that went to its mouth, whilst one speaks through it at a good distance' (Houghton, 1942: 202).

The Royal Society, although ostensibly a national institutional body, still retained strong features of the gentlemen's club from which it had stemmed. The Fellows showed a disproportionate tendency to come from the fashionable medical elite and to be based on friendship groups (Hunter, 1982: 8). Most of the members were located in London, with very few provincial Fellows (ibid: 7). As a voluntary group without an endowment, it was important to recruit social support where possible. The membership of the eminent and the aristocratic was therefore thought very desirable, and members with this social background received a far less rigorous scrutiny in respect of their intellectual credentials than other humbler aspirants.

The Repository had emerged in the early days of the Royal Society with ambitious aims, and had played a significant part in the activities of the Society at this time (Simpson, 1984: 187). Later, as scientific and linguistic endeavours moved apart from each other, the Repository had less import-ance. Complaints of neglect were consistent throughout the early eight-eenth century (Hunter, 1981: 189) and in 1779 the collection of the Repository was offered to the British Museum, ostensibly because of lack of space in the new premises of the Society. A voluntary society could not generate the resources required to maintain the collection, nor was it any longer sensible or rational to try to construct a visual grammar of things.

Conclusions

The discussion of the Repository of the Royal Society reveals a number of important points.

Firstly, the aim of the institution would appear to be unusual in 'museums' during this period. Although there is no in-depth research which seeks to relate the intentions of collections to the epistemic thrust of Foucault's classical *episteme*, no other collection has come to light which seeks to provide a grammar of words and things in quite the same way. Other collections 'systematised' their things in relation to their form, and made new classifications which divided rather than united material things, but further research would be necessary to discover how far these divisions related to a grammar of things, and how far the individual institutions had specific 'Classical' epistemic intentions.

The failure to achieve the 'grammar of words and things' is in itself interesting. This failure can be explained partly because the aim was too ambitious and based on a philosophical principle with a very limited application, and partly because the technologies that would have enabled the achievement of the aims were not yet developed. In effect, other non-epistemic factors that were present as part of the Repository combined to make a powerful thrust in directions that effectively sabotaged the scientific aims.

The aim of cataloguing the whole of nature was too ambitious. The taxonomic work of the Natural History Museum in London at the present time is based on exactly the same intention, but with the resources of a very large state institution, modern computing facilities, and developed taxonomic systems (Whitehead, 1981: 20). The naming of specimens at the present time is limited to placing the specimen on a taxonomic table which describes their place in a family, but where the name used does not also physically describe the features of the specimen involved. The aims of the Royal Society have been broken down into discrete areas, some of which are seen as appropriate to the discipline of science and some of which are placed within other disciplines, such as linguistics. The comprehensive unity of the Repository's intentions held failure within their complexities.

The theory of the sign that underpinned the linguistic work of the early classical age meant that a transparent relationship was presupposed between word and thing. The polysemia that characterised the Renaissance *episteme* was cut away from the classificatory tables of knowledge of the classical *episteme*. Things could only be constituted as meaningful objects in one relation at any one time, and their place on the table was defined in respect of only a few of their attributes. Thus, vast semiological areas were ignored, and conversely, meanings and things which did not have a material identity could not be included on the classificatory table. The move from a lexical to a syntactical linguistic schema in the eighteenth century demonstrates this very basic philosophical flaw in the Classical *episteme*.

Any discussion of this case-study must include some comment on the unification of the classical *episteme*. Foucault states in *The Archaeology of Knowledge* that the *episteme* is 'something like a world-view' and that it is not a motionless figure, but is in constant oscillation as a series of articulations and shifts (Foucault, 1974: 191–2). Nonetheless there is a sense in *The Order of Things* (Foucault, 1970) in which the characteristics of one *episteme* are not expected to continue for long during the time of another. In the third case-study, positioned at the end of the seventeenth century and therefore well into Foucault's classical age, some aspects of the older Renaissance *episteme* appear to be still active, and to operate in an apparently contradictory relationship with the new. Wilkins, for example, although formulating his universal language that was intended to restructure knowledge through a new relationship of words and things premised on the transparent nature of language in relation to things, was also the owner of 'magical curiosities' (Hartley, 1960: 51).

The belief that everything could be reduced to mathematics was typical of the thought of some at the time, as is demonstrated by the attempts to reduce politics and morality to geometry (Hunter, 1981: 16). Nonetheless, new mathematical and mechanistic explanations of the world coexisted with a whole range of other contradictory philosophies that had older roots, and were linked back to the occult explanations of the fifteenth and sixteenth centuries (Ornstein, 1938: 20). In part, the things collected by the Royal Society were seen in this way. Seventeen 'aetites' or 'eagle-stones' were catalogued (Bromehead, 1947b: 17). This dual classification places the material things on the 'scientific' table of knowledge but also acknowledges their magical powers. The new insistence on testing and experimentation was extended to old ideas (Hunter, 1981: 18). Thus there were papers on magnetic and sympathetic cures (Ornstein, 1938: 104). The unity of the epistemological framework was not totally seamless.

A further point in relation to the classical *episteme* is made by Cohen (1977: xxiv), who states that his discovery of the move from lexical to syntactic linguistic schemes constitutes the discovery of a major epistemological shift which had been overlooked by Foucault. He explains that his focus is more local, less overarching than Foucault's, but, notwithstanding, this linguistic shift is an important discovery. Certainly, the shift in relationship from words and things to words and mind deserves further exploration from the historians of 'museums'.

This case-study reveals the limitations of the *episteme* as an analytical concept, but nonetheless, without the insight provided by its discussion, the specific practices of this particular case-study would not have been noticed.

The third case-study demonstrates that the idea of an 'institutional museum' was emerging in seventeenth-century England, but for a variety of reasons, including the organisational and financial weakness of the institution, the social aspirations of its members, and the failure to develop appropriate technologies, the Repository was unable to fulfil the aims that would have established it as a new prototype, and a new programme. The position of the knowing and perceiving subject had not changed (Foucault, 1976: 51), new subject positions had not emerged, and the practices which would have enabled the fulfilment of the original aims were not established. The epistemological ambitions could not be achieved.

Most interesting perhaps is the fact that this 'museum' is very little known. Most general 'histories of the museum' give space to the Tradescants, and ignore the Repository of the Royal Society. This is partly explained by the fact that the Tradescant collection was transformed from a private collection into a university museum which still has a separate identity at the present time as the Ashmolean Museum, and institutional pressures ensure the research of its 'origins' (MacGregor, 1983; Impey and Mac-Gregor, 1985). The collections of the Royal Society were subsumed into the British Museum, and the Repository remains as a rather quaint, early practice of the Royal Society. However, this quaint and misguided failure illuminates the efficacy of the focus of effective history on the history of error. The nature of 'truth', of present-day rational structures and forms of knowledge, are revealed through the analysis of these practices which appear to us today as irrational. The dismissal of all those things that have failed to continue through the years to the present time may well be the dismissal of that which demonstrates the difference of the past from the present.

A final point should be made. The understanding of the limitations of the classificatory table of knowledge is critical in relation to the work of the present-day museum. Much curatorial work is concerned with 'completing the collection' and 'filling the gaps', as though a complete tabulation of knowledge is possible. The presentation of material things as if they relate to only one space on a limited classificatory table leads on the one hand to the museum whose displays look like a three-dimensional trade catalogue (Foucault's 'books furnished with structures' (1970: 137)), and on the other to the constitution of a unilinear meaning in relation to only one of the many contexts in which any material things may be made meaningful. The articulations of relations of advantage (acquisition policies, selection grids, display technologies), through which a single selected meaning is offered as the natural, authoritative, and complete meaning-potential of material things, constitute some of the micro-processes of power in the present-day museum, instrumental technologies with the functionality of enshrining the specialist, academic knowledge of the 'curator' as 'truth' (Hooper-Greenhill, 1987a: 21-2).

The disciplinary museum 7

The revolution in France led to the conditions of emergence of a new museological programme which radically transformed collecting practices and subject positions. In the place of intensely personal, private collections housed in the palaces of princes and the homes of the scholars, public collections in spaces open to the whole population were established. The subject in the Renaissance had accumulated collections according to their individual choice (Foucault, 1986: 26) in their own private, domestic spaces. Now the gaze that surveyed an extended geographical space initially for military purposes surveyed that same space for cultural purposes. Material things, 'works of art' (*objets d'art*), were deployed in the same way as other strategic commodities.

Modelled on the military deployment of resources, museums were established across Europe. An intersecting 'curatorial' gaze emerged that paralleled the contemporary medical gaze (Foucault, 1976: 31); a 'curatorial' gaze constituted through a network of institutions articulating a constant, mobile, differentiated supervision. New technologies emerged to enable this large-scale supervision. Collections were gathered together, filtered, redispersed, and reorganised. In the name of the newly formed Republic, the spaces and things belonging to the king, the aristocracy, and the church were appropriated and transformed, at first in France and later across Europe.

The revolution in France marked the end of the society of the hierarchic and inegalitarian type, and at the same time the end of the old way of imagining the world, as a fixed order ruled by a theological-political logic (Laclau and Mouffe, 1985: 155). The French Revolution was founded on the legitimacy of the people, which was something entirely new. For Napoleon, the state was the centralised, nationalistic state enhanced by the revolution and based on the social dominance of the bourgeoisie (Bronowski and Mazlish, 1970: 461).

An abrupt discontinuity can be identified, the invention of democratic culture. The 'museum' was created as one of the instruments that exposed both the decadence and tyranny of the old forms of control, the *ancien régime*, and the democracy and public utility of the new, the Republic.

A further discontinuity can be identified in the theory of government (Foucault, 1979: 17). Previously, government had been conceived on the model of the family, with economy understood in terms of family management; now population, and the control of health, wealth, and education came to be seen as the ultimate end of government, with the family understood as a (privileged) segment in the larger model. The public museum emerged as one of the campaigns of the state to direct the population into activities which would, without people being aware of it, transform the population into a useful resource for the state.

At the same time, the 'disciplinary museum' gave rise to a complex interaction of both new and old subject positions that positioned the 'visitor' as beneficiary (the population enabled to know); the 'curator' as knowing subject with specialist expertise (who enables the knowing of others); and the subject-emperor, newly poised as the source of public benefaction and liberation. This new position, however, could not help but recall those older renditions of the prince who represented the world, which centred himself, through the organisation of meaningful objects.

The theme of the three-dimensional encyclopedia was replaced by that of constantly revised information, where, rather than enclosing knowledge in a closed, static, and systematic form, it was to become a question of totalising events: centralising information; conveying it from one part of the country to another; discussing questions that still remained obscure; and indicating what research needed to be carried out (Foucault, 1976: 29). The 'museum' was transformed from a localised and limited site to a programme at once disciplinary and fully extended, both spatially and socially. Foucault has described the way in which disciplinary technologies operated at the end of the classical age in both the school and the prison: these technologies can equally be identified in the 'museum', which can, therefore, be viewed as another of those apparatuses that create 'docile bodies'.

Disciplinary technologies in the 'classical age'

Foucault describes the emergence of the disciplinary technologies of power towards the end of his classical age. The disciplines (methods that divided and controlled time, space, and movement, which had long been in existence in the monasteries, the armies, and in workshops) became general formulas during the seventeenth and eighteenth centuries for domination and control (Foucault, 1982b: 137). The classical age discovered the body as object and target of power (ibid.: 136). An art of the human body was born.

Discipline as a power/technique operates through hierarchical observation, normalising judgement, and examination. The concept of hierarchical observation indicates the connection between visibility and the establishment of deep-seated relations of advantage/disadvantage, and introduces the idea of an apparatus designed for observation, which induces the effects of these relationships deployed through the visibility of those subject to it.

Disciplinary technologies depend on the distribution of individuals in space and in visibility. Historically, this required the emergence of the specification of a space heterogeneous to all others and closed in upon itself (Foucault, 1982b: 141). Schools, hospitals, and military barracks, as specialised spaces, confined and controlled the inhabitants, separating and differentiating them from the mass of the population. The principle of the enclosure of space extended to individual partitioning. Each individual should have his or her own place, and each space should have its individual. This cellular arangement of individuals in space permitted constant surveillance.

The space of the hospital, and Foucault's example is the military hospital at the port of Rochefort, acts as a filter, a mechanism that pins down and partitions the swarming mass of sailors, epidemics, and goods. The medical supervision of diseases and contagions is inseparable from a whole series of other controls: military control over deserters; fiscal control over commodities; and administrative control over remedies, rations, cures, and deaths. The first steps that were taken concerned things rather than people. Fiscal and economic supervision preceded medical observation. Medical technologies were put into operation later; medicines were put under lock and key, and their use recorded; a system was worked out to verify the real number of patients, their identity, and the units to which they belonged. Their comings and goings were regulated; they were forced to remain in their wards; to each bed was attached the name of its occupant; each individual treated was entered in a register that the doctor had to consult on his visit. Later came the isolation of contagious patients and separate beds. Gradually, an administrative and political space was articulated upon a therapeutic space and this individualised bodies, diseases, symptoms, lives, and deaths. The space constituted a real epistemological table of juxtaposed and carefully distinct singularities. Out of discipline, a medically useful space was born (Foucault, 1982b: 144).

The principle of individualising partition operated in other spaces. In the school and the army, for example, bodies were visibly separated into ages, abilities, skills, and levels of achievement. Through separation and observation, differences became visible and thereby classifiable. The differences were judged and evaluated, entailing the production of a norm through the exercise of rewards and penalties. Normalising judgement, combined with hierarchical observation, enabled the use of spaces to expose differences and to display identities.

Through the organisation of 'cells', 'places', and 'ranks', the disciplines create complex spaces that are at once architectural, functional, and hierarchical. Spaces fix positions and permit circulations; they mark places and assign values. They individualise things and individuals in a vast table of discrimination and distinction. The division of spaces and bodies entailed the establishment of records: day-books, ledgers, inventories, filing cabinets, and archives, were all required to document the spatial distribution of bodies and things. Thus, in the eighteenth century, the classificatory table became both a technique of power and a procedure of knowledge (Foucault, 1982b: 281).

Individualising and normalising space at the level of bodies and institutional spaces found its corollary in the division, observation, and supervision of geographical space. In *The Birth of the Clinic* (Foucault, 1976) Foucault describes the emergence of the French medical profession as part of the conjuncture of events during the revolutionary period. Many elements – political, military, economic, and ideological – articulated to create the conditions of emergence for new medical practices. A medical network was established, a medical gaze that surveyed the entire country through the building of hospitals and the geographical deployment of staff. The new medical discourse was supported by the political ideology of the French Revolution with its conception of the free citizen of the Republic as clean, pure, and healthy. The theme of 'medicine in liberty' was structured in a precise historical context that enabled the definition of its institutional and scientific structures (ibid.: 69).

Within the space of fifty years, at the turn of the eighteenth century, a new medical discourse was established where medical space coincided with social space: 'One began to conceive of a generalised presence of doctors whose intersecting gazes form a network and exercise at every point in space, and at every moment in time, a constant, mobile, differentiated supervision' (Foucault, 1976: 31).

Disciplinary technologies survey, classify, and control time, space, bodies, and things. As the subject is surveyed, classified, and exposed to examination, he or she becomes his or her own self-regulator. It becomes unnecessary

> to use force to constrain the convict to good behaviour, the madman to calm, the schoolboy to application, the patient to the observation of the regulations. He who is subjected to a field of visibility, and who knows it, assumes reponsibility for the constraints of power; he makes them play spontaneously upon himself; he inscribes in himself the power relation in which he simultaneously plays both roles: he becomes the principle of his own subjection.
>
> (Foucault, 1982: 209)

Thus human subjects, enmeshed in impersonal power relations which separate, survey, and judge, become their own overseers in the ongoing process of normalisation.

How does the emergence of the museum relate to the emergence of other disciplinary technologies? The French Revolution provided the conditions of emergence for a new programme for 'museums'. The 'programme' is a set of calculated, reasoned prescriptions in terms of which institutions are meant to be reorganised, spaces arranged, behaviours regulated (Foucault, 1981a: 3–14). The programme grounds and enables the rationality on which 'regimes of truth' are contingently constructed (Foucault, 1977b: 14). The ruptures of revolution created the conditions of emergence for a new truth, a new rationality, out of which came a new functionality for a new institution, namely the public museum. The old collecting practices of the king, the aristocracy, and the church were radically revised, taken over, and rearticulated in a new field of use. The collections themselves were torn out of their earlier spaces and groupings and were rearranged in other contexts as statements that proclaimed at once the tyranny of the old and the democracy of the new.

In France the museum as a public, democratic, state institution was born from the articulation of three general elements: republicanism, anti-clericalism, and successful aggressive war (Gould, 1965: 13). The concurrent forces of these three elements (all of which existed in fields other than that of the museum, and none of which was new in itself) produced an apparatus with two deeply contradictory functions; that of the elite temple of the arts, and that of a utilitarian instrument for democratic education (Nochlin, 1972: 8). This new, fundamentally fragmented institution entailed the development of technologies based on existing military administrative practices. The institution that emerged was to prove decisive in the rearticulations of collecting practices across Europe during the course of the nineteenth century.

The 'museum': a new apparatus for the production of knowledge

On 27 September, 1792, it was decreed that a 'museum' should be created in the galleries of the old royal palace of the Louvre, to be called the 'Museum Français'. The 'museum' opened late in 1793. In 1796 its name was changed to 'Musée Central des Arts' (Seling, 1967: 109). In 1803 the name was changed again to 'Musée Napoléon' (Alexander, 1983: 90).

'Effective' history recognises that immanent ruptures and discontinuities that can radically change practices are able to exist alongside the long slow movements of events. The accumulation and exposition of objects can be seen as an enduring activity with a long history, although the identities and uses of these accumulations have been subject to abrupt changes. The form and target of the articulations of subject, object, space, and power have no essential 'nature'; 'collections' and 'museums' take on contingent identities according to shifts and reversals in both the relations of forces and the random play of events.

Plans to create a 'museum' in the Louvre had been in existence for many years, and considerable efforts had been made during the *ancien régime* to develop the royal collection into a more useful resource, but to no conclusion (Bazin, 1959: 40; Gould, 1965: 22). It was not until the revolution that new forces propelled a radically new institution, with completely new powers and potentials, into existence. Previously, Diderot in 1765 in volume IX of his *Encyclopédie* had proposed a comprehensive scheme to use the collections as a 'museum', with distinct separations made between different types of artefact. The ground floor was to contain the sculptures, brought in from the garden where they were gradually deteriorating, and the paintings were to hang in the Grande Galerie. Other spaces were to contain the plans of the fortresses of the kingdom, the coins, and the natural material (Bazin, 1959: 39–40). New separations and new categories were in evidence here.

Other plans were to follow, although only small, piecemeal changes actually took place (Bazin, 1959: 40–5; Gould, 1965: 20–2). However, although the older plans had not come to completion, much of the work that had begun in preparation for a new 'museum' based on the royal collections laid the foundation for the new technologies that were to emerge during the revolutionary period. This preparatory work included partial reorganisation of both the palace building and the material contents (paintings were labelled and given uniform framing, for example) (Bazin, 1959: 40–4). As it happened, the earlier project, which would have meant a 'museum' constituted through the French royal collections alone, and which probably would have been administered and organised as a private collection with limited public access, was completely outstripped by the events precipitated by the ruptures and discontinuities of the revolution (ibid.: 46). A new institution with new functions and new targets was born.

The decree of 1789 nationalising ecclesiastical property brought a new urgency to the plans for the 'museum' (Hemmings, 1987: 74; Gould, 1965: 22). Later the property of the aristocracy and of the royal family was confiscated, detaching many thousands of things from their previous contexts. As Napoleon conquered Europe, large amounts of material were removed from their former spaces, appropriated in the form of war indemnities (Seling, 1967: 109). The accumulations of these trophies were to make the museums in Paris, and particularly the museum in the Louvre, the largest and most spectactular ever seen (ibid.: 109).

In France the organisation of the transfer of enormous quantities of material from private ownership to the ownership of the state was fraught with problems. The state risked the loss of material that would be untraceable without firm identification and documentation (Hemmings, 1987: 75). New procedures were therefore instituted. A 'Commission of Monuments' was established with an initial aim of drawing up an inventory of the entire 'art treasures' of France; and thereby to prevent the destruction of works of art through ignorance or anti-royalist sentiment.

This Commission was replaced in 1793 by another, the 'Commission Temporaire des Arts', which was more motivated by republican sentiments than anxiety to preserve objects of aesthetic interest. The artistic heritage of France had been admired by foreigners, and the revolutionaries had no wish to be identified with the fifth-century vandals who had laid waste the cities of the empire through brutish ignorance. 'Vandalism' was a key term in the reports laid before the Commission in late 1794. Any acts of 'vandalism' that were acknowledged were blamed on the British and on counter-revolutionaries (Hemmings, 1987: 77). The 'museum' in the Louvre, already acquired as a repository for the confiscated property of the church and the aristocracy, soon became an apparatus that could position the revolutionary government in triumphant opposition to former powerful formations.

The 'Commission du Museum', writing in the summer of 1793 'Considérations sur les Arts et sur le Museum National' put forward the argument that the arts could blossom under any kind of government, and drew attention to the flourishing state of the arts under Augustus, the Medici, and Louis IV, all of whom were despots. It then discussed Belgium and Holland, where on the one hand the oppression of a foreign power and on the other the exhilaration of a newly enfranchised republic had equally produced great works (Gould, 1965: 28). The National Museum was to demonstrate this creative potential enabled by the revolutionary government of France.

A new discourse emerged which both legitimated and effected the articulations of the 'museum'. The decision to levy war indemnities in the form of precious material things was justified by the Minister of Justice in a letter to Napoleon: 'The reclamation of works of genius and their safe-keeping in the land of Freedom would accelerate the development of Reason and human happiness' (Wittlin, 1949: 233). Other official statements similarly celebrated the actions of the Republic and spelt out the justification for 'museums':

> By means of courage the Republic has succeeded in obtaining what Louis XIV was unable to obtain for enormous sums of money. Vandyke and Rubens are on their way to Paris and the Flemish School en masse will adorn our museums ... France will possess inexhaustible means of enlarging human knowledge and of contributing to the perfection of civilization.
>
> (quoted in Wittlin, 1949: 233)

The pure courage of the Republic is celebrated both as a greater moral force and also as more useful than the power of the inherited wealth of the overturned sovereign. 'Museums' are seen as apparatuses for public rather than private consumption. The education of the population through 'museums' emerged as a new form of population management, targeted at the collective good of the state rather than for the benefit of individual knowledge. The 'museum' was to be used to support the Republic by offering an opportunity to all citizens to share in what would previously have become the private possessions of the king. The 'museum' is a crucial point in this articulation. It enables the triumph of 'liberty over tyranny' and 'philosophy over superstition' (Quynn, 1945: 243).

The officer in charge of the convoy of Italian works of art wrote announcing their impending arrival in Paris:

> Citizens of all classes of the population ought to be aware that the Government has given them consideration and that all will have their share of the great booty. People will be able to judge what a Republican Government means if compared with the rule of a monarch who makes conquests merely for the pleasure of his courtiers and the satisfaction of his personal vanity.
>
> (Wittlin, 1949: 233)

INSTRUCTION

Sur la manière d'inventorier et de conserver, dans toute l'étendue de la République, tous les objets qui peuvent servir aux arts, aux sciences, et à l'enseignement,

P R O P O S É E

PAR LA COMMISSION TEMPORAIRE DES ARTS,

E T   A D O P T É E

PAR LE COMITÉ D'INSTRUCTION PUBLIQUE

D E   L A   C O N V E N T I O N   N A T I O N A L E.

L A Convention nationale a présenté au peuple français une constitution républicaine, fondée sur les principes éternels de l'égalité.

Le peuple français l'a acceptée avec enthousiasme ; il la fera respecter au-dehors par la force de ses armes, mais il ne peut la maintenir au-dedans que par l'ascendant de la raison.

Le peuple n'oubliera point que c'est par une instruction solide et vraie que la raison se fortifie. Déja, mise à sa portée, l'instruction est devenue pour lui le moyen le plus puissant de régénération et de gloire ; elle a placé dans ses mains un levier d'une force immense, dont il se sert pour soulever les nations, pour ébranler les trônes et renverser à jamais les monumens de l'erreur. Quelques-uns de nos philosophes avoient dit qu'il seroit dangereux de présenter à-la-fois toutes les vérités aux hommes. Plus hardi que ses philosophes, le peuple français a poursuivi toutes les vérités ensemble ; celles qu'on lui cachoit avec le plus d'art, sont celles qu'il a recherchées avec le plus d'empressement : maintenant il les possède toutes entières ; il les chérit ; il a versé son sang pour elles, et il veut conserver une conquête que ses législateurs sauront mettre à profit.

Nécessité d'une instruction généralement répandue.

A

27   First page of the Instructions prepared on the order of the National Convention for the Preservation of Cultural Objects. These instructions, prepared in 1794, were distributed throughout France.

The public 'museum' was constituted to share what had been private and expose what had been concealed.

New technologies and new subject positions

New technologies and new subject positions were constituted through the administration and care of the newly acquired material. Works confiscated from the whole of France were assembled in a few key warehouses, which were in fact often the newly vacated, newly secularised spaces of the convents (Bazin, 1967: 170). The seriated spaces which had divided and controlled religious personnel were particularly useful for the task of collecting, storing, dividing, and sorting works of art. These art depots acted as classifying and filtering points. The confiscated works were assembled, identified, catalogued, documented, repaired, and assessed for their seditious potential. Works that had feudal, religious, or royal connections were destroyed (ibid.: 170). Special deputies were appointed for this work. Later the Commission on the Arts drew up instructions for the care and conservation of artefacts for the directors of art depots. Inventories identified the individual items, reports assessed their physical condition, and they were separated out into various groupings to enable their later dispersal to designated cultural centres. Cultural control was both enmeshed with and enabled by other forms of control: military control over confiscations and travel arrangements; administrative and bureaucratic control over appointments of personnel. Through administrative and documentary procedures, the religious spaces were rearticulated as administrative cultural spaces.

New technologies also emerged to facilitate the identification and removal of works from the conquered territories. These included techniques for physical removal in times of violent disruption, legal provision for the transfer of ownership, and methods of identification and selection of material. The artistic conquest was organised as systematically as the military (Wescher, 1964: 180). In the summer of 1794 the Committee of Instruction laid down the main features of the policy of 'organised art pillage' that was to have far-reaching effects over the next twenty years. The Committee proposed to:

despatch secretly in the wake of our brothers in arms artists and men of letters with a solid educational background. These honest citizens of proven patriotism will remove with all due care such masterpieces that exist in the territories into which republican arms have penetrated. The riches of our enemies are, as it were, buried in their midst. Arts and letters are friends of liberty. The monuments erected

28 *Entrée triomphale des Monuments* (*6 February 1798*), engraving by Pierre Gabriel Berthault from a drawing by Girardet. The Napoleonic Wars resulted in the massive redistribution of the contents of princely cabinets, churches, menageries, and other collections of all sorts. This engraving shows the arrival in Paris of a variety of goods, in the centre of which can be seen the four bronze horses from St Mark's Basilica in Venice, closely followed by camels.

by slaves will acquire, when set up among us, a splendour which a despotic government could never confer on them.

(Hemmings, 1987: 78)

It was recognised that in order to remove the works most efficiently, this should be done as soon as possible after the arrival of the shock troops, when conditions were still chaotic and before the owners could hide their property (Alexander, 1983: 91; Wescher, 1964: 184). Any delay would be likely to lead to difficulties (Gould, 1965: 90). The cultural appropriations were both facilitated and constrained by military imperatives. Thus, in 1806, Vivant Denon, then Director of the Musée Napoléon in the Louvre and thereby *de facto* official collector for the empire, was given a free hand in selecting material from the princely galleries of Brunswick, Hesse-Cassel, Mecklenburg-Schwerin, Berlin, and Potsdam. He was prevented, however, from breaking up the collection in the Green Vaults in Dresden, the most famous, and therefore the most desirable to Denon, because the king of Saxony had changed sides after the defeat of the Prussian–Saxon armies at Jena, and Napoleon needed his military aid (Alexander, 1983: 91; Wescher, 1964: 183).

The transfer of property was legalised by inclusion in the various peace treaties (Wescher, 1964: 180). For example, the Treaty of Tolentino (17 February 1797) forced the Pope, Pius VI, to relinquish one hundred pictures from the Vatican Gallery, seventy-three statues, five hundred manuscripts, and hundreds of other gems, coins, vases, mosaics, and other items (Wescher, 1964: 180; Alexander, 1983: 89). Artists, naturalists, and other technical experts were appointed to accompany the invading forces, to carry out the task of removing material whose destination was the Louvre, the Jardins des Plantes, or the Bibliothèque Nationale (Gould, 1965: 31, 32, 40). The commissioners studied carefully such books as the *Voyage de deux Bénédictins* which described the things seen in the churches, libraries, and collections of the conquered countries (Quynn, 1945: 443). The development of expertise in the knowledge of which things were in which spaces was crucial for the success of the removal of material in times of war. Advance planning and organisation was essential for success. This led to the constitution not only of new technologies of identification and documentation, but also to the emergence of new subject positions of dealers and experts, those people who knew where things were, and which things were worth removing. New criteria of worth were evolved as selections were made. The forcible removal of material from the battlefield led to new classifications of material things. In the appropriations, reversals of values occurred: thus paintings were preferred to sculpture because they were lighter, more portable, and less susceptible to damage in transit (Hudson, 1987: 41).

Much of the work acquired both in France and in the conquered territories was transported to the Louvre. The official historian of the Louvre describes the immense work of 'requisition, selection, distribution, installation, removal, reinstallation, classification, restoration, inventories, exhibitions, catalogues, for thousands upon thousands of works' (Bazin, 1959: 52). A general archive was being created (Foucault, 1986: 26). This can be seen as part of an organised policy of accumulating in Paris the 'archives of civilisation', all those documents, papers, and material things that bear traces of the events of the past. The aim of this vast collection of the historic material of politics, the arts and the sciences, was to enable the scholars of the revolution to rewrite their histories in the spirit of the liberation of all nations (Bazin, 1959: 55). Thus, for example, the dossier of the trial of Galileo was taken to Paris from the archives of the popes in order to be reinterpreted.

The histories of the disciplines were to be transformed, reconstructed, rearticulated, and reiterated in a new field of use. New groups of statements were to be made, in conjunction with new divisions of the perceptual field (Foucault, 1974: 33).

Rearticulations in 'museum' practices

At first, the 'museum' in the Louvre contained many of the items that had been removed from the older collections, and they were articulated as they might have been in some of the sixteenth-century collections, with tables in the centre of the room containing mixed, three-dimensional material, and with paintings in multiple tiers on the walls between the windows. An immediate separation, however, was made between the works of living and dead subjects, on the grounds that the living would argue over the relative spatial positioning for their work.

The Grande Galerie (where things other than the work of living artists were displayed) was rather dark, a very long space with a continuous barrel vault, and with small windows along both walls (Gould, 1965: 27). Paintings were placed between the windows, and along the centre were tables on which were arranged bronzes, busts, *objets d'art*, clocks, and other 'curiosities': 'spoils' taken from 'tyrants', or 'enemies of our country' (Bazin, 1959: 47). The 'museum', however, was soon to rearticulate its collections and methods of display. The selection of items that were to be displayed and the separation of these from the items that would be stored or otherwise disposed of led to the development of new categories of inclusion/exclusion, and to new 'curatorial' processes.

The organisation of light and space played a crucial role in the rearticulation of the old palace as a new, public, democratic space, and the opening to the gaze of that which had been hidden. The space was partitioned and illuminated. Plans for top lighting which had been designed during the *ancien régime* but had not been carried out were revived, although the work in the Grande Galerie was not completed until 1938 (Seling, 1967: 109). The immense perspective was divided into nine bays or cells separated by great transverse arches supported on double columns (Bazin, 1959: 51) with overhead and side lighting alternating (Alexander, 1983: 90). New staircases were built (Seling, 1967: 109).

Artists' lodgings had been jammed into the unused rooms of the Louvre, where whole houses had been built in the vacant spaces, holes had been cut in the walls between the rooms, and chimneys installed projecting through the windows of the palace (Quynn, 1945: 442). These were removed. New spaces were constructed and the newly rationalised spaces were all decorated in a unified way, in the taste of the period (Wescher, 1964: 183).

New classifications were made and objects were made meaningful in new ways. Representative samples were selected to be displayed from the vast mass of material available (Gould, 1965: 21) and these selections were changed from time to time. The concepts of 'storage' and 'reserve collections' emerge. Spaces are divided into 'repositories' and 'exhibition spaces'.

The concept of the 'temporary exhibition' surfaced. Special exhibitions were mounted in relation to current events, celebrating especially, for example, the birthday of Napoleon. Exhibits changed as new pieces arrived at the museum. The displays were altered to underline military procedures: when Napoleon was planning to invade England, for example, the Bayeux Tapestry was put on display to remind visitors to the museum of earlier successes. Napoleon's wedding celebrations were held in the Louvre, although this necessitated demounting some of the large paintings for fear of damage during the proceedings. The curators of the Louvre were concerned to prove the value of the museum to both the court circle and the general public, and thus special galas were held (Alexander, 1983: 94). These new 'curatorial' practices were, as can be seen, contingently related to political, military, and social moments.

Material things were reorganised in new series of relations. The tables and their contents (which perhaps had come from the old princely cabinets of Hesse-Cassel or Mecklenburg-Schwerin), those 'miscellaneous' three-dimensional things (*objets d'art*), were removed into separate spaces. Any possibility of the older relationships that might have existed between the objects, articulated either through the art of memory and the structures of the Renaissance *episteme*, or even through the two-dimensional table of classification, were invisible to the 'modern' eye and the resulting unrelated and jumbled things were separated out again into divisions that made more sense, and that fitted newer rationalities.

The work of living artists was separated out and displayed separately. Previously, collections had displayed both older pieces and the work of living artists/craftsmen together. At first the paintings were mixed together, with the attractiveness of the painting being the only criterion of inclusion, on the grounds that: 'The museum ... is a flower-bed where we must assemble the most brilliant colours' (Gould, 1965: 24). Later the paintings would be hung in 'schools' and to show 'histories'.

The conservation of the collections became a specialist activity as new techniques were developed and older ones improved. Works of art were cleaned and repaired, paintings were relined, and in some cases transferred from wood to canvas. Reports were drawn up to describe and document the processes. Thus in 1801 a ten-page report described the process of transferring a painting by Raphael from wood to canvas (Alexander, 1983: 95; Gould, 1965: 20). The work of conserving the paintings was used to justify further appropriations during the conquests, on the grounds that the previous owners had been negligent, and that the work would be far better looked after in France.

The scale of these new activities demanded new subject positions. The work of conservation required the development of specialist expertise, but in addition the scale of the entire operation required permanent personnel. Up until 1802, the work of administering the collections as they arrived in Paris, and directing the acquisitions (including appointing and instructing the agents) had been carried out by successive commissions. In 1802, the volume of work was such that a director was appointed to oversee the development of the 'museum'. The post extended to the oversight of the entire artistic production of the empire, including the decoration of imperial Paris, the commissioning of paintings of the emperor and his battles, and the supervision of the former royal factories of Sèvres, Beauvais, and the Gobelins (Wescher, 1964: 183). The policies of the 'museum' were thereby directly enmeshed with the other cultural policies of the new state.

The new director, Vivant Denon, had organised the production of works that celebrated the new history of the revolution and its greatest heroes (Alexander, 1983: 97). Notes and sketches were provided for the paintings that provided the required images. Remuneration was standardised according to size of painting and expertise of the artist (ibid.: 97). A new race of dealers and 'art historians' was born (Hudson, 1987: 6, 41).

The training of artists was radically altered. Previously, artists had worked as apprentices, as in the medieval guild system, in the studio of a master. Now the 'museum' took the place of the master (Bazin, 1959: 51), and students worked in the galleries, faithfully following the master painters step by step.

The appointment of one individual, a differentiated and specialised 'eye', to oversee the work of the 'museum' led to further and more rigorous systematisation of processes and techniques both in the 'museum' itself and in its procedures for acquisition. A *catalogue raisonné* was proposed by the new director, which would document the history of the Musée Napoléon (Wescher, 1964: 182, 183). Henri Beyle (Stendhal), as auditor for the Council of State, made an inventory of the existing collections and assisted in the decisions relating to further requisitions. Comprehensive financial accounts were kept and a registration system was devised for the documenting of the works (Alexander, 1983: 93–4).

New practices emerged as the 'museum' attempted to fulfil its function of transforming the population into a useful resource for the state. Explanatory texts were attached to the works displayed (Hudson, 1987: 42; Seling, 1967: 109). Some teaching took place in the gallery housing the antiquities (Seling, 1967: 109). Cheap catalogues and guides to the collections on display were produced specifically to inform the visitors to the museum and these were quite distinct from the complete inventories of the collections produced for purposes of identification, documentation, and control of the objects. The catalogues were written for the visiting 'citizens', not for the curators of the collections or for scholars (Hudson, 1987: 186). These catalogues were cheap to purchase (Seling, 1967: 109) and were reproduced in translation (Bazin, 1959: 51). As the collections were divided, documented, and placed in new spaces, so the population was to be constituted as citizens of the state, by means of their propulsion through the newly public spaces and their exposure to the newly available symbols of civilisation.

Administratively and legally, the museum formed part of the state education system. This had profound implications and produced practices of access that were discontinuous in relation to other institutions, other 'museums', where hitherto entry had been restricted to educated people from higher social classes whose behaviour and correct demeanour could be relied upon (Hudson, 1987: 42). Methods for controlling access in other 'museums' varied from issuing tickets in advance that enabled a check on identity and reputation, as at the British Museum, to requirements in terms of dress worn, as at the Hermitage (Wittlin, 1949: 113, 131). In every ten-day period the 'Museum Français' was opened exclusively to artists and copyists for the first five days, the next two were reserved for cleaning, and on the last three the 'museum' was open free of charge to the public (Alexander, 1983: 88).

New subject positions emerged. The new director, Vivant Denon (Alexander, 1983), had a small specialist staff to work in the museum (Wescher, 1964: 183). This included one general secretary and three 'curators', personnel experienced in the artefacts that the museum contained. One of these three curators, Ennius Quirinus Visconti, who was in charge of the sculptures, had worked with the same objects in Rome. He had been Minister of the Interior and Consul of the Roman Republic in 1798. When the sculptures were removed to Paris, he went with them (Bazin, 1959: 52). The work of the curators was divided according to the material nature of the artefacts; Visconti cared for the sculptures and a colleague was in charge of the paintings.

Subject positions were also split according to different classifications of 'care'. In addition to the three curators who cared for the collections in relation to specialist knowledge (of their individual general histories, and the condition of each artefact), a greater number (maybe as many as thirty) of guards or 'attendants', possibly uniformed (Gould, 1965: 27), cared for the security of the collections and watched over the spaces open to the public (Alexander, 1983: 93). These attendants were, of course, necessitated by the openness of the institution. Thus, at the same time as the 'museum' is represented as open and free to all, the idea of patrolled, surveyed, and controlled public spaces emerges. The 'museum', placed within the sovereignty–discipline–government triangle (Foucault, 1979: 19), becomes one among many apparatuses of security and surveillance.

The accessibility of the collections to the general mass of the population led to a new dispersal of subject positions. This accessibility was in itself quite a new notion and it was initially the cause of much comment. It was as much the openness of the collections as the collections themselves that made the 'museum' a target for foreigners. After the Treaty of Amiens in 1802, English and German artists, writers, and others came in large numbers to visit the museum (Hudson, 1987: 4). The painter Lawrence noted that 'everything was laid out to the public with a degree of liberality unknown elsewhere' (Alexander, 1983: 105).

Following the establishment of the Louvre as a 'museum' in Paris, 'museums' were established on a regional basis across France (Alexander, 1983: 92). This policy of decentralisation, based on educational principles, used existing resources, but extended them into a conscious network. By

1814, twenty-two departmental 'museums' had been established, mainly art 'museums' founded in relation to existing schools of art, where it was judged that the people would be already sufficiently educated and numerous to produce adequate numbers of students (Bazin, 1967: 180). Paintings were sent to these 'museums' from the Louvre. The paintings were exhibited in Paris before being sent to the regions (Wescher, 1964: 182). Curators and lecturers were appointed to care for the works and to explain them to the people (Bazin, 1967: 180).

Once 'museums' had been set up in a regular geographical network in France, they were established in other parts of Europe. Revolutionary principles led to rationalisation of 'museums' and artefacts in relation to the greatest access for the people. Large 'museums' were formed through-out Europe to allow the people to enjoy the collections that had previously been reserved for the elite (Bazin, 1959: 55).

A new cultural space was articulated on the existing military space of the empire. The museological map of Europe was superimposed on to the military map: thus Brussels, a military port, and hitherto not a centre for collections, was designated a museological centre and received thirty-one important paintings. Antwerp, however, seen as little more than a marginal city, a small military outpost on the outskirts of the empire, lost many of its 'historic treasures' (Bazin, 1967: 183).

Other central 'museums' were created that paralleled the Musée Napoléon in France. Milan was the capital of Italy and therefore the Brera was created as the most important 'museum'; its collections built up by removing items from elsewhere in Italy, mainly the depots which con-tained the confiscated works from the religious houses (Bazin, 1959: 55). Academies of fine art had been established by a decree of 1801, and 'museums' were attached to these (Bazin, 1967: 55). Later, the depots themselves, both in Italy and in France, opened as 'museums' (Bazin, 1959: 55; 1967: 173). Through the deployment of the new technologies, these spaces for storage and accumulation were rearticulated as spaces for exposure and exhibition.

Once the institutions were established with their full complement of objects, exchanges were proposed between 'museums' both nationally and internationally, although the collapse of the imperial government in 1814 meant that many of these plans did not come to fruition. Denon, however, effected an exchange with the Brera in 1812–13, sending paint-ings of the Northern School from the Louvre to offset a weakness in the collections of the Brera (Bazin, 1967: 183).

The overall plan for the redistribution of works to the 'museums' was conceived on an international scale; the Louvre in Paris, capital of 130 departments of the Empire, would represent a faithful reflection of all European art and each European city would do so on a smaller regional scale (Bazin, 1967: 183). Thus a vast intersecting museological gaze was established that judged and surveyed collections in the regions of France and in the conquered domains. Interconnections were established both in and out of the centres and across the regions.

The 'museum' and the modern *episteme*

> The ever more complete preservation of what was written, the establishment of archives, then of filing systems for them, the reorganization of libraries, the drawing up of catalogues, indexes and inventories, all these things represent, at the end of the classical age, not so much a new sensitivity to time, to its past, to the density of history, as a way of introducing into the language already imprinted on things, and into the traces it has left, an order of the same type as that which was being established between living creatures. And it is in this classified time, in this squared and spatialized development, that the historians of the nineteenth century were to undertake the creation of a history that could at last be 'true' – in other words, liberated from Classical rationality, from its ordering and theodicy: a history restored to the irruptive violence of time.
>
> (Foucault, 1970: 132)

A great discontinuity in the space of knowledge occurred in the last years of the eighteenth century. During the early years of the seventeenth century, 'the great circular forms in which similitude was enclosed were dislocated and opened so that the table of identities could be unfolded' (ibid.: 217); but now this flat table of difference mutated into a three dimensional space where

> the general area of knowledge was no longer that of identities and differences, that of non-quantitative orders, that of a universal characterization, of a general taxinomia, of a non-measurable mathesis, but an area made up of organic structures, that is, of internal relations between elements whose totality forms a function.
>
> (Foucault, 1970: 218)

These organic structures were discontinuous, and did not therefore form a table of unbroken similarities and differences. The organising principles of this new space of empiricities were analogy and succession. The link between one organic structure and another was not the identity of several elements, but the identity of the relation between elements (and here visibility no longer played a role) and of the functions that they perform. In the classical age the space of the table presented all the possibilities in advance, which were then scanned in order to identify the sequence of chronologies; but from the nineteenth century, History was to deploy, in a temporal series, the analogies that connected distinct organic structures to one another.

In the nineteenth century, philosophy was to reside in the space between history and History, between events and the Origin (Foucault, 1970: 219). Explanations of the world were to be based on the probing of deep structural relationships. This necessarily led thought back to the question of knowing what it meant for thought to have a history. The third dimension that Foucault suggests opened up at this stage in western culture is the dimension of philosophical questioning, and analysis of relationships.

This cultural shift can be identified in the 'museum'. Paintings are hung together such that the functional relation between them constitutes identities – a 'history of art' was created. During the closing of the Musée Central des Arts for repairs in 1796, for example, the paintings were rehung by 'schools' (Bazin, 1967: 172). 'Schools' in this case meant by country, and specifically by country conquered through war. (Thus there was no 'English School' as England did not form part of the empire. To all intents and the purposes, English painting did not exist (Hudson, 1987: 42)). The different schools were hung in separate bays, the first bay containing 107 French paintings, the next four bays containing Dutch, Flemish, and German paintings, and the last four bays containing Italian paintings (Alexander, 1983: 95).

This method of according meaning to objects was in marked contrast to earlier eighteenth-century display arrangements, which grouped items by theme, material, or size, and which put together the works of both living and dead artists from all countries (Bazin, 1967: 159). The intention behind the innovative new hang was explained in the catalogue by the curator who had organised it:

> The purpose was to use this beautiful building, so suitable by its many rooms, so that the arrangement should be as far as possible a visual history of art. Such a large, public collection intended for instruction more than for fleeting pleasure, is like a rich library in which those eager to learn are glad to find works of all kinds and all periods.
>
> (Seling, 1967: 109)

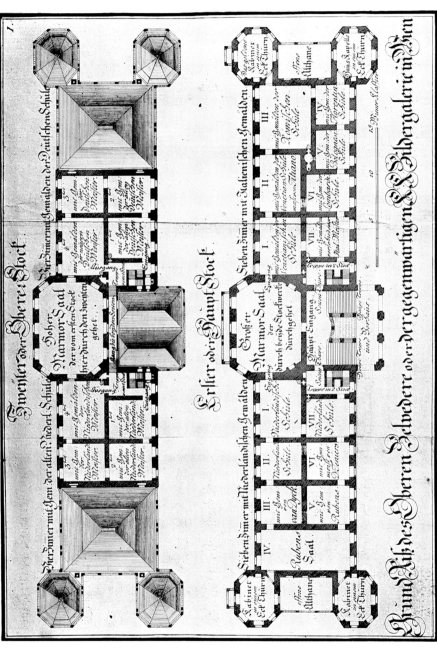

29 Histories of Art were created in many of the galleries of Europe. This plan of the paintings gallery in the Schloss Belvedere in 1778, shows how the works were grouped by country, and within that, by date, by (geographical) school, or by individual artist. This is in marked contrast to the form of display shown in Plate 23.

In the laying out of paintings by geographical and historical divisions into 'schools' of artists, a 'picture-book' of art history is presented. The relationships of the paintings depend on the country of origin of the artist rather than the physical appearance of the work itself. The visible surface of things is no longer the determining factor in the creation of order in the 'museum'.

In fact, 'museums' had already acted as a site for the representation of chronology. One of the depots to which material was sent during the acquisitioning of church property during the 1790s, the former monastery of the Petits Augustins, had been opened as the Musée des Monuments Français. The fragments of church sculpture and architecture, tombs and decorations were assembled in the seriated rooms of the convent by centuries, with periodisation being the unifying factor (Seling, 1967: 110). Material things were arranged by chronology, or temporal sequence, rather than by hidden, secret resemblances, or by the relationships of visible features.

Other individual 'histories' were also created: on his appointment as director of the Musée Napoléon, Denon immediately rehung one of the bays of the Grande Galerie with sixteen paintings by one artist, Raphael, rearranged in such a way as to show the development of the artist (Alexander, 1983: 95). Successive identities and differences began to replace the visual identities and differences of the classical age.

Conclusions

The fourth case-study, the 'disciplinary museum', represented a trans-formation of previous 'museum' practices. This new institution was constituted through the articulations of several elements: the great rupture of people and things at the time of the revolution in France; the emergence of a state that conceived the population as a resource; and the reworking of earlier models of princely positions, created and supported by collections of precious material things. A new cultural matrix emerged, that enmeshed the 'museum' within a network of state patronage and art production. New subject positions and new disciplinary technologies were required.

This new 'disciplinary museum' was on a far greater scale than in the past, and required specialised subject positions to maintain its momentum as an instrument of the state. These positions were defined partly by the type of artefact accumulated, partly by the need to oversee the security of these things while open to the public gaze, and partly by the need to position the emperor as prince.

The open availability of the collections led to the emergence of a secure and surveyed apparatus that acted initially to articulate the conjunction of people and things in a new freedom, but which also had the potential of becoming an instrument through which the people could be controlled. The 'museums' in France were underpinned by ideals of the liberation of both human subjects and material things from tyranny and ignorance, but this democratic impetus, born from the ideas of liberty and fraternity, led to the emergence of an apparatus that, through its articulations, also operated to reform the population as a resource for the state. This disciplinary apparatus could be rearticulated and reworked in other times and spaces, where the balance between freedom and control could be altered as required. During the modern age, museums shape both knowledge and bodies.

In Britain, for example, where the arts were seen as 'those softeners of human life. Those refiners of the rough drossy ore of humanity', one of the functions of the newly founded National Gallery was to civilise the mass of people, who 'get a taste when exposed to art'. Later, the aim of the National Portrait Gallery in London was the assemblage of a collection of images of the heroes of the British state which would lead the beholder to 'mental exertion, noble actions, to good conduct' (Hooper-Greenhill, 1980: 21–3). History, represented as a temporal progression of the great and the good, was held up as an example to be imitated through intellectual endeavour, through heroic acts, or (failing both of these) merely by behaving well.

The physical organisation of immense numbers of artefacts across large geographical spaces, combined with the need to ensure the integrity both of the things and of their new owners, led to new administrative measures and techniques. During the appropriations and requisitions, collections were subject for the first time to legal strictures. Public ownership was enshrined in new codes. These new Napoleonic codes were fundamentally discontinuous with those that had indicated ownership in the past (Bronowski and Mazlish, 1970: 461).

The processes of collecting became more dynamic. The old passive collecting of the style of the Repository of the Royal Society, where a reliance on gifts led to an uneven and irregular collection, was demonstrated as haphazard and 'unprofessional' in comparison with the well-researched and thoroughly organised collecting practices that this new institution demonstrated. The network of records that emerged positioned the collections in a financial, cognitive, spatial, and legal framework. Material objects were constituted as meaningful, therefore, through a number of interlocking discourses.

Museums and the Shaping of Knowledge

The 'museum' as a disciplinary apparatus articulated a new ensemble of oppositions within a new regime of truth. The oppositions included private/public, closed/open, tyranny/liberty, superstition/knowledge, inherited wealth/courage. The museum was a crucial instrument that enabled the construction of a new set of values that at once discredited the *ancien régime* and celebrated the Republic. The collections, the confiscations from the tyrants and the trophies of war, accumulated together within one space, previously the property of the king and now available to all, materially demonstrated the historic shift in power.

New technologies for administering and curating the vast collections and the vast spaces had been developed. These technologies entailed the emergence of new values, new functions, and new subject positions. The 'museum' became part of the network of constant and mutiple relations between population, territory, and wealth (Foucault, 1979: 180).

Within this new institution, new functional divisions emerged. Earlier, collecting and viewing were different aspects of the same practices and were carried out by the same small group of people, whether aristocracy, scholars, or merchants. Objects were obtained and shown largely within the same social network. Now, with the concept of the museum as an instrument for the democratic education of the 'masses', or the 'citizen', the exposition moves onto a larger platform. The display is offered to those who would know nothing about the processes of collecting, and who would not necessarily belong to the same social group.

A division was drawn, therefore, between knowing subjects, between the producers and the consumers of knowledge, between expert and layman. This division held within it relations of advantage and disadvantage. In the public museum the producing subject 'works' in the hidden spaces of the museum, while the consuming subject 'works' in the public spaces. Relations within the institution are skewed to privilege and enable the hidden, productive 'work' of the museum, the production of knowledge through the compilation of catalogues, inventories, and installations (Hooper-Greenhill, 1987a). The seriated public spaces, surveyed and controlled, where knowledge is offered for passive consumption, are emblematic of the museum as one of the apparatuses that created 'docile bodies' through disciplinary technologies.

A useful past for the present 8

The successes and failures of history

Museums have been active in shaping knowledge over (at least) the last 600 years. During the period of the Renaissance *episteme*, the classical age, and the modern age, a variety of both structures of knowledge and rules for the production of truth can be observed to have been in operation. Accumulation of material things, both natural and artificial, have always been one of the ways in which it has been possible to know the world, but cabinets, *studioli*, *Theatrum sapientiae*, repositories, and 'museums' have been constituted according to the prevailing epistemological context, and have, therefore, enabled different possibilities of knowing according to the rules and structures in place at the time.

There is no essential museum. The museum is not a pre-constituted entity that is produced in the same way at all times. No 'direct ancestors' (Taylor, 1987: 202), or 'fundamental role' (Cannon-Brooks, 1984: 116) can be identified. Identities, targets, functions, and subject positions are variable and discontinuous. Not only is there no essential identity for museums, as the case-studies demonstrate, but such identities as *are* constituted are subject to constant change as the play of dominations shifts and new relations of advantage and disadvantage emerge. 'Truth is of the world: it is produced by virtue of multiple constraints' (Foucault, 1977b: 13).

> The successes of history belong to those who are capable of seizing these rules, to replace those who had used them, to disguise themselves so as to pervert them, invert their meaning, and redirect them against those who had initially imposed them; controlling this complex mechanism, they will make it function so as to overcome the rulers through their own rules.
>
> (Foucault, 1977c: 151)

Museums and the Shaping of Knowledge

An 'effective' history of museums has discovered a long story of collection, confinement, and classification of material things, but there have been radical shifts in what things have been seen as desirable, how classifications and meanings have been made, why collections have been put together, and how these collections, once constituted, have been used. The production of 'truth' or 'knowledge' is a process that can be found to be operating at all times, and the selection, confinement and organisation of material things has been only one of the modalities of this production. However, the forms of truth and knowledge that *have* been constituted have not followed a continuous identity.

Truth in the Medici Palace was simply the truth that positioned the prince (Cosimo/Piero/Lorenzo de Medici) at the apex of a fixed hierarchical structure, closer to the Creator-God than others, and legitimately so placed because the visible splendour of his material existence marked a relation of exteriority. The production of this knowledge was abruptly ended when Florence was invaded by the French and the first generation of Medici were thrown out of the city. The collections that were still remaining were abruptly removed, physically altered, reorganised, and re-presented: rearticulated to constitute a new regime of truth to legitimise a new form of relations of advantage/disadvantage.

Knowledge in the 'cabinet of the world' was the revelation of the hierarchical unification of an occultised, magical, centripetal, fixed world both revealed and concealed through the interpretation of the signatures of the world, and at the same time the positioning of the subject (prince/ scholar/consumer) at the centre of this partly objectified world. The shaping of this truth could no longer be sustained on the collapse of the Renaissance structures of knowing. Those collections which remained intact could no longer maintain the rational structures of the interpretation of hidden knowledges. Once the relationships revealed by the links between material things were lost, the unity of the collections could no longer be perceived and they became 'irrational', 'confused', and 'miscellaneous'.

'Knowing' in the Repository of the Royal Society was the pure tabulated relationship of words and things constituted through differentiation and separation, where the original ordering of nature was demonstrated through simple, visible, physical juxtapositions. The production of this truth could not be achieved because of a lack of instrumental technologies. With a change in the target of language from the ordering and naming of the material world to the representation of mental processes, the production of this knowledge became irrelevant, the project declined, and the collection was neglected until the British Museum was established with its own regime of practices, and producing its own truths.

Knowledge in the 'disciplinary museum' was the truth of liberation from tyranny, the egalitarian and democratic opportunity to gaze on a history of man liberated from oppressors and free to constitute history in his own image. At the same time, an old form of knowing was reactivated in a new context; the knowledge of the position of the prince. This complex structure of knowledge had both specific short-term political dimensions, which were abruptly ended in 1814, but long-term cultural and political dimensions. The establishment of such a system of museum practices acted as a programme and a stimulus to further museum estab-lishment across Europe during the nineteenth century where new relations of advantage/disadvantage, new princes, and new histories were produced.

Each society has its 'general politics' of 'truth' (Foucault, 1977b: 13). This knowledge is produced through regimes of practices, of which the museum is one. The knowledge so produced is radically discontinuous and subject to abrupt reversals.

The histories of the museum successes and failures demonstrate that the use of knowledge is contingent upon other power practices. When the Medici were reinstalled in Florence in the sixteenth century, the idea of the golden age in Florence as a reactivation of their own specific past, presented in a specific way, was used to legitimise their rule. History was rewritten and re-presented. The suppression of the truth of the cabinet of the world, and the redesignation of its rational knowledge as irrational and disordered, came about because this older way of knowing the world conflicted with a new scientific truth that positioned the subject in control of the world and his own destiny. Occult and magical explanations could not be accommodated within such explanations.

'Effective' history places the museum in its constitutive context. Previously this has not been the case. All writers of 'normal', all-encompassing museum histories (Wittlin, 1949; Bazin, 1967; Van Holst, 1967) write about museums by tracing a line that moves from museum to museum, across time and space, drawing out the features of an essential museum.

This attempt at effective history has worked with specific case-studies with the aim of drawing out the particular and detailed features of each one. The case-studies were chosen because of their differences rather than their similarities. At the same time, effective history recognises that the social is open, only partially fixed, and that therefore, any case-study, any site of the production of knowledge, is equally only partially fixed and thus that external/internal relations are subject to movement and change. The social includes material things, subject positions, spaces, and values. Through the analysis of the elements of several 'museums', it has become clear that none of these things has an essential identity. A radically contingent, differential fluid identity was revealed in each case.

The identity and meaning of material things is seen to be constituted in each case according to the articulations of the epistemological framework, the field of use, the gaze, technologies, and power practices. If the same object had been held as part of the collection of each of the 'museums' that have been discussed, the meaning of the object would have radically changed as it moved from one institution to the next. The way in which the object would have been both understood and enjoyed would have shifted. Neither what counted as knowing, nor what counted as pleasurable, remained the same.

Thus a painting of a 'Madonna and Child' would be understood in the Medici Palace as both a magical and a religious thing, something that could give protection against evil forces, and something that should be held in awe. The value of the painting would have some relation to both the quality and quantity of precious material (gold leaf or lapis lazuli) expended in its production and to the skill of the artist who had painted it. This painting might well have been an integral part of the decorative scheme of a room, or executed upon an item of furniture. It would probably have been produced specifically for consumption within the Medici Palace.

The modality of knowing the painting in the Medici Palace would have been constructed through the reading, evaluative, and calculating gaze which operated within a pre-existing, fixed, theological-political order. Pleasure would have been produced through the exercise of both the evaluative gaze and the gaze sensitive to the spiritual qualities of colour and light.

In the second case-study, 'the cabinet of the world', a painting of a 'Madonna and Child' would be understood as part of the representation of the hierarchical structure of the world. It would be one thing among other things both old and new that were placed together in the cosmological picture, and it might possibly be linked to other things of very disparate nature through resemblance and signatures. It would probably have been painted in allegorical form. The painting would possibly have been acquired by agents on behalf of the collector and might therefore have belonged to more than one owner. Its value would have increased had this owner been a person with a certain social position. It would be detached from a specific site of production and consumption. The modality of knowing this painting would be constructed through the occultised interpretive gaze which placed it in an objectified cosmological framework. Pleasure would be produced through reading the hierarchies and correspondences (which might be extremely personalised) in attempting to bring together and represent a world picture, which might be highly secretive and occultised.

In the third case-study, the Repository of the Royal Society, a painting of a 'Madonna and Child' would be seen as something that did not fit with a complete picture of nature. Nonetheless it would be valued as a gift from a specific donor. If it had been painted by a specific artist or if it had previously belonged, or been seen by, specific people, its value would increase. It might well have been purchased in a 'curiosity' shop, and if it had hung in another collection, could have been formatised to fit. The modality of knowing was constructed through the classificatory gaze that separated and divided but that also evaluated the painting according to social structures, and possibly even magical notions. Pleasure would more likely reside in contemplating the status of the donor (or of being the donor) than in fitting the painting into the classificatory framework.

In the fourth case-study, the 'disciplinary museum', the painting would be part of a constellation of objects that represented liberation from tyrants and oppressors. In being seen, it took its place among the technologies designed to create docile bodies, and to reform the population as a resource for government. The painting might be part of a hang that had specific educational functions. It might be grouped with other paintings by the same artist, or from the same geographical location, to demonstrate a personal history, or a geographical 'school'. The painting might equally be in store, part of a reserve collection, or it could have been subjected to restoration.

The painting would have been perceived and known through the causal philosophical gaze that was beginning to understand man as both subject and object of analysis. The gazer might have used the painting as a starting point for the consideration of the psychology of man. Pleasure would have varied radically in relation to subject position: subjects internal to the museum practices might have taken pleasure from the production of knowledge and truth (exhibitions, catalogues, research) from the painting, while subjects external to these productive processes might have taken pleasure from the consumption of this knowledge and truth. Or, of course, they might not. In this case-study, the breadth of consumers and the function of truth at the level of population, introduces to museum practices for the first time the question of the acceptance or rejection of specific forms of truth. Museum practices become enmeshed in the constitution of the politics of pleasure. As such, the identities of collected material things, previously constituted within a small social group, become of political relevance on a large scale.

The use of effective history is that it reveals that material things have no essential identity, that meaning is not constant, and that the processes of 'keeping and sorting' (Impey and MacGregor, 1985: 1) have not remained the same. The search for rupture shows no unbroken continuity, but on the contrary constant discontinuity, breaks, ruptures, and reorganisations of material things and their meanings. Effective history also reveals the intimate articulations of the constitutions of identities through relations of advantage and disadvantage.

A constant flux of meaningful objects is revealed: manuscripts are broken up and rebound, reassembled, retranslated, becoming new forms of inscription; sculpture is repositioned in different spaces, and pieces are added or removed; images carved on to one thing are reproduced in another medium, on another scale, to make new historical and political points; jewels are melted down, remade, sold, given as gifts, according to current needs; things are discarded, thrown away for lack of relevance, broken up on new ownership, brought across vast spaces by agents of all sorts (missionaries, sailors, travellers, colonisers, cultural agents); things are cherished, nourished, or neglected according to the play of the factors that constitute them as objects. The identity of meaningful objects remains open, and is constantly shifting as other aspects of the social shift around them, as elements are transformed. Effective history reveals the 'unstable assemblage of faults, fissures, and heterogeneous layers that threatens the fragile inheritor from within or from underneath' (Foucault, 1977c: 146).

The constitutive elements of the various case-studies were found to be in a constant state of flux due on the one hand to violent reversals such as invasions, imperial wars, revolutions, and civil wars, and on the other to smaller discontinuities such as management techniques, problems of changing monies, or the need to cultivate social support. All of these changes operate on their own time-scale which leads to non-correspondences and discrepancies within small areas of the social. Specific manifestations and their constituent factors also change at varying rates. In spite of the collapse of the Renaissance *episteme*, for example, some 'cabinets of the world' (Dresden) remained intact until the Napoleonic wars; some (Francesco I in Florence) were rearticulated almost immediately after their initial establishment.

Discontinuity can be identified in the separations and classifications made of meaningful objects. Changes in the valorisation of the old, the real, and the complete can be seen. Up until the end of the eighteenth century, old and new objects were placed together; in museums at the present time radical separations are made on the basis on periodisation. For a long time there was no distinction between the real and the replica; where it was the series that mattered, this distinction was not important. Now the integrity of the 'real thing' is crucial. The need for a series meant that things were made complete; the ethics of restoration was not an issue as it is at the present time. Many museums up until fairly recently were focused exclusively on the representaton of the past. Indeed, even today, many people assume that this is the major function of museums. This was not the function of the collections of the Medici Palace, the cabinets of the world, or the Repository of the Royal Society. The values and priorities that are taken for granted in museums today are not the same as the values and priorities that were important in the past.

Museums in the modern age

The modern *episteme* is constituted by the emergence of the human sciences. A human science exists 'wherever there is an analysis – within the dimension proper to the unconscious – of norms, rules, and signifying totalities which unveil to consciousness the conditions of its forms and contents' (Foucault, 1970: 364). A human science is understood as a form of knowledge which takes knowledge itself, and knowing, as problematic. A human science questions that which forms its target of study. Thus sociology problematises society, and asks 'how is the social possible?'. The answers may come from a variety of perspectives, and the relationships between these answers also form part of the content of sociology.

The human sciences 'address themselves to that mode of being of man which philosophy is attempting to conceive at the level of radical finitude, whereas their aim is to traverse all its empirical manifestations' (Foucault, 1970: 347). Where philosophy searches for analytical purity, abstract concepts and refined systems of mental activity, sociology, for example, is far more concerned with studying how people relate together in specific locations (school, industry); how practices and relations are constituted through systems of power (in the family or the professions); how many people act in specific ways at specific times (go to museums or football matches, shop at Harrods). The analytical and descriptive mapping of experience is the basis for the formulation of ideas, problems, and concepts in the human sciences. Sociology, psychology, anthropology, archaeology, history, art history, biology, and geology tell the stories of the history of the earth, of life, of man, and of civilisation. The interrelationships of these forms of knowing constitute a totalising order of things and of knowledge, which is historicised through and through (Bennett, 1990: 43).

'The domain of the Modern episteme should be represented as a volume of space open in three dimensions' (Foucault, 1970: 347). Deductive sciences such as maths and physical sciences are situated in the first dimension, the sciences of language, life, and economics are placed in the second dimension; while the third dimension is the site for the space of philosophical questioning. The human sciences do not exist in any of these dimensions, and are in fact, very difficult to locate. They have their existence in the three-dimensional space that is formed by this epistemological trihedron, and they borrow methods from each of the sciences at their boundaries. The existence of the human sciences is tenuous and perilous, positioned as they are between, and borrowing from, the deductive sciences, the empirical sciences, and philosophical reflection. Nonetheless, the human sciences have succeeded in establishing themselves as the most characteristic mode of knowing in the modern age.

In the modern age, it was to be no longer enough for material things to present themselves on a table of knowledge: the way in which things would be understood was in their relationship to man; 'it is no longer their identity that beings manifest in representation, but the external relation they establish with the human being' (Foucault, 1970: 313). The stories of man, life, and civilisation were to become more important than the physical identities of material things.

The basic structures of knowledge of the modern *episteme* are totality (a story, a theme, a history, organic relationships) and experience (relationships of things to people, knowledge evolved through the study of and activity in empirical events). Knowing and knowledge have become three-dimensional, all-involving, and all-encompassing. The main themes of knowledge are people, their histories, their lives, and their relationships.

These themes and structures underpin the shifts and changes in museums and galleries that can be observed today. New technologies, and new articulations of space, individual subjects, and objects, have emerged to enable the new themes and structures of knowledge to do their work. The functions and targets of this work have perhaps changed less. Museums and galleries are still able to subdue and to control bodies, and to establish social and cultural divisions. Today, however, these actions are not unfrequently documented and contested and museums have become sites for active and visible ideological struggles. Many of the new technologies and micro-processes of power demanded by the new structures of knowledge hold within them new possibilities for intervention in power processes and for the fragmentation of monolithic messages. This potential for intervention and for new perspectives has called forth its own response in terms of totalising and all-encompassing 'experience'.

Although the modern age began to emerge at the beginning of the nineteenth century, developments did not occur at the same time and in the same way across all the various knowledges that can be grouped under the term 'human sciences'. Shifts and changes in the constitutive elements of museums could no doubt be charted as they responded to the developments of the individual sciences, although the responses might not always be found to be in step with the modalities of knowing. Thus the relationship between space and knowledge in the Natural History Museum as conceived by its first director, Richard Owen, was more in tune with the out-of-date theories of Georges Cuvier, than the modern ideas of Lamarck, Darwin, and Wallace. Owen had visited Cuvier in the Natural History Museum in Paris as a young man, and had worked with Cuvier shortly before his death in 1832. Cuvier's concepts of the relationships of groups in the animal kingdom as variations on an archetype were to be given material expression in the spaces of the 'Index Museum' which was proposed by Owen in 1859. In the event, the 'Index Museum' was incorporated into the central, cathedral-like hall of the museum, and is described by Owen in a report of 1880 (Stearn, 1981). The bays of the 'Index Museum' would be labelled 1–12, and would 'convey an outline … of the divisions of Natural History, which would be fully and systematically illustrated in the several Galleries of the Museum'. The central core of the museum, therefore, opened to the public at the end of the nineteenth century (1881), expressed through its spaces knowledge that looked back to the end of the eighteenth century, and which had not yet fully made the shift into the modern age. The two-dimensional classification of the classical age offered principles of three-dimensional layout (Peponis and Hedin, 1982). The exhibition on human biology that opened at the end of the 1970s rearticulated the space of the museum, incorporating ideas informed by several divisions of the human sciences, including human biology (exhibition content), educational technology (exhibition design), and sociology (visitor studies). A very different spatial environment emerged, where convex spaces, curved lines, smooth transitions, and several choices of route shaped both the physical and intellectual experience of the museum visitor.

The technologies and micro-processes of museums can be discussed in relation to space, material things, and individual subjects. The identities and interrelationships of each of these elements will have changed many times during the period designated by Foucault as constituted through the modern *episteme*, and the current discussion will, therefore, focus on museums at the present time. How do spaces, material things, and individual subjects, at the end of the modern age, articulate with the primary themes and structures of knowledge?

Technologies in the modern museum

At the birth of the public museum, a division was drawn between the private space where the curator, as expert, produced knowledge (exhibitions, catalogues, lectures) and the public space where the visitor consumed those appropriately presented products. A deep cleft was formed that separated out the practices of the museum workers from those of the visitor. The experience of the museum, its collections, and its specialist processes, was different on either side of this divide. The lack of knowledge of the work of the curator constituted the visitor as ignorant and the curator as expert in respect of the collections. Conversely, the lack of knowledge of the visitor's reactions and responses constituted the curator as ignorant in respect of the audience for whom the musem's intellectual products were intended. Now, the closed and private space of the early public museums has begun to open, and the division between private and public has begun to close.

This opening of the space of the museum can be observed at a number of different levels. Conceptually, some curators are inclined to see themselves as facilitators for learning rather than as sole dispensers of knowledge. Shifts in the understanding of the learning process in schools, and the consequent recasting of the role of the teacher as facilitator, can be observed in museums. Exhibitions, and even collections, are now sometimes the product of joint efforts between audience and museum worker. An adult education project on history in a local community in Southampton resulted in an exhibition at the local art gallery of photographs brought by local people (Jones and Major, 1986). Getting together an art exhibition in a small village in Sweden involved the art adult education group in decisions about inclusion and exclusion, presentation, levels of text, and so on. This was followed by a visit to the art gallery in the nearby town, where the adult students experienced a new interest in the art gallery because they had themselves been through the processes of making an exhibition (Riksutstallningar, 1976).

The private spaces and processes are sometimes opened quite literally through inviting visitors on 'open days' to see 'behind the scenes'. Storage areas, conservation and photographic laboratories, and archives are demonstrated and explained. Sometimes the activities that, in the past, would always have been carried out behind closed doors, are pursued in the public spaces. Thus the preparation of exhibitions, previously a hidden process, is sometimes now open to view. At Leicester Museum an exhibition of large historic paintings which had not often been displayed before, was prepared in the large open spaces of the art gallery; partly because the objects themselves were so large that this was the only space where they could be displayed, but partly also as an educational opportunity for the public. Discussions on the condition of the paintings and the conservation work required were held equally between the curator and the conservator and the curator and the visitor.

The idea of open storage has emerged in the last few years (Ames, 1985). Conceived with a democratic end, several museums in western Canada found ways to redisplay their collections so that not only were the objects always accessible, but so also was the information held by the curator. At the University Museum of British Columbia, for example, the collections previously held in stores closed to the public were rearticulated in newly open spaces redesignated 'Research Collections'. The data held on the collections was made accessible through the use of computer documentation and print-outs collated in books positioned near the relevant objects. This attempt to 'deschool' the museum meant that new display cases had to be designed, so that, for example, those objects which were small and therefore liable to loss or damage were placed in cabinets with glass-topped drawers. At the Children's Museum of Boston, the curators work in glass-fronted offices next to the public galleries. The private work of the museum is visually accessible.

The architecture of museum buildings is now being adapted to enable information of all sorts to flow through more smoothly. Where the Natural History Museum in London, for example, was constructed to enable objects to be laid out in a typology, new museums in Japan are being built to allow channels of information to be installed. These cables and optical fibres carry information on all aspects of the work of the museum, including documentation on the collections, demographic and other information on the visitors, and data concerning the security and the internal environment of the museum. The 'intelligent' museum (Mizushima, 1989) requires adequate information-transmission capability; thus the quality of the electrical supply and the electrical wiring method is all-important.

The 'intelligent' museum controls its own environment through air-conditioning, and factors such as the thermal quality of the structure, the heat emission from equipment, changes in the number of visitors, and the characteristics of both exhibition and conservation environments must all be understood as part of the same general framework. The 'intelligent' museum monitors its own security through a strong system of information provision concerning the protection against fire, floods, or earthquakes; against penetration of boundary security; and against theft and burglary. Devices can be installed which inspect temperature, humidity, carbon-monoxide and carbon-dioxide intensity, dust quantity, wind speed, luminescence, and light.

Museums and the Shaping of Knowledge

Information on the collections can now be moved around the museum space itself, and also can be made available in other collections across the world or down the road. The space of the museum and the space of the object are no longer as they were.

The visitor, too, is connected to the museum space and its information-carrying function. Computer terminals distributed about the museum building offer guidance to the space itself, and information on various collection-related topics. Visual exhibits and simulation games are on the menu. The computers can be linked together and to central information banks. As the visitor works with the computer, it is possible to interrogate the nature of the interaction. Demographic information is recorded, such as the age and sex of the operator, the length of the interaction, how often an individual will use a terminal, what path of enquiry is followed, and how accurate are the reponses of the visitor when tested (Mizushima, 1989). As the subject and the information terminal interact, so the one generates the other: the subject generates information at the same time as consuming it; the terminal both gives and takes at once.

The entrances to museums often now look more like hotel lobbies than the prisons they perhaps resembled in the past. Large green plants, thick-pile red carpets, bubbling, sparkling waterfalls, and cheerful smiling faces are to found in the spaces that were formerly austere, bare, colourless, and peopled by warders in military-style uniforms.

Museum spaces have been rearticulated in other ways too. Shops, restaurants, rest and orientation areas occupy space that in the past would have contained objects and displays. The percentage of space within the building allowed for the display of objects is reduced in favour of spaces to display people. Thus, in La Villette in Paris, lounges with a group of sofas, a television monitor, and a nearby counter from which to buy food and drink are to be found at regular intervals. People can be found sleeping among the displays, and are, in many ways, much more entertaining. In some museums, specialist facilities are available for adults with babies, and the recent large-scale exhibition in Glasgow, namely 'Glasgow's Glasgow', contained a play area for children.

As shops take over gallery spaces, museum exhibits are returned to storage, and items for sale take their place. Objects for looking at are replaced by objects for purchase. Museum visitors as lookers and learners are repositioned as consumers. The merchandise in the shop is selected to relate as closely as possible to the collections of the museum, and may include replicas of three-dimensional objects, or prints of paintings. Patterns and designs from the material things in the collections are reproduced to 'museumise' ordinary items such as tablemats, diaries, pens, pencil cases, wrapping paper, small boxes, and calendars. Images are detached from their original sites of inscription and reassembled in new ways. Thus a book in the British Museum on the subject of 'cats' consists of images of cats from Ancient Egypt, the Classical World, the Middle Ages, and any other attractive cat that can be seen on a 'real' object from the collections. Cats from a Walter Crane ink drawing appear on the page next to cats from a seventeenth-century woodcut of three witches, the broadsheet reporting on their trial. A cat is abstracted from *The Historie of Foure-footed Beasts* by Edward Topsell, written in 1607, and reused as one of many cats in ancient times.

The contents of shops relate to the nature of the collections, but shops are sometimes even more specialised. At the British Museum, for example, a general shop with three-dimensional objects such as replicas of the Harris chessmen and Egyptian sculptures, T-shirts, posters, and silk scarves, is to be found in the main entrance; a general bookshop in a side gallery; a more specialised bookshop in the galleries of the British Library; and a small stall, with cheap items for children, in the Egyptian galleries.

Many museums and galleries have allocated space for their visitors to eat and drink. These spaces vary from elitist and expensive restaurants to sandwich bars. Some museums contain both, so that business people and families can both be suited. Meals, and other events too, are sometimes carefully selected also to relate to the collections; thus at an open day as part of an exhibition on the Caribbean at Leicester Museum and Art Gallery, Caribbean food was served, and, if visitors wanted, it was even possible to obtain a Caribbean hair-do during the evening.

With a reorientation in the funding of museums and galleries (Hooper-Greenhill, 1990: 65–6), the appeal to business sponsorship includes the use of space for corporate entertaining, either in the galleries or in special hospitality suites. The Museum of Science and Industry in Manchester which occupies a building that was recently converted from a station to a museum, includes a conference and entertainment suite sited next to the spaces used by the education department.

Many museums have begun to define their image more carefully, and this can be seen in the way in which their spaces are articulated. Along with new attentions to segmentation of the customers, the products have themselves become more segmented and specialised. Individual identities are heightened to compete in the marketplace. Thus the Science Museum in London has become more like a giant playground with the installation of Launchpad, a space entirely filled with large-scale exhibits that invite participation. Historic houses become more historic and more 'real' by employing actors to 'live' for a period on the premises. Oakwell Hall, in

Batley, Yorkshire 'came to life' when a team of actors in seventeenth-century costume ate, drank, cooked, talked, walked about, surveyed the land, fired guns, and cut down a tree, all in period style (and ignored the vast crowds that threatened to test the strength of the balcony over their heads as they ate in the hall). The National Gallery of Scotland was recently redesigned with dark, rich, and heavy wall-coverings, apparently intended to recall Victorian decor, although for any visitor who is not a specialist in Victorian style or the history of design, the atmosphere is more likely to evoke impressions of an extremely wealthy present-day house, or a large stately home.

Museums have now become part of a 'total destination'; part of a holiday package that might include two nights in a hotel, a trip through the local countryside, and a visit to the museum. Museums sell themselves in the same brochure along with other local tourist attractions. Ironbridge Gorge Museum, long a successful tourist destination with its river, town, shops, and variety of sites, many with costumed 'interpreters', is now considering acquiring a hotel to complete its universal appeal.

Today's 'universal' museum is one where all the various needs of visitors can be satisfied: a museum with well-displayed and enlivened collections, with a shop in which desirable and well-packaged objects can be purchased, with several places to eat according to one's taste and pocket, with a rest area, and with space for the children to be cared for and to play. Open, intelligent spaces offer increased access to subject and object.

'Objects' in the modern age are no longer presented on the table of classification, where their morphology defined both their identity and their interrelationships. During the classical age, a thing became an object through its visible features. Now material things present themselves in their relation to human beings (Foucault, 1970: 313). Material things are now constituted as objects through organic, historic links, through stories, and through people. In the museum, the three-dimensional display case was evolved to show the artefact or specimen in its physical dimension. Display cases seem to us now as, on the one hand, a metaphor for our understanding of what counts as a museum, but on the other hand, as curiously outdated. How can organic relationships, histories, and links to people be shown in display cases? What strategies are museums and galleries inventing to incorporate anthropology, sociology, and psychology as part of the knowledge of museums?

New technology is being used in displays to fragment the meaning of the artefact and to introduce many perspectives, many points of view. In the past, the object on display was accompanied with a label that fixed it in a monolinear frame of reference. A chair was 'Oak, Seventeenth

Century'; a gun was identified by its firing capacity; a feather head-dress from the Solomon Islands was presented as an exotic item from the colonies. The human, social, and cultural contexts of these artefacts were rendered invisible by these strategies. Now the many frames of reference that can contextualise material things are displayed along with the things themselves.

In Birmingham Museum and Art Gallery for example, a new exhibition, known as the 'Gallery 33 Project' focuses on cultural assumptions. The exhibition's name indicates its new approach: 'Gallery 33. A meeting ground of cultures. An exhibition about the way people live: beliefs, values, customs and art from around the world.' The exhibition draws on the museum's extensive holdings of art and artefacts from the Americas, Africa, Asia, and the Pacific, some of which have been in store for twenty years. Artefacts in everyday use in Birmingham, and in other parts of the world, are displayed alongside historical objects, with the past and the present both represented. There are opportunities for active involvement through handling and through the use of interactive video. A performance space is included as part of the gallery space, where musicians, dancers, storytellers' and craftspeople can work, thus enabling what the curator calls ' a true meeting ground of cultures'.

The interactive video is used as an opportunity to fracture and augment the meanings of four key artefacts, through the presentation of different perspectives and experiences. Four individuals who collected artefacts from the Solomon Islands are profiled: Ida Wench, a missionary, and Arthur Wilkins, a collector, both active in the 1920s; then from the contemporary scene, a fictional American tourist, N. S. Jones, and Law-rence Fontana, the director of the Solomon Islands National Museum. These four people offer a variety of views that contrast in terms of time, gender, race, and professional interest. The visitor is offered a number of routes through the various perspectives, according to choice. The interactive video itself can be experienced at a variety of levels, depending on knowledge and interest. The video is incorporated into the gallery spaces in such a way that those who are working with the touch screen can be observed, and their choice of study route through the material can be shared with other visitors. In the display of the artefacts many different opportunities are made for relationships with people to emerge.

In the past, museum classification systems offered very limited frames of reference for the sorting of objects. Even where more than one reference was possible for each object, many curators insisted on using only one (Porter, 1990: 81). Thus a domestic item (a kitchen chair, say) would be classified under the heading 'furnishing', and would not also be cross-referenced in relation to design, production, or material. Systems which enable the positioning of the item in more than one structure are now required, but even these systems (design, production, material), which consider the chair in terms of its intrinsic features, will very soon be felt to be insufficient. Where it is necessary, as it is today, to present objects in relation to people, the chair may well be related to its use in a human context. For example, it might be considered as one of the first pieces of furniture of a couple setting up home for the first time. At the Geffrye Museum in London in 1990, an exhibition 'Putting on the Style: Setting up Home in the 1950s' consisted of a number of room sets, all of which related to specific typical local groups, including immigrants from the West Indies (sitting-room); young single people (bedsitter); a young wife (kitchen); and so on. The memories and experiences of local people were researched as part of the exhibition planning, and local objects were acquired, often through donation. During the exhibition a questionnaire asked visitors which room they found the most meaningful in order for the curators to decide which of the room sets potential visitors might most like to see as a permanent room display. This approach to collection and documentation demands a sensitive and sophisticated system that goes beyond mere classification.

Until recently, research on the collections was carried out after the object had entered the collection (Porter, 1990: 79). Acquisition and research were seen as two separate processes. Now these are seen as part of the same process. Ideas are now more important than objects. Now the idea is to tell a specific story, and objects are gathered as they relate to the story. The person-related context is gathered at the same time, sometimes through the processes of oral history. The words that are collected along with the objects are often displayed together with the objects, inscribed either on a panel, through writing, or in the air, through an audio system. In 'The People's Story', for example, in Edinburgh, a fishwife is reconstructed life-size as part of a display. She is, however, not just any fishwife, but based on a specific individual whose actual words appear in the accompanying panel and are broadcast, along with sea-gulls, through an audio system, from time to time. The research for displays such as these is meticulously carried out; representative types of people are chosen, and then from within the type, a particular individual example is documented. The criteria for inclusion are historical and scholarly, rather than enter-tainment related. However, once the choice of content is made, the method of communication is as active and interactive as possible. Human experience forms both the basis for the research, and the basis for the mode of communication.

Other forces are at work here, too. 'The People's Story' deliberately takes an oppositional stance in terms of which history is told, and the experience of the telling. In contrast to the National Gallery of Scotland, for example,

30 A choice screen from the interactive video *The Collectors* made by New Media for Gallery 33 at Birmingham Museum and Art Gallery.

which is nearby, this story is not of the elite, but of the everyday, and the experience of the museum is noisy, active, and friendly. 'The People's Story' is housed in a small building with a narrow entrance off the pavement, like many small houses. In contrast, the National Gallery of Scotland is in a large building, overlooking a public park. A flight of steps leads through an entrance portico into the large, heavy, quiet, closely guarded rooms. People walk through this museum slowly, maintaining an upright stance, talking quietly, looking quietly, keeping their own personal space inviolate. At 'The People's Story', the small spaces soon lead to the development of a crowd who jostle together to peer in through the narrow window of a cell containing a reconstructed scene; different noises can be heard all the time, including the sea-gulls, the real broad speech of the reconstructed individuals who form the bulk of the displays, and the exclamations of the visitors as links and connections are made to their own lives and experiences.

This museum in Edinburgh comes close to the 'total museum', where ideas not objects are most important (Sola, 1987: 47; Weil, 1989). This focus on themes, ideas, and relationships can be identified as one of the guiding forces of the modern museum. The Musée de la Civilisation in Quebec, for example, states:

> While many museums focus on the artefact, the *Musée de la Civilisation* focuses on the human being. Artefacts, however important they may be, are only so because of their meaning and use. They are seen above all as evidence of human activity.
>
> (Trudel, 1989: 68)

New technologies and practices are evolving in museums to display ideas. In the past, the curator, as object-expert, played the most important role in the production of exhibitions. The exhibition process itself tended to be disjointed, consisting of several different activities which happened sequentially, but generally without much discussion of exhibition objectives or targets. Thus the curator worked on the topic and the content of the exhibition; the designer received the brief and found a way of presenting the ideas in a visual form (generally rewriting the labels, and thinning out the number of objects in the process); and once the process had come to an end, the education officer taught in the exhibition spaces (generally using the objects, but finding a new order for their presentation, and completely disregarding the texts). Now, exhibition teams have emerged, and project-leaders are appointed from within the team to manage the exhibition process. The project-leader need not be the curator, the 'power-brokers' in the earlier model (Miles, 1985).

In the past, the knowledge of the object was the most important

31 Peggy Livingstone worked as a fishwife and bought and sold her fish in Edinburgh. She is shown in 'The People's Story' at Edinburgh City Museum as a working woman aged 39. Currently 77, Peggy worked closely with the museum in its research for this display.

knowledge required to make an exhibition; now, knowledge about the audience is equally important. Information gathered through the disciplines of sociology and psychology is incorporated into the exhibition process: sociology offers knowledge about demographics (who comes to the museum), and about who might be interested in the subject matter of the exhibition; psychology offers information about learning styles and approaches, with particular reference to learning in museums. As museums develop new ways of finding out about audiences and their attitudes, beliefs, values, and habits in so far as these affect museum-going habits, so new practices are developing to incorporate the findings into museum work.

In the past, exhibitions were prepared by curators and when they were finished, they were 'opened to the public'. The process of production was closed, and the completed display allowed no point of entry for the consumer, the visitor. The consuming subjects, the visitors, were constituted firstly as separate from the professional processes of the museum, and secondly as a general, undifferentiated mass. The 'general public' was offered carefully designed exhibitions which had been researched with scholarly precision, and which presented themes and topics of complete absorption to the curator. Those people who did not share this fascination (often fostered through long years of specialist education and work with collections) were regarded as somehow deficient. No help was offered in the deciphering of the concepts or the ideas for those that did not possess the specialist knowledge. In some museums these processes still remain, but in many, radically new approaches can be observed.

At the present time, in many museums, the curator has been decentred, and instead of one point of view, many voices are encouraged to speak. Thus in an exhibition on Caribbean history in Leicester Museum in the mid-1980s, a Caribbean historian was asked to write the texts of the exhibition. In Sheffield, a travelling caravan took a touring exhibition to areas of the city not immediately accessible to museums and art galleries. The exhibition was a taster for, and introduction to, an exhibition to be held in the Mappin Art Gallery 'Reflections to the Future: Black Lifestyles in Sheffield 1955–88'. The form and content of the final exhibition was not decided until reactions to the exhibition had been assessed, alterations had been made, and some new objects had been temporarily collected (Robinson and Toobey, 1989).

The potential audience for the exhibition is encouraged to contribute to the display techniques and the subject matter. At the same time, a curatorial consciousness has emerged which highlights those audiences that have been omitted in the past. Exhibitions in the past tended to attract an audience with a very similar demographic profile to that of many curators:

white, middle- or upper-class, able-bodied, and male. Now, the perspectives of women, different ethnic groups, and people with disabilities are actively incorporated. The contributions of these groups are often small, but very significant. For example, a group of blind sculptors visited an exhibition of sculpture, intended specifically for the blind and partially sighted, before its opening, and it was discovered that many of the objects that had been placed on the floor by the young, able-bodied curator were difficult for the group to appreciate. Many of them suffered not only from impaired vision, but also from old age. The pre-visit was able to reveal major defects that could be improved without difficulty, and which made the exhibition much more accessible for its intended audience.

It is generally expected that audiences wish to be much more active and physically involved in museums today. The age of the passive visitor has passed, to be superseded by the age of the active and discriminating 'consumer' or 'client' (Henley Centre, 1989). The terminology is significant. 'Visitors' are present in a space by permission; they enter an alien space, akin to someone else's home. The museum or art gallery has in the past been very much the territory of the professional staff, with the 'public' allowed in on suffrance, if their behaviour was appropriate. Now the 'client' demands active rights and expects good service. A 'client' has a contract for the delivery of goods or services, and is in a negotiated situation where he or she has an equal position of power.

The subject as 'client' or 'consumer' is offered numerous opportunities for involvement – to the extent of complete immersion – in museums and galleries today. Where in the past, the experience of visiting a museum was two-dimensional, an experience of a slow, controlled, surveyed walk past completed displays designed without the needs or interests of the visitor in mind, now experiences are three-dimensional. A museum visit can include theatre or 'living history' in social history collections; science centre exhibits that are only complete when the visitor/client operates or uses them; or discussions with artists that are in residence in art galleries. Many of these experiences depend on the visitor's participation to be effective: the actors offer food to the visitors; the artists are expected to talk as they work in their public studios; science demonstrators ask questions as they carry out experiments in the open gallery spaces.

The concept of 'target audiences' has emerged, partly to facilitate this process, but partly in response to the introduction of marketing techniques to museums. During the last five years, new subject positions have emerged in museums. Marketing managers, development officers, and fund-raisers are all now to be found working in museums. In the 1950s, 1960s, and 1970s, education officers and designers were employed in addition to curators. These professionals improved the experience of the

32 'The People's Show' at Walsall Museum in 1990 offered local people the opportunity...

... to display their own
collections.

museum for those who happened to visit. In the 1990s, however, audiences are actively recruited through the techniques of the salesman and the advertising executive. The technologies of mass marketing and mass communication have begun to be adapted for the museum environment and as the technologies become incorporated, significant changes can be observed.

The marketing of a 'product' (the museum) that is not for financial gain but for educational and entertainment value, means an adaptation of the 'sell' from hard to soft, with an emphasis on less immediate and more intangible gains. The British Museum, for example, has evolved a cookbook based on the collections: 'Feast with the Pharaohs!'; 'Dine with a Renaissance Prince!' it suggests.

> To return home after a visit to the British Museum and to relive the experience by reading your guidebook or admiring your postcards is wonderful, but how much better if you could also 'taste' your visit by recreating the dishes that the ancient civilisations, whose art works and artefacts are now displayed in glass cases, actually ate and enjoyed?
> (Johnson, 1987)

In the modern age, knowledge is no longer shaped by the secret, enclosed, circulating structures of the Renaissance *episteme*; nor by the flat, classificatory table of difference of the classical *episteme*; now knowledge is structured through a three-dimensional, holistic experience which is defined through its relationship to people. The act of knowing is shaped through a mix of experience, activity, and pleasure, in an environment where both the 'learning' subject and the 'teaching' subject have equal powers. Subject positions are more closely related than in the past; former divisions are now bridged in a number of diferent ways. Where both the object and the curator are decentred, the visitor/client/customer has new opportunities.

New articulations of space, object, and subject create the conditions for the emergence of new technologies. However, although targeted at 'enjoyment' and 'pleasure', the uses of this pleasure cannot be accepted uncritically. In the museum environment where equal rights offer (and indeed require) multiple perspectives, and thereby the articulation of many potentialy conflictual points of view, newly pleasurable technologies of discipline and control have evolved to soften the contradictions and to disguise the inequalities. The total experience (in living history or interactive exhibits), the total immersion (in gallery workshops and events), can have the function, in the apparently democratised environment of the museum marketplace, of soothing, of silencing, of quieting questions, of closing minds.

What is the use of museums in the age of the 'experience', the unified total approach to knowledge? Where museums seek to emulate theatres, cinemas, pageants, and funfairs, what is left of unique and specific value?

An 'effective' history has shown us how the meanings that are construed from objects are many, variable, and fragile. Meanings are not constant, and the construction of meaning can always be undertaken again, in new contexts and with new functions. The radical potential of museums lies in precisely this. As long as museums and galleries remain the repositories of artefacts and specimens, new relationships can always be built, new meanings can always be discovered, new interpretations with new relevances can be found, new codes and new rules can be written.

> The successes of history belong to those who are capable of seizing these rules, to replace those who had used them, to disguise themselves so as to pervert them, invert their meaning, and redirect them against those who had initially imposed them; controlling this complex mechanism, they will make it function so as to overcome the rulers through their own rules.
>
> (Foucault, 1977c: 151)

The radical potential of material culture, of concrete objects, of real things, of primary sources, is the endless possibility of rereading. In contemporary culture, where contextualised and mediated messages surround us, and where reality and hyper-reality (Eco, 1986b) can barely be distinguished, the potential of a return to the concrete material evidence is of overriding importance. Effective history teaches us that, because meanings and interpretations are endlessly rewritten, we too can seize the opportunity to make our own meaning, and find our own relevance and significance.

Does this individual and intensely personal interpretation of artefacts stand in opposition to the experiential and contextualising efforts that many museums are making, as part of their new destiny as totalising institutions? Is it the case that the more the museum contextualises artefacts, places them in narrative displays, and demonstrates the links that these objects make with other objects and with people, the more difficult it becomes even to perceive the possibility of a personal interpretation? Foucault suggested that the modern age, which began at the end of the eighteenth century, would not continue much beyond the present time. Can the end of the modern age be glimpsed in the contradictions revealed by contemporary museums? And if so, what is the future of museums?

Bibliography

Ackermann, H.C. (1985) 'The Basle cabinets of art and curiosities in the sixteenth and seventeenth centuries', in Impey, O. and MacGregor, A. *The Origins of Museums*, Clarendon Press, Oxford, pp.62–8.

Aeliume, J.M. (1983) 'The Riviere beast, or the unfinished trial of the creature who tortured birds and frogs', *October*, 24, pp.63–82.

Aimi, A., de Michele, V. and Morandotti, A. (1985) 'Towards a history of collecting in Milan in the late Renaissance and baroque periods', in Impey, O. and MacGregor, A. *The Origins of Museums*, Clarendon Press, Oxford, pp.24–8.

Alexander, E.P. (1979) *Museums in Motion*, The American Association for State and Local History, Nashville.

Alexander, E.P. (1983) *Museum Masters: their Museums and their Influences*, Association for State and Local History, Nashville.

Alpers, S. (1983) *The Art of Describing: Dutch Art in the Seventeenth Century*, John Murray, London.

Alsop, J. (1982) *The Rare Art Traditions: the History of Art Collecting and its Linked Phenomena*, Thames and Hudson, London.

Alt, M.B. (1980) 'Four years of visitor surveys at the British Museum (Natural History) 1976–1979', *Museums Journal*, 80 (1), pp.10–19, Museums Association, London.

Altick, R.D. (1978) *The Shows of London*, Harvard University Press.

Ambrose, T. and Kavanagh, G. (eds) (1987) *Recording Society Today*, Scottish Museums Council, Edinburgh.

American Association of Museums (1984) *Museums for a New Century*, American Association of Museums, Washington, D.C.

Ames, M.M. (1983) 'How should we think about what we see in a museum of anthropology?', Transactions of the Royal Society of Canada, series 4 (21), pp.93–101.

Ames, M.M. (1985) 'De-schooling the museum: a proposal to increase public access to museums and their resources', *Museum*, 145, pp. 25–31.

Arac, J. (1980) 'The function of Foucault at the present time', *Humanities in Society*, 3 (1), pp.73–86.

Arnell, U., Hammer, I., and Nylöf, G. (1976) *Going to Exhibitions*, Ritsutstallningar/ Swedish Travelling Exhibitions, Stockholm.

Attridge, D. and Bennington, G. (eds) (1987) *Post-Structuralism and the Question of History*, Cambridge University Press, Cambridge.

Ayers, J. (1985) 'The early China trade' in Impey, O. and MacGregor, A. *The Origins of Museums*, Clarendon Press, Oxford, pp.259–66.

Barrell, J. (1980) *The Dark Side of the Landscape: the Rural Poor in English Painting 1730–1840*, Cambridge University Press, Cambridge.

Barthes, R. (1973) *Mythologies*, Paladin, St Albans.

Barthes, R. (1977) *Image–Music–Text*, Fontana/Collins, Glasgow.

Bassani, E. and McLeod, M. (1985) 'African material in early collections', in Impey, O. and MacGregor, A. *The Origins of Museums*, Clarendon Press, Oxford.

Baudrillard, J. (1968) *Le Système des objets*, Denoel/Gonthier, Editions Gallimard.

Baudrillard, J. (1980) 'Forgetting Foucault', in *Humanities in Society*, 3 (1), pp.87–111.

Baudrillard, J. (1982) 'The Beaubourg-effect: implosion and deterrence', *October*, 20, Spring, pp.3–13.

Baxandall, M. (1972) *Painting and Experience in Fifteenth-Century Italy*, Oxford University Press, Oxford.

Baxandall, M. (1985) *Patterns of Intention: on the Historical Explanation of Pictures*, Yale University Press, New Haven and London.

Bazin, G. (1959) *The Louvre*, Harry N. Abrams, New York.

Bazin, G. (1967) *The Museum Age*, Desoer, S.A. Publishers, Brussels.

Becker, H.S. (1974) 'Art as collective action', *American Sociological Review*, 39 (6), December, pp.765–76.

Becker, H.S. (1982) *Art Worlds*, University of California Press.

Bedini, S. (1965) 'The evolution of science museums', *Technology and Culture*, 6, pp.1–29.

Bennett, J.A. (1972) 'Wren's last building', *Notes and Records of the Royal Society*, 27, pp.107–18.

Bennett, T. (1990) 'The political rationality of the museum', *Continuum, an Australian Journal of the Media*, 3 (1), pp.35–55.

Berger, J. (1972) *Ways of Seeing*, British Broadcasting Corporation, London.

Berger, J. (1980) *About Looking*, Writers and Readers Publishing Cooperative, Ltd, London.

Bernal, J.D. (1940) *The Social Function of Science*, George Routledge & Sons Ltd, London.

Bernal, J.D. (1969) *Science in History, vol.I: The Emergence of Science; vol II: The Scientific and Industrial Revolutions*, C.A. Watts & Co. Ltd, London.

Bernheimer, R. (1956) 'Theatrum mundi', *Art Bulletin*, 38, pp.225–47.

Binford, L.R. (1962) 'Archaeology as anthropology', *American Antiquity*, 28 (2), pp.217–25.

Bostrom, H.-O.(1985) 'Philip Hainhofer and Gustavus Adolphus's *Kunstschrank* in Uppsala', in Impey, O. and MacGregor, A. *The Origins of Museums*, Clarendon Press, pp.90–101.

Bourdieu, P. and Darbel, A. (1966) *L'Amour de l'art: les musées et leur public*, Les Editions de Minuit, Paris.

Bourdieu, P. (1968) 'Outline of a sociological theory of art perception', *International Social Science Journal*, 20 (4).

Bourne, R. (1985) 'Are American Indians museum pieces?', *New Society*, 29, November, pp.380–1.

Bove, P.A. (1980) 'The ends of humanism: Michel Foucault and the power of disciplines', *Humanities in Society*, 3 (1), pp.23–40.

Braudel, F. (1977) *Afterthoughts on Material Civilization and Capitalism*, Johns Hopkins University Press, Baltimore and London.

Bromehead, C.N. (1947a) 'Bottle imps, notes and news', *Antiquity*, 21 (82), June, pp.105–6.

Bromehead, C.N. (1947b) 'Aetites or the eagle-stone', *Antiquity*, 21 (81), March, pp.16–22.

Bronowski, J. and Mazlish, B. (1970) *The Western Intellectual Tradition*, Penguin Books, Middlesex.

Brown, B. and Cousins, M. (1986) 'The linguistic fault: the case of Foucault's archaeology', in Gane, M. *Towards a Critique of Foucault*, Routledge & Kegan Paul, pp.33–60.

Bryson, N. (1984) *Vision and Painting: the Logic of the Gaze*, Macmillan, London.

Burcaw, G.E. (1975) *Introduction to Museum Work*, The American Association for State and Local History, Nashville.

Bibliography

Buren, D. (1973a) 'Function of the museum', *Art Forum*, September, pp. 67–8.

Buren, D. (1973b) 'Function of an exhibition', *Studio International*, December, p.216.

Burke, P. (1969) *The Renaissance Sense of the Past*, Edward Arnold, London.

Burke, P. (1974) *Tradition and Innovation in Renaissance Italy*, Fontana/Collins, London.

Burrett, G. (1985) 'After Rayner', in Cossons, N. (ed.) *The Management of Change in Museums*, National Maritime Museum, London, pp.5–7.

Cannon-Brookes, P. (1984) 'The nature of museum collections', in Thompson, J. (ed.) *Manual of Curatorship*, Butterworth, London.

Carroll, D. (1978), 'The subject of archaeology or the sovereignty of the episteme', *Modern Language Notes*, 93, pp.695–722.

Cavalari, H.M. (1980) 'Savoir and pouvoir: Michel Foucault's theory of discursive practice', *Humanities in Society*, 3 (1), pp.55–72.

Caygill, M. (1981) *The Story of the British Museum*, British Museum Publications, London.

Centre for Contemporary Cultural Studies (1982) *Making Histories: Studies in History-Writing and Politics*, Hutchinson, London and Centre for Contemporary Cultural Studies, University of Birmingham.

Chamberlin, R. (1983) *Loot! The Heritage of Plunder*, Thames & Hudson, London.

Chiapelli, F. (ed.), (1976) *First Images of America*, University of California Press.

Cohen, M. (1977) *Sensible Words: Linguistic Practice in England 1640–1785*, Johns Hopkins University.

Comito, T. (1971) 'Renaissance gardens and the discovery of paradise', *Journal of the History of Ideas*, 32, pp.483–506.

Coomans, H.E. (1985) 'Conchology before Linnaeus', in Impey, O. and MacGregor, A. *The Origins of Museums*, Clarendon Press, Oxford, pp.188–92.

Cossons, N. (1987) 'Dangers of a dinosaur mentality', *The Listener*, 16 April, pp.18–20.

Cousins, M. and Hussain, A. (1984) *Foucault*, Macmillan, London.

Crimp, D. (1985) 'On the museum's ruins', in Foster, H. *Postmodern Culture*, Pluto Press, London, pp. 43–56.

Crook, J.M. (1972) *The British Museum*, Allen Lane, The Penguin Press, London.

Crow, T.E. (1985) *Painters and Public Life in Eighteenth Century Paris*, Yale University Press, New Haven and London.

Cunningham, H. (1980) *Leisure in the Industrial Revolution*, Croom Helm, London.

Dabydeen, D. (1987) 'High culture based in black slavery', *The Listener*, 24 September, pp.14–15.

Dallmayr, F.R. and Hinkle, G.J. (1987) *Human Studies*, 10 (1), Foucault Memorial Issue.

Davidson, A.I. (1986) 'Archaeology, genealogy, ethics', in Hoy, D.C. (ed.), *Foucault: A Critical Reader*, Blackwell, Oxford.

Davies, S. (1985) 'Collecting and recalling the twentieth century', *Museums Journal*, 85 (1), pp.27–9.

Defert, D. (1982) 'The collection of the world: accounts of voyages from the sixteenth to the eighteenth centuries', *Dialectical Anthropology*, 7, pp.11–20.

Digby, P.W. (1974) *Visitors to Three London Museums*, HMSO, London.

Dijksterhuis, E.J. (1961) *The Mechanization of the World Picture*, Clarendon Press, Oxford.

Dimaggio, P. (1978a) *Audience Studies of the Performing Arts and Museums: a Critical Review*, Research Division Report no. 9, National Endowment for the Arts.

Dimaggio, P. (1978b) 'Elitists and populists: politics for art's sake', *Working Papers for a New Society*, 6, pp.23–31.

Dimaggio, P. (1983) 'The American art museum director as professional: results of a survey', *Bullet*, January, pp.5–9.

Dimaggio, P. and Useem, M. (1978a) 'Cultural property and public policy: emerging tensions in government support for the arts', *Social Research*, 45 (2), pp.356–89.

Dimaggio, P. and Useem, M. (1978b) 'Social class and arts consumption – origins and consequences of class differences in exposure to the arts in America', *Theory and Society*, 5 (1), pp.141–61.

Dimaggio, P. and Useem, M. (1982) 'Cultural entrepreneurship in nineteenth-century Boston: (Part I) the creation of an organizational base for high culture in America. (Part II) The classification and framing of American art', *Media, Culture and Society*, 4, pp.33–50, 303–22, London.

Distelberger, R. (1985) 'The Habsburg collections in Vienna during the seventeenth century', in Impey, O. and MacGregor, A. *The Origins of Museums*, Clarendon Press, Oxford, pp. 39–46.

Dixon, B., Courtney, A., and Bailey, R.H. (1974) *The Museum and the Canadian Public*, Arts and Culture Branch, Department of the Secretary of State, Toronto.

Donnelly, M.J. (1982) 'Foucault's genealogy of the human sciences', *Economy and Society*, 11 (4), pp.363–80.

Donnelly, M.J. (1986) Foucault's genealogy of the human sciences, in Gane, M. (ed.) *Towards a Critique of Foucault*, Routledge & Kegan Paul, London.

Donzelot, J. (1980), *The Policing of Families*, Hutchinson, London.

Doughty, P.S. (1968) 'The public of the Ulster Museum: a statistical survey', *Museums Journal*, 68 (1), pp.19–25; 68 (2), pp.47–53.

Drew, A. (1985) 'The Presidential Address', *Museums Journal*, 85 (3), pp.115–18.

Dreyfus, H.L. and Rabinow, P. (1982) *Michel Foucault: Beyond Structuralism and Hermeneutics*, Harvester Press, Brighton.

Drier, F.A. (1985) 'The *Kunstkammer* of the Hessian Landgraves in Kassel', in Impey, O. and MacGregor, A. *The Origins of Museums*, Clarendon Press, Oxford, pp.102–9.

Eco, U. (1984) *The Name of the Rose*, Book Club Associates, London.

Eco, U. (1986a) *Art and Beauty in the Middle Ages*, Yale University Press, New Haven and London.

Eco, U. (1986b) *Travels in Hyper-Reality*, Picador, London.

Edwards, E. (1870) *Lives of the Founders of the British Museum*, Trubner & Co., London.

Eisenbeis, M. (1972) 'Elements for a sociology of museums', *Museum*, 24 (2), pp.110–19.

English Tourist Board (1982) *Visitors to Museums Survey 1982*, English Tourist Board, London.

Evans, E.P. (1987) *The Criminal Prosecution and Capital Punishment of Animals: The Lost History of Europe's Animal Trials*, Faber & Faber, London.

Evans, R.J.W. (1973) *Rudolf II and his World: a Study in Intellectual History 1576–1612*, Clarendon Press, Oxford.

Evans, R.J.W. (1979) *The Making of the Hapsburg Monarchy 1550–1700*, Clarendon Press, Oxford.

Feest, C. (1985) 'Mexico and South America in the European *Wunderkammer*', in Impey, O. and MacGregor, A. *The Origins of Museums*, Clarendon Press, Oxford, pp.237–44.

Fewster, C. (1990) 'Beyond the show-case', *Museums Journal*, 90 (6), pp. 24–7.

Foucault, M. (1961) *Madness and Civilization*, Tavistock Publications, London.

Foucault, M. (1970) *The Order of Things*, Tavistock Publications, London.

Foucault, M. (1972) 'History, discourse, and discontinuity', *Salmagundi*, 20, Summer/Fall, pp.241–8.

Foucault, M. (1974) *The Archaeology of Knowledge*, Tavistock Publications, London.

Foucault, M. (1976) *The Birth of the Clinic*, Tavistock Publications, London.

Foucault, M. (1977a) *Language, Counter-Memory, Practice: Selected Essays and Interviews*, ed. D.F. Bouchard, Blackwell, Oxford.

Foucault, M. (1977b) 'The political function of the intellectual', *Radical Philosophy*, 17, pp.12–14.

Foucault, M. (1977c) 'Nietzsche, genealogy, history', in Bouchard, D.F. *Language,*

Bibliography

Counter-Memory, Practice: Selected Essays and Interviews, Blackwell, Oxford.

Foucault, M. (1979) 'Governmentality', *Ideology and Consciousness*, 6, pp.5–21.

Foucault, M. (1980a) *Power/Knowledge: Selected Interviews and Other Writings 1972–1977*, ed. C. Gordon, Harvester Press, Brighton.

Foucault, M. (1980b) 'The history of sexuality: interview', *Oxford Literary Review*, 4 (2), pp.3–14.

Foucault, M. (1981a), 'Questions of method: an interview with Michel Foucault', *Ideology and Consciousness*, 8, pp.3–14.

Foucault, M. (1981b) 'Omnes et singulatim', in McMurrin, S.M. (ed.) *The Tanner Lectures on Human Values*, 2, Cambridge University Press, Cambridge, pp.225–54.

Foucault, M. (1981c) 'The order of discourse' (inaugural lecture at the Collège de France, 2 December 1970), in Young, R. *Untying the Text: A Post-Structuralist Reader*, Routledge & Kegan Paul, London, pp.49–78.

Foucault, M. (1982a) 'Afterword: the subject and power', in Dreyfus, H.L. and Rabinow, P. (eds) *Michel Foucault: Beyond Structuralism and Hermeneutics*, Harvester Press, Brighton.

Foucault, M. (1982b), *Discipline and Punish: The Birth of the Prison*, Penguin Books, Middlesex.

Foucault, M. (1984) *The History of Sexuality: Vol. 1, An Introduction*, Peregrine, Penguin Books, Middlesex.

Foucault, M. (1986) 'Of other spaces', *Diacritics*, 16 (1), pp.22–7.

Foucault, M. (1987) *The Use of Pleasure: The History of Sexuality, Vol. 2*, Penguin Books, Middlesex.

Foucault, M. and Sennett, R. (1982), 'Sexuality and solitude', *Humanities in Review*, 1, pp.3–21.

Fucikova, E. (1985) 'The collection of Rudolf II at Prague: cabinet of curiosities or scientific museum?', in Impey, O. and MacGregor, A. *The Origins of Museums*, Clarendon Press, Oxford, pp.47–55.

Fuller, P. (1978) 'Mighty opposites', *New Society*, 22 June, pp.667–8.

Gane, M. (ed.) (1986) *Towards a Critique of Foucault*, Routledge & Kegan Paul, London.

George, W. (1985) 'Alive or dead: zoological collections in the seventeenth century', in Impey, O. and MacGregor, A. *The Origins of Museums*, Clarendon Press, Oxford, pp.179–87.

Gilbert, C.E. (1980) *Italian Art 1400–1500: Sources and Documents*, Prentice-Hall, Inc., New Jersey.

Glasgow University Media Group (1972) *Bad News*, Routledge & Kegan Paul, London.

Glasgow University Media Group (1980) *More Bad News*, Routledge & Kegan Paul, London.

Glasgow University Media Group (1982) *Really Bad News*, Writers and Readers, London.

Godwyn, J. (1979) *Robert Fludd: Hermetic Philosopher and Surveyor of Two Worlds*, Thames & Hudson, London.

Gombrich, E.H. (1963) *Meditations on a Hobby Horse*, Phaidon Press, Oxford.

Gombrich, E.H. (1968) 'Should a museum be active?', *Museum*, 21 (1), pp.79–82.

Gombrich, E.H. (1985a) *Norm and Form: Studies in the Art of the Renaissance I*, Phaidon Press, Oxford.

Gombrich, E.H. (1985b) *Symbolic Images: Studies in the Art of the Renaissance II*, Phaidon Press, Oxford.

Gordon, C. (1980) 'Afterword' in Gordon, C. (ed.) *Power/Knowledge: Selected Interviews and Other Writings 1972–1977, Michel Foucault*, Harvester Press, Brighton.

Gould, C. (1965) *Trophy of Conquest: the Musée Napoléon and the Creation of the Louvre*, Faber & Faber, London.

Gould, R.A. and Schiffer. M.B. (1981) *Modern Material Culture: The Archaeology of Us*, Academic Press, London.

Grana, C. (1972) 'The private lives of public museums', in Stone, G.P. *Games, Sport and Power*, Transaction Books, New Brunswick, New Jersey.

Green, O. (1985) 'Our recent past: the black hole in museum collections', *Museums Journal*, 85 (1), pp.5–7.

Greene, J.P. (1978) 'A visitor survey at Norton Priory Museum', *Museums Journal*, 78 (1), pp.7–9.

Greenwood, E.F. (1971) 'Botany and English provincial museums', *Museums Journal*, 70 (4), pp.164–8.

Grew, N. (1681) *Musaeum Regalis Societatis or A Catalogue and Description of the Natural and Artificial Rarities Belonging to the Royal Society and Preserved at Gresham College*, London.

Gunestrup, B. (1985) 'From royal *Kunstkammer* to the modern museums of Copenhagen', in Impey, O. and MacGregor, A. *The Origins of Museums*, Clarendon Press, Oxford, pp.128–33.

Hacking, I. (1979) 'Michel Foucault's immature science', *Nous*, 13, pp.39–51.

Hacking, I. (1986) 'The archaeology of Foucault', in Hoy, D.C. (ed.) *Foucault: a Critical Reader*, Blackwell, Oxford.

Hajos, E.M. (1958) 'The Concept of an Engravings Collection in the Year 1565: Quiccheberg, "Inscriptiones vel tituli theatri amplissimi"', *Art Bulletin*, 40, pp.151–6.

Hajos, E.M. (1963) 'Samuel Quiccheberg's "Inscriptiones vel tituli theatri amplissimi"', *Bibliothèque d'Humanisme et Renaissance*, 25, pp.207–11.

Harris, M. (1980) *Cultural Materialism: The Struggle for a Science of Culture*, Vintage Books (Random House), New York.

Harris, N. (1978) 'Museums, merchandizing and popular taste', in Quimby, I. M. (ed.) *Material Culture and the Study of American Life*, Winterthur Museum, Norton and Co., New York.

Hartley, H. (1960) *The Royal Society – Its Origins and Founders*, Royal Society, London.

Harvey, B. (1987) *Visiting the National Portrait Gallery*, OPCS, HMSO, London.

Heady, P. (1984) *Visiting Museums*, OPCS, HMSO, London.

Heidegger, M. (1951) 'The age of the world view', *Measure*, 2, pp.269–84.

Heikamp, D. (1972) *Mexico and the Medici*, Editrice Edam, Florence.

Heikamp, D. (1976) 'American objects in Italian collections of the Renaissance and baroque: a survey', in Chiapelli, F. (ed.) *First Images of America*, University of California Press, Berkeley, pp.455–82.

Heikamp, D. (1981) 'A bronze bust of Cosimo I de Medici for the courtyard of the Pitti Palace', in Barasch, M. and Sandler, L. F. *Art the Ape of Nature*, Harry N. Abrams, New York.

Hemmings, F.W.J. (1987) *Culture and Society in France 1789–1848*, Leicester University Press, Leicester.

Henley Centre (1989) 'The discerning consumer', *Leisure Management*, 9 (5), pp. 34–6.

Hesse, M.B. (1966) 'Hooke's philosophical algebra', *Isis*, 57, pp.67–83.

Hewison, R. (1986) 'The future of museums', *The Listener*, 26 June, pp.11–12.

Hewison, R. (1987) *The Heritage Industry*, Methuen, London.

Hill, C.R. (1986) 'The cabinet of Bonnier de la Mosson (1702–1744)', *Annals of Science*, 43, pp.147–74.

Hindess, B. (1985) 'Actors and social relations', in Wardell, M. and Turner, S. (eds) *Sociological Theory in Transition*, Allen and Unwin, London.

Holst, N. von (1967) *Creators, Collectors and Connoisseurs*, Thames & Hudson, London.

Hood, M. (1981) 'Adult attitudes toward leisure choices in relation to museum participation', PhD thesis, Ohio State University, University Microfilms International.

Hood, M. (1983) 'Staying away – why people choose not to visit museums', *Museum News*, 61 (4), pp.50–7.

Hooper-Greenhill, E. (1980) 'The National Portrait Gallery – a case-study in cultural reproduction', MA thesis, University of

Bibliography

London, Department of Sociology of Education.

Hooper-Greenhill, E. (1982) 'Some aspects of a sociology of museums', *Museums Journal*, 82 (2), pp.69–70.

Hooper-Greenhill, E. (1985) 'Art gallery audiences and class constraints', *Bullet*, January, pp.5–8.

Hooper-Greenhill, E. (1987a) 'Knowledge in an open prison', *New Statesman*, 13 February, pp.21–2.

Hooper-Greenhill, E. (1987b) ' Museums in education; towards the twenty-first century' in Ambrose, T. (ed). *Museums in Education: Education in Museums*, Scottish Museums Council, HMSO, London.

Hooper-Greenhill, E. (1988a) 'Counting visitors or visitors who count?', in Lumley, B. (ed.) *The Museum Time Machine*, pp.213–32, Routledge, London.

Hooper-Greenhill, E. (1988b) 'The art of memory and learning in the museum: museum education and GCSE', *International Journal of Museum Management and Curatorship*, 7, pp. 129–37.

Hooper-Greenhill, E. (1988c) 'Museums in education: working with other organisations', in Ambrose, T. (ed.) *Working with Museums*, Scottish Museums Council/HMSO.

Hooper-Greenhill, E. (1989a) 'The museum in the disciplinary society', in Pearce, S. (ed.), *Museum Studies in Material Culture*, Leicester University Press, Leicester.

Hooper-Greenhill, E. (ed.) (1989b) *Initiatives in Museum Education*, Department of Museum Studies, University of Leicester, Leicester.

Hooper-Greenhill, E. (1990) 'The space of the museum', *Continuum: an Australian Journal of the Media*, 3 (1), pp.56–69.

Hooper-Greenhill, E. (1991) *Museum and Gallery Education*, Leicester University Press, Leicester.

Horne, D. (1984) *The Great Museum*, Pluto Press, London and Sydney.

Houghton, W.E. (1942) 'The English Virtuoso in the seventeenth century', *Journal of the*

History of Ideas, 3, Part 1, pp.51–73; Part 2, pp.190–219.

Hoy, D.C. (1986) *Foucault: A Critical Reader*, Blackwell, Oxford.

Hudson, K. (1987) *Museums of Influence*, Cambridge University Press, Cambridge.

Hunt, C. (1978) 'Museums in the Pacific Islands: a metaphysical justification', *Museum*, 30 (2), pp.69–75.

Hunt, J.D. (1985) '*Curiosities* to adorn *Cabinets* and *Gardens*', in Impey, O. and MacGregor, A. *The Origins of Museums*, Clarendon Press, Oxford, pp.193–203.

Hunter, M. (1981) *Science and Society in Restoration England*, Cambridge University Press, Cambridge.

Hunter, M. (1982) *The Royal Society and its Fellows 1660–1700*, British Society for the History of Science, Chalfont St Giles.

Hunter, M. (1985) 'The cabinet institutionalized: the Royal Society's "Repository" and its background', in Impey, O. and MacGregor, A. *The Origins of Museums*, Clarendon Press, Oxford, pp.159–

Impey, O. (1985) 'Japan: trade and collecting in seventeenth-century Europe', in Impey, O. and MacGregor, A. *The Origins of Museums*, Clarendon Press, Oxford, pp.267–73.

Impey, O.R. and MacGregor, A.G. (eds) (1985) *The Origins of Museums*, Clarendon Press, Oxford.

Johnson, M.B. (1987) *The British Museum Cookbook*, British Museum Publications Ltd, London.

Jones, D. (1987) 'Hidden peoples of the Amazon', *Museum Ethnographers Group Newsletter*, 20, pp.103–10.

Jones, S. and Major, C. (1986) 'Reaching the public: oral history as a survival strategy for museums', *Oral History Journal*, 14 (2), pp.31–8.

Kaplan, S.L. (1984) *Understanding Popular Culture: Europe from the Middle Ages to the Nineteenth Century*, Mouton Publishers, New York.

Kaufmann, T. da C. (1976) 'Arcimboldo's

imperial allegories', *Zeitschrift für Kunstgeschichte*, 39 (4), pp.275–96.

Kaufmann, T. da C. (1978) 'Remarks on the collection of Rudolph II: the *Kunstkammer* as a form of *Representatio*', *Art Journal*, 38, pp.22–8.

Keenan, T. (ed.) (1987) *Political Theory*, 15 (1).

Klein, R. (1974) 'Who goes to museums?', *Illustrated London News*, April, pp.27–9.

Klessmann, R. (1971) *The Berlin Gallery*, Thames & Hudson, London.

Knowlson, J. (1975) *Universal Language Schemes in England and France 1600–1800*, Toronto University Press, Toronto.

Kristeller, P.O. (1951) 'The modern system of the arts (I)', *Journal of the History of Ideas*, 12, pp. 496–527.

Kristeller, P.O. (1952) 'The modern system of the arts (II)', *Journal of the History of Ideas*, 13, pp. 17–46.

Laclau, E. and Mouffe, C. (1985) *Hegemony and Socialist Strategy: Towards a Radical Democratic Politics*, Verso, London.

Laclau, E. and Mouffe, C. (1987) 'Post-Marxism without apologies', *New Left Review*, 166, Nov./Dec.

Lash, S. (1984) 'Genealogy and the body: Foucault/Deleuze/Nietzsche', *Theory, Culture and Society*, 2 (2), pp.2–17.

Laurencich-Minelli, L. (1985) 'Museography and ethnographical collections in Bologna during the sixteenth and seventeenth centuries', in Impey, O. and MacGregor, A. *The Origins of Museums*, Clarendon Press, Oxford.

Lemert, C.C. and Gillan, G. (1982) *Michel Foucault: Social Theory as Transgression*, Columbia University Press, New York.

Levidow, L. and Young, B. (1984) 'Exhibiting nuclear power: the Science Museum cover-up', *Radical Science Journal*, 25 (1), pp.53–79.

Lewis, G. (1984) ch.1, 'Introduction', pp.5–6; ch.2, 'Collections, collectors and museums: a brief world survey', pp.7–22; ch.3, 'Collections, collectors and museums in

Britain to 1920', pp.23–37; ch.4, 'Museums in Britain: 1920 to the present day', pp.38–53, in Thompson, J.M.A. (ed.) *Manual of Curatorship*, the Museums Association/Butterworth, London.

Lewis, G. L. (1986) 'The term "Museum" and related words', Museum Studies Notes I, 1.1.0.c, Department of Museum Studies, University of Leicester, Leicester.

Lewis, G. (1987) 'Museums', *The New Encyclopedia, Vol.24, Macropedia: Knowledge in Depth*, Encyclopedia Britannica Inc., Chicago, pp.478–90.

Lilla, M. (1982) 'Art and anxiety: the writing on the museum wall', *Public Interest*, 66, Winter, pp.37–54.

Lowe, D.M. (1982) *History of Bourgeois Perception*, Harvester Press, Brighton.

Lumley, B. (ed.) (1988) *The Museum Time-Machine*, Routledge, London.

Lyons, H. (1944) *The Royal Society 1660–1940*, Cambridge University Press, Cambridge.

Macdonell, D. (1986) *Theories of Discourse*, Blackwell, Oxford.

MacGregor, A. (ed.) (1983) *Tradescants Rarities: Essays on the Foundation of the Ashmolean Museum 1683 with a Catalogue of the Surviving Early Collections*, Clarendon Press, Oxford.

MacGregor, A. (1985) 'The cabinet of curiosities in seventeenth-century Britain', in Impey, O. and MacGregor, A. *The Origins of Museums*, Clarendon Press, Oxford, pp.147–58.

Major-Poetzl, P. (1983) *Michel Foucault's Archaeology of Western Culture: Toward a New Science of History*, Harvester Press, Brighton.

Mann, P. (1986) *Visitors to the British Museum (1982–1983)*, British Museum Occasional Paper 64, London.

Meltzer, D.J. (1981) 'Ideology and material culture', in Gould, R.A. and Schiffer, M.B. *Modern Material Culture – The Archaeology of Us*, Academic Press Inc., London.

Menzhausen, J. (1970) *The Green Vaults*, Druckerei Fortschritt, Erfurt, Leipzig.

Bibliography

Menzhausen, J. (1985) 'Elector Augustus's *Kunstkammer*: an analysis of the inventory of 1587', in Impey, O. and MacGregor, A. *The Origins of Museums*, Clarendon Press, Oxford, pp.69–76.

Merquior, J.G. (1985) *Foucault*, Fontana Modern Masters, London.

Merleau-Ponty, M. (1962) *Phenomenology of Perception*, Routledge & Kegan Paul, London.

Merriman, N. (1989) 'The social basis of museum and heritage visiting', in Pearce, S. (ed.) *Museum Studies in Material Culture*, Leicester University Press, Leicester.

Meyer, K.E. (1977) *The Plundered Past: the Traffic in Art Treasures*, Penguin Books, Middlesex.

Miles, R. (1985) 'Exhibitions: management, for a change', in Cossons, N. (ed.) *The Management of Change in Museums*, National Maritime Museum, London, pp.31–3.

Miller, E. (1973) *That Noble Cabinet*, Andre Deutsch, London.

Minson, J. (1985) *Genealogies of Morals*, Macmillan, London.

Mizushima, E. (1989) 'What is an intelligent museum? A Japanese view', *Museum*, 164, pp.241–3.

MORI (1982) *Visitors to the Royal Academy*, MORI.

Mullaney, S. (1983) 'Strange things, gross terms, curious customs: the rehearsal of customs in the late Renaissance', *Representations*, 3, pp.40–67.

Murray, D. (1904) *Museums, their History and their Use*, 3 Vols, J. Maclehose & Sons, Glasgow.

Neverov, O. (1985) 'His Majesty's Cabinet and Peter I's *Kunstkammer*', in Impey, O. and MacGregor, A. *The Origins of Museums*, Clarendon Press, Oxford, pp.54–61.

Nicholson, S. and Warhurst, M. (1984) *Joseph Mayer, 1803–1886*, Merseyside County Museums Occasional Papers, no. 2.

Nisbet, H.C. (1971) 'The Geological Museum of Edinburgh University', *Museums Journal*, 70 (4), pp.169–72.

Nochlin, L. (1972) 'Museums and radicals: a history of emergencies', in O'Doherty, B. and Hanks, N. *Museums in Crisis*, George Braziller, New York.

O'Doherty, B. and Hanks, N. (1972) *Museums in Crisis*, George Braziller, New York.

Olmi, G. (1985) 'Science – honour – metaphor: Italian cabinets of the sixteenth and seventeenth centuries', in Impey, O. and MacGregor, A. *The Origins of Museums*, Clarendon Press, Oxford.

Ornstein, M. (1938) *The Role of Scientific Societies in the Seventeenth Century*, Chicago.

Parshall, P.W. (1982) 'The print collection of Ferdinand Archduke of Tyrol', *Jahrbuch der Kunsthistorischen Sammlungen in Wien*, 78, pp.139–84.

Pearce, S. (1985) 'Thinking about things', *Museums Journal*, 85 (4), pp.198–202.

Pearce, S. (1986a) 'Objects high and low', *Museums Journal*, 86 (2), pp.79–82.

Pearce, S. (1986b) 'Objects as signs and symbols', *Museums Journal*, 86 (3), pp.131–5.

Pearce, S. (1986c) 'Objects in structures', *Museums Journal*, 86 (4), pp.178–81.

Pearce, S. (1987) 'Museology, museums and material culture: some thoughts', *Museology and Museums*, ICOFOM Study Series 12, Helsinki, pp.233–58.

Pearce, S. (ed.) (1989) *Museum Studies in Material Culture*, Leicester University Press, Leicester.

Peirson-Jones, J. (1990) 'Interactive video and the Gallery 33 Project', *Museum Development*, June, n.p.

Peponis, J. and Hedin, J. (1982) 'The layout of theories in the Natural History Museum', *9H*, (3), pp.21–5.

Porter, G. (1990) 'Gender bias: representations of work in history museums', *Continuum: an Australian Journal of the Media*, 3 (1), pp. 70–83.

Poster, M. (1984) *Foucault, Marxism and History*, Polity Press, Cambridge.

Prince, D.R. (1983) 'Behavioural consistency and visitor attraction', *The International*

Journal of Museum Management and Curatorship, 2 (3), pp.235–48, Butterworth, London.

Prince, D.R. (1984) 'The museum as dreamland', *The International Journal of Museum Management and Curatorship*, 4 (3), pp.243–50, Butterworth, London.

Prince, D.R. (1987) *Museums UK*, Museums Association, London.

Prince, D.R. and Schadla-Hall, R.T. (1985) 'The image of the museum: a case-study of Kingston upon Hull', *Museums Journal*, 85 (1), pp.39–45.

Prini, P. (1981) 'Florence and the Tuscany of the Medici in sixteenth-century Europe', *Museum*, 33 (2), pp.99–114.

Purver, M. and Bowen, E.J. (1960) *The Beginning of the Royal Society*, Clarendon Press, Oxford.

Quimby, I.M. (ed.) (1978) *Material Culture and the Study of American Life*, Winterthur Museum, Norton and Co., New York.

Quynn, D.M. (1945) 'The art confiscations of the Napoleonic Wars', *The American History Review*, L (3), pp.437–60.

Rabinow, P. (1982), 'Space, knowledge and power', *Skyline*, March, pp.16–20.

Rabinow, P. (1984) *The Foucault Reader*, Penguin Books, Middlesex.

Raby, J. (1985) 'Exotica from Islam', in Impey, O. and MacGregor, A. *The Origins of Museums*, Clarendon Press, Oxford, pp.251–8.

Racevskis, K. (1980) 'The discourse of Michel Foucault: a case of an absent and forgettable subject', *Humanities in Society*, 3 (1), pp.41–53.

Rajchman, J. (1983) 'Foucault, or the ends of modernism', *October*, 24, pp.37–62.

Raulet, G. (1983) 'Structuralism and post-structuralism: an interview with Michel Foucault', *Telos*, 55, pp.195–211.

Read, H. (1921) 'Museums in the present and future', *The Antiquaries Journal*, 1 (3), pp.167–82.

Reay, B. (ed) (1985) *Popular Culture in 17th Century England*, Croom Helm, London and Sydney.

Ricoeur, P. (1965) 'Hermeneutics: restoration of meaning or reduction of illlusion?' in Connerton, P. (ed.) (1976) *Critical Sociology*, Penguin Books, Middlesex.

Riksutstallningar (1976) *Going to Exhibitions*, Swedish Travelling Exhibitions, Sweden.

Rinehart, M. (1981) 'A document for the Studiolo of Francesco I', in Barasch, M. and Sandler, L. F. *Art the Ape of Nature*, Harry N. Abrams, New York.

Robinson, A. and Toobey, M. (1989) 'Reflections to the future', *Museums Journal*, 89 (7), pp. 27–9.

Roover, R. de (1948) *The Medici Bank – Its Organization, Management, Operation and Decline*, New York University Press, New York.

Roover, R. de (1963) *The Rise and Decline of the Medici Bank*, Harvard University Press, Cambridge, Mass.

Roth, M. (1981) 'Foucault's history of the present', *History and Society*, 20, pp.32–46.

Said, E.W. (1974) 'The problem of textuality: two exemplary positions', *Critical Inquiry*, 4 (4), pp.673–714.

Salmon, V. (1974) 'John Wilkins's essay 1668: critics and continuators', *Historiographica Linguistica* I, pp.147–63.

Scheicher, E. (1985) 'The collection of Archduke Ferdinand II at Schloss Ambras: its purpose, composition and evolution', in Impey, O. and MacGregor, A. *The Origins of Museums*, Clarendon Press, Oxford, pp.29–38.

Schepelern, H.D. (1985) 'Natural philosophers and princely collectors: Worm, Paludanus, and the Gottorp and Copenhagen collections', in Impey, O. and MacGregor, A. *The Origins of Museums*, Clarendon Press, Oxford, pp.121–7.

Schlereth, T.J. (1982) *Material Culture Studies in America*, The American Association of State and Local History, Nashville.

Schlereth, T.J. (1989) 'Material culture research and North American social history',

Bibliography

in Pearce, S. (ed.) *Museum Studies in Material Culture*, Leicester University Press, Leicester.

Schupbach, W. (1985) 'Some cabinets of curiosity in European academic institutions', in Impey, O. and MacGregor, A. *The Origins of Museums*, Clarendon Press, Oxford.

Scottish Office (1981) *A Survey of Visitors to the Scottish National Museums and Galleries*, Central Research Unit Papers, Edinburgh.

Seelig, L. (1985) 'The Munich *Kunstkammer*, 1565–1807', in Impey, O. and MacGregor, A. *The Origins of Museums*, Clarendon Press, Oxford, pp.76–89.

Seling, H. (1967) 'The genesis of the museum', *Architectural Review*, 141, pp.103–14.

Sheridan, A. (1980) *Michel Foucault: The Will to Truth*, Tavistock Publications, London.

Simcock, A.V. (1984) *The Ashmolean Museum and Oxford Science, 1683–1983*, Museum of the History of Science, Oxford.

Simpson, A.D.C. (1984) 'Newton's telescope and the cataloguing of the Royal Society's Repository', *Notes and Records of the Royal Society*, 38 (2), pp.187–214.

Singleton, C.S. (ed.) (1967) *Art, Science, History in the Renaissance*, Johns Hopkins University Press, Baltimore.

Skeat, W.W. (1912) 'Snakestones and stone thunder bolts as subjects for systematic investigation', *Folklore*, 23, pp.45–80.

Skelton, R. (1985) 'Indian art and artefacts in early European collecting', in Impey, O. and MacGregor, A. *The Origins of Museums*, Clarendon Press, Oxford, pp.274–81.

Slater, D. (1983) 'The object of photography', *Camerawork*, 2, pp.4–9.

Slaughter, M.M. (1982) *Universal Languages and Scientific Taxonomy in the Seventeenth Century*, Cambridge University Press, Cambridge.

Smart, B. (1982), 'Foucault, sociology, and the problem of human agency', *Theory and Society*, 11 (2), pp.121–41.

Smart, B. (1985a) *Foucault, Marxism and Critique*, Routledge & Kegan Paul, London.

Smart, B. (1985b) *Michel Foucault*, Ellis

Horwood, Chichester; Tavistock Publications, London.

Smyth, M. and Ayton, B. (1985) *Visiting the National Maritime Museum*, OPCS, HMSO, London.

Sola, T. (1987) 'The concept and nature of museology', *Museum*, 153, pp.45–9.

Sontag, S. (ed.) (1983) *Barthes: Selected Writings*, Fontana Paperbacks, London.

Sprat, T. (1667) *The History of the Royal Society*, London; (1959) Cope, J. and Jones, H.W. (eds), Routledge, London.

Sprinkler, M. (1980) 'The use and abuse of Foucault', *Humanities in Society*, 3 (1), pp.1–21.

Stalker, D. and Glymour, C. (1982) 'The malignant object: thoughts on public sculpture', *Public Interest*, 66, pp.3–21.

Stearn, W.T. (1981) *The Natural History Museum at South Kensington: a History of the British Museum (Natural History), 1753–1980*, Heinemann, London.

Stimson, D. (1949) *Scientists and Amateurs: History of the Royal Society*, Sigma, London.

Stocking, G.W. (ed.) (1985) *Objects and Others: Essays on Museums and Material Culture*, History of Anthroplogy, vol. 3, The University of Wisconsin Press.

Strong, R. (1973) *Splendour at Court: Renaissance Spectacle and Illusion*, Weidenfeld & Nicolson, London.

Strong, R. (1984) *Art and Power, Renaissance Festivals 1450–1650*, The Boydell Press, Suffolk.

Sturrock, J. (ed.) (1979) *Structuralism and Since*, Oxford University Press, Oxford.

Suggitt, M. (1985) 'Heals to Habitat; museums and modern interiors', *Museums Journal*, 85 (1), pp.13–16.

Taborsky, E. (1981) 'The socio-structural role of the museum', PhD thesis, Department of Educational Theory, University of Toronto, Canada.

Taborsky, E. (1982) 'The socio-structural role of the museum', *The International Journal of*

Museum Management and Curatorship, 1, pp.339–45.

Taborsky, E. (1983) 'The "syntax" and the museum', *Recherches Sémiotiques/Semiotic Inquiry*, 3 (4), pp.364–75.

Taylor, F.H. (1948) *The Taste of Angels: A History of Art Collecting from Rameses to Napoleon*, Little, Brown & Company, Boston.

Taylor, F.S. (1945) *Science Past and Present*, Heinemann, London.

Taylor, M. A. (1987) 'Mr. George Ruthven's Cabinet', *Museums Journal*, 84 (4), pp.202–4.

Teather, J.L. (1983a) 'Some brief notes on the problems of museological research', unpublished paper, Ottowa.

Teather, J.L. (1983b) 'Museology and its traditions: the British experience, 1845–1945', PhD thesis, University of Leicester.

Thomas, K. (1973) *Religion and the Decline of Magic*, Weidenfeld, London.

Thompson, J.M.A. (ed.) (1984) *Manual of Curatorship*, The Museums Association, Butterworth, London.

Thorndike, L. (1941) *A History of Magic and Experimental Science, vol iv: Fourteenth and Fifteenth Centuries; vols v and vi: The Sixteenth Century*, Columbia University Press, New York.

Tillyard, E.M. (1943) *The Elizabethan World Picture*, Chatto & Windus, London.

Torrens, H. (1985) 'Early collecting in the field of geology', in Impey, O. and MacGregor, A. *The Origins of Museums*, Clarendon Press, Oxford, pp.204–13.

Trudel, J. (1989) 'The first generation of exhibitions at the Musée de la Civilisation in Quebec City', *Muse*, 7 (2), pp.67–71.

Turner, G. l'E. (1985) 'The cabinet of experimental philosophy', in Impey, O. and MacGregor, A. *The Origins of Museums*, Clarendon Press, Oxford, pp.214–22.

Van Holst, N. (1967) *Creators, Collectors and Connoiseurs: The Anatomy of Artistic Taste from Antiquity to the Present Day*, Thames & Hudson, London.

Vickers, M. (1985) 'Greek and Roman antiquities in the seventeenth century', in Impey, O. and MacGregor, A. *The Origins of Museums*, Clarendon Press, Oxford, pp.223–31.

Wackernagel, M. (1981) *The World of the Florentine Renaissance Artist: Projects and Patrons, Workshop and Art Market*, Princeton University Press, New Jersey.

Weil, S. (1989) 'The proper business of museums: ideas or things?', *Muse*, 7 (1), pp.28–38.

Weiss, R. (1969) *The Renaissance Discovery of Classical Antiquity*, Blackwell, Oxford.

Welch, M. (1983) 'The Ashmolean as described by its earliest visitors', in MacGregor, A. (ed.) *Tradescant's Rarities*, Clarendon Press, Oxford.

Weld, C.R. (1975) *History of the Royal Society, vols I and II*, Arno Press, New York.

Wescher, P. (1964) 'Vivant Denon and the Musée Napoléon', *Apollo*, 80, pp.178–86.

White, H. (1973) 'Foucault decoded', *History and Theory*, 12 (1), pp.23–54.

Whitehead, P.J.P. (1970) 'Museums in the history of zoology (part I)', *Museums Journal*, 70 (2), pp.50–7.

Whitehead, P.J.P. (1971) 'Museums in the history of zoology (part II)', *Museums Journal*, 70 (4), pp.155–60.

Whitehead, P. (1981) *The British Museum (Natural History)*, Scala, London.

Wickham, G. (1986) 'Power and analysis: beyond Foucault', in Gane, M. (ed.) *Towards a Critique of Foucault*, Routledge & Kegan Paul, London.

Williams, R. (1974) *Television: Technology and Cultural Form*, Fontana, London.

Williams, R. (1976) *Keywords: a Vocabulary of Culture and Society*, Fontana/Croom Helm, London.

Wilson, D. (1982) 'Public interest versus conservation', *Museum*, 34 (1), pp.65–7.

Wilson, D.M. (1984) 'National museums', in Thompson, J.M.A. (ed.) *Manual of Curatorship*, Museums Association, Butterworth, London.

Bibliography

Wilson, J. (1975) 'Little gifts keep friendship alive: an historic dessert service', *Apollo*, 102, pp.50–60.

Winner, L. (1980) 'Do artifacts have politics?' *Daedalus*, 109, Journal of the American Academy of Arts and Sciences.

Wittlin, A.S. (1949) *The Museum: its History and its Tasks in Education*, Routledge & Kegan Paul, London.

Wittlin, A.S. (1970) *Museums: in Search of a Usable Future*, MIT Press, Cambridge, Mass.

Woolley, L. (1952) *Ur of the Chaldees*, Penguin, Middlesex.

Woolley, L. and Moorey, P.R.S. (1982) *Ur 'of the Chaldees'*, Book Club Associates, London.

Wright, G. and Rabinow, P. (1982) 'Spatialization of power: a discussion of the work of Michel Foucault', *Skyline*, March, pp.14–16.

Wright, P. (1985) *On Living in an Old Country*, Verso, London.

Yates, F.A. (1966) *The Art of Memory*, Routledge & Kegan Paul, London.

Yates, F.A. (1967) 'The hermetic tradition in Renaissance science', in Singleton, C.S. (ed.) *Art, Science and History in the Renaissance*, Johns Hopkins University Press, Baltimore.

Yates, F.A. (1969) *Theatre of the World*, Routledge & Kegan Paul, London.

Yates, F.A. (1972) *The Rosicrucian Enlightenment*, Routledge & Kegan Paul, London.

Yates, F.A. (1979) *The Occult Philosophy in the Elizabethan Age*, Routledge & Kegan Paul, London.

Yates, F.A. (1983) *Renaissance and Reform: the Italian Contribution*, Routledge & Kegan Paul, London.

Yorke, D.A. and Jones, R.R. (1984) 'Marketing and museums', *European Journal of Marketing*, 18 (2), pp.90–9.

Young, M.F.D. (1975) 'An approach to the study of curricula as socially organised knowledge', in Golby, M., Greenwald, J., and West, R. *Curriculum Design*, Croom Helm, London, and the Open University Press.

Young, R. (1981) *Untying The Text: a Post-Structuralist Reader*, Routledge & Kegan Paul, London.

Zolberg, V. (1981) 'Conflicting visions in American art museums', *Theory and Society*, 10 (1), pp.103–25.

Index

Index

Index